FACING ME IS YOU

Bridging the Divide Between China and the Foreign Press

FU YING

Translated by
Dr Chen Chunhua and **Fu Ying**

ACA

Published by ACA Publishing Ltd
London - Beijing
✉ info@alaincharlesasia.com ☎ +44 20 3289 3885
www.alaincharlesasia.com

Published by ACA Publishing Ltd in arrangement with the China Translation & Publishing House

Author: Fu Ying **Translators:** Dr Chen Chunhua and Fu Ying
Editor: Martin Savery

Original Chinese Text © 我的对面是你，新闻发布会背后的故事 *(Wo de Duimian Shi Ni, Xinwen Fabuhui de Gushi)* 2018, CITIC Press Group,
Beijing, China

The greatest care has been taken to ensure accuracy but the publisher can accept no responsibility for errors or omissions, or for any liability occasioned by relying on its content.

Paperback ISBN: 978-1-83890-021-2
eBook ISBN: 978-1-83890-022-9

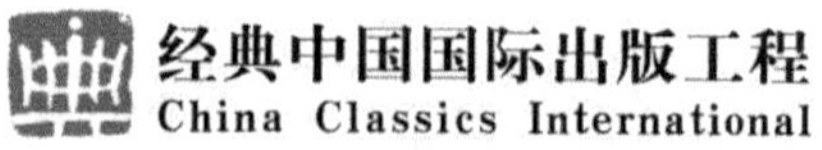

FACING ME IS YOU

BRIDGING THE DIVIDE BETWEEN CHINA AND THE FOREIGN PRESS

FU YING

Translated by
CHEN CHUNHUA AND FU YING

ACA PUBLISHING LTD

CONTENTS

Section I
THE NPC PRESS CONFERENCE 2017

Section II
STORIES BEHIND THE PRESS CONFERENCES

Section III

STORIES OUTSIDE THE NEWS CONFERENCE

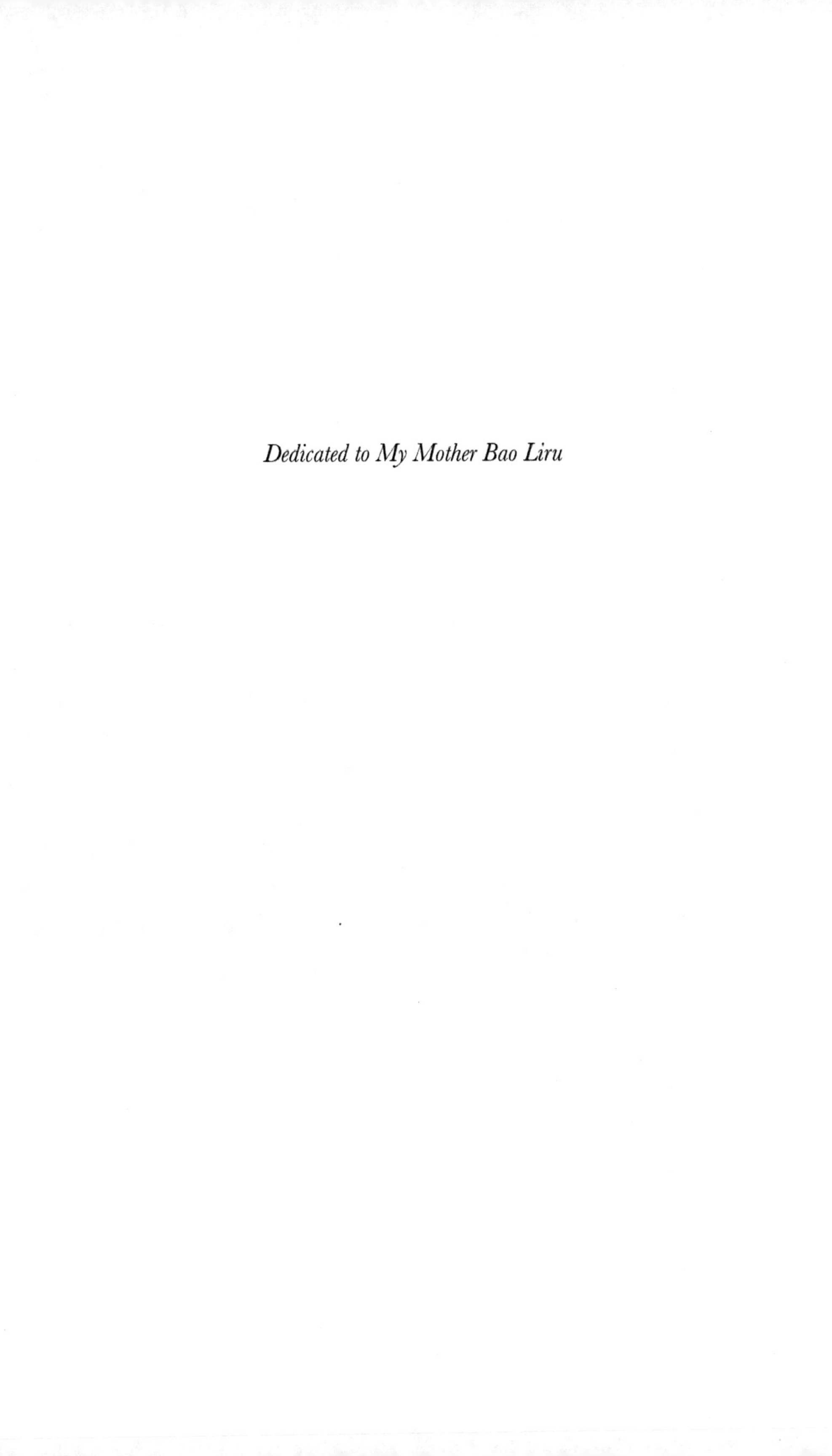

Dedicated to My Mother Bao Liru

PREFACE TO THE ENGLISH EDITION

FU YING

The United Kingdom was one of the first European countries to recognize the People's Republic of China (PRC) and March 13, 2022 marks the 50th anniversary of its establishment of diplomatic relations at the Ambassadorial level with China in 1972. In the context of major changes in the international arena in the 1970s, the two countries increased communication and cooperation in economic, trade and cultural areas. Despite twists and turns, our overall relations have moved forward in the ensuing decades with ever growing cooperation.

In the 30-plus years of my diplomatic career, I have had close association with the UK. I studied at the University of Kent as a postgraduate student in 1985 and served as Chinese Ambassador to the UK from 2007 to 2010. I have witnessed and got personally involved in some of the progress in the relationship and have made friends among the people I met and the counterparts I worked with. Their understanding and advice gave me much support which enabled me to learn more about the country and its people. No matter whether it was becoming immersed in a beautiful opera at a West End theatre, joining the cheering crowd at a football game, or attending a traditional and elegant horse racing event, I have been able to experience and better appreciate the British people's passions and pastimes. Looking back on my three-year term in the UK, while I did have some hard times dealing with frictions between the two countries, my general impression has been positive and I kept fond memories of both my work and life. Before leaving London, at my farewell reception at the Mandarin Oriental Hyde Park Hotel in January 2010, I confessed during my speech that I was already missing the country.

I have continued to follow the bilateral relations in the years after I left the UK and I kept a strong interest in the progress of cooperation. I also noted with concern the difficulties arising in the relationship. As far as I could see, many issues affecting our relations were derived from conflicting views about China's domestic politics and policies, not matters affecting the interests of the British people. Fundamentally speaking, it revealed the reality that the two countries have differing values and world outlook which were shaped by their different political systems and historical experience. Therefore, it is important that the two sides gain mutual understanding through communication, so that the differences do not hinder the normal development of China-UK relations.

As Chinese President Xi Jinping told the then British Prime Minister Boris Johnson during a phone conversation on October 29, 2021, "For China-Britain relations to fare well, mutual trust is the foundation, understanding is the precondition, and proper management of differences is the key."

China-UK relations have come a long way, thanks to the tenacious efforts of generations of leaders and diplomats as well as contributions by people from all walks of life in the two countries. In 1972, bilateral trade was about US$300 million. I remember doing research on China-UK trade as my thesis at the University of Kent in 1986. I came up with a very optimistic projection about the trade growth prospects. Years later, the actual trade growth was much more robust than I had expected and when I left London in early 2010, it had risen to US$39.15 billion from US$760 million in 1980, registering a 50-fold increase in 29 years.

The UK has become China's third-largest trade partner, second-largest investment destination, and second-largest source of foreign investment from Europe. In the meantime, China has become the largest trade partner and the largest source of imports for the UK in Asia. In 2021, bilateral trade grew by 22% year on year to US$112.6 billion. More than 500 Chinese enterprises created over 80,000 job opportunities in the UK. London has become the world's biggest hub for offshore trading of China's renminbi (RMB) currency. Financial cooperation initiatives, including the Shanghai-London Stock Connect and currency swaps, have shown impressive progress. New energy has emerged as a new growth point including such green energy projects as battery storage, offshore wind power, and electric vehicles. In February 2022, Hualong One (HPR1000, China's nuclear power technology, passed the UK's Generic Design Assessment (GDA). This project, once completed, is expected to provide the British people with more reliable and clean energy.

The UK was also one of the first countries to open educational cooperation with China. It is now the most popular destination for Chinese students pursuing studies in Europe. When I went to the UK for overseas study in 1985, there were only a few dozen of us in that year. By 2020, the UK was the top destination for overseas Chinese students. Currently, there are about 200,000 Chinese students in UK schools and universities, and around 10,000 British students studying in China. It can be expected that, when the pandemic is over, bilateral people-to-people exchanges will recover with new vigor.

China and the UK share some common views on international issues. For instance, both countries support multilateralism and believe in an open international economy. We agree that mutually beneficial cooperation between our countries contributes to a peaceful and prosperous world. President Xi Jinping calls for building a community with a shared future for humankind. Nurturing the friendship among our peoples helps foster an enabling environment for achieving that objective.

This book is, to some extent, inspired by my experiences in the UK. 2008 was seen as the year China rose to major country status on the world stage. But for many of us in China, it was a year of overwhelming sorrow because of the severe earthquake in Wenchuan, followed by great joy at the Beijing Olympic Games. It was also a year in which China's international image went through ups and downs. The experience made me realize that people in the UK, as well as in the Western world at large, lacked sufficient knowledge of modern-day China. Prejudice and misinformation about China were easy to sell. China was often portrayed in the media with biased tones and poorly researched stories, which tended to influence public opinion negatively. As a result, efforts to expand bilateral cooperation often ran into obstacles.

The public receives information from the media. In the West, ordinary people have little chance to gain first-hand knowledge of China. For example, for a British truck driver or a housewife, when they learn about the world through TV programs in a bar or in the kitchen, they rarely see or hear Chinese talking about China.

During my three-year term as Chinese Ambassador to the UK, I gave much priority to promoting understanding. I spent time learning how to respond to critical views, how to inform audiences of China's stand on some of the issues, and how to promptly and effectively provide the Chinese view when problems occurred. I came to understand the British media, particularly the history and underlying logic of media-government relations. For me, these efforts went a long way to improving our communication with British society and making Chinese information more accessible to more people. This experience also proved useful when I moved on to be a spokesperson of the National People's Congress (NPC) of China.

Facing Me is You recounts my experiences as a spokesperson for five sessions of the NPC since 2017. In this book, I have gone into great detail about my work while on that job. I hope, by sharing the stories behind my press conferences, I can help people get a closer look at the NPC. Some of the experience and lessons I learnt may also be useful for my peers and those to come.

Now that this book is published in the UK, I hope it can provide a fresh perspective for the world in learning about China, and help to increase understanding on how China's political system operates. For instance, how does the Chinese government run a country of more than 1.4 billion people? China's governance is based on the NPC and the local peoples' congresses at all levels. They are created through democratic elections and are responsible to the people and subject to their oversight. The NPC is China's highest organ of power. It exercises the power conferred by the people in accordance with the Constitution under the leadership of the Communist Party of China (CPC). The NPC formulates laws to safeguard social stability and the rights of individuals. Meanwhile, it ensures that the government acts under the framework of the Constitution and laws, and ensures strict law enforcement.

This book starts with the press conference I gave for the Fifth Session of the 12th NPC, which was held on March 4, 2017. Section I of the book tries to reveal the thinking behind this press conference by deconstructing some of the Q & A process. Flashbacks from the previous press conferences are also given to reinforce some of the points. Section II tells stories behind the scenes, revealing the preparatory process not only for my press conferences but also for the NPC Session's overall communications work. It details how I fulfilled my role as a spokesperson. Section III retraces my experience in international interactions including the exercises I went through in order to sharpen my communications skills during my tenure as Chinese Ambassador to the UK.

China's international image needs to be proactively shaped and reinforced by the Chinese people themselves. This is both necessary and achievable. It is not impossible for us to communicate with the international community, including with the people of Western countries. I have learnt through experience that we should also be equipped with the necessary skills when interacting with Western media. I hope more and more people will join the effort to advance China's international communications and exchanges.

It is important that the Chinese people learn how to tell our own story to the world. The way to do so, in my view, is to communicate, communicate and communicate, which is particularly important for China and the UK. As the significance of China-UK ties has gone beyond bilateral relations, it has become increasingly important for both countries to enable closer cooperation on global issues. We should draw on historical experience and lessons, cast off outdated misconceptions, learn to respect and accommodate each other, and expand bilateral cooperation through dialogue and consultation no matter what difficulties lie ahead.

INTRODUCTION

WRITTEN BY ANOTHER WITNESS OF THIS EMERGING WORLD

STEPHEN PERRY

This introduction is something that tells not just about the book but its setting and Fu Ying's unique place to see from. Her vantage point of this new world is unique and reading her writings is a chance to see the future from her past. From her own ingrained ways and ideas. Some not even perceived by Fu Ying, as we all only know something of who we are.

Inner Mongolia where Fu Ying grew up is a mysterious place I have flown over 400 or more times. Hohhot is one of the most remote cities of the world. Between Russia and China, Inner Mongolia is a golden part of the history of China over centuries and millennia. This is the base from which to see the emergence of modern China in the new world. I would recommend visiting Inner Mongolia in a good climate season and enjoy the amazing land miles from the seas. It is a fascinating place.

But the main story is the changing world that Mme Fu Ying has walked across from a little Mongolian girl to a major global diplomat.

The world has changed in front of her eyes and let's see some of those changes that are the backdrop to this fine work.

Eurasia is changing and we know not yet to where and to what. China changed from 1978 to 2020 beyond anyone's expectations. China is now changing again and it will be so different by 2049, the next centenary target of China. Asia is changing also. From one end of the world to the other change is happening, and yet policy makers are mainly addressing the challenges of today.

Mme Fu Ying entered diplomatic service in 1976, rising to be Vice Minister of Foreign Affairs and Chair of the Foreign Relations Committee of the Chinese Parliament, the National People's Congress (NPC). Mme Fu Ying was Ambassador of the PRC to the UK in the middle of the first decade of this century.

The origin of the changes that are altering the world so much in the next 30-50 years and into the next century have been the daily life of Fu Ying, an ethnic Mongol and a representative of China in Asia and the UK.

Fu Ying has worked through the roots of change in Eurasia and helps us understand what has happened, and has given us an insight into what might happen.

Chinese philosophy is quite different from ours. It spans 3,000 years or more and change is seen as natural, like the seasons, and the contact with other systems is seen as normal.

We are looking at a China which fell behind from 1840 and began its return in 1949. Stabilising but yet poor by 1978, it was then to start a journey back to the much changed world. Its peasant class was to be replaced by an emerging middle income system, a manufacturing system to change the world, and a service sector that has transformed many features of the modern world.

Fu Ying drove the same streets in Beijing that many of us travelled in the 1970s as the Cultural Revolution was fast being left behind. Soon the Reform and Opening Up Era was to begin, as the Party led the people to an Economic Reform priority in the great changes of 1978 and 1981. Until then the peasantry was the largest part of China, comprising over 85% of the people. Within just 30 years they were to be changed by mechanisation into an advanced agricultural sector, and its population reduced to 25% of the nation. Manufacturing peaked at 60% and dropped back towards 30% and the new service sector rose to 60% of the nation. The cities transformed as the peasantry of China moved to the Eastern seaboard and soon sky scrapers announced the change of urban China.

Looking ahead, China is now into the next stage of change and four great metropolitan regions are the core of new China leading the changes across China from North to South and East to West. China's new Silk Road – BRI (Belt & Road Initiative) – has lasted only nine years and has transformed the roads and rail from the East of Asia to the West of Europe. Until now the passage from Asia to Europe has mainly been by ship. Carrying the cargoes and travellers from both continents. The land passage was dominated by huge camel trains but was lengthy and treacherous. The routes were dominated by the sea routes as the main carrier of colonialism was the ship.

BRI is changing this to a road and rail transport system not only changing the passage of goods but also heralding the change of focus of the great movement of goods and services from the Pacific to the Atlantic. The high speed change will add to this transformation in the years to come but already new nations are upon the map of the world. New forms of ribbon development are happening in this new Eurasia, as they did in Europe and the USA in the 19th and 20th centuries.

Towns and cities are growing in this vast new transportation system opening markets in both directions. The Middle East is seeing itself as the new centre of transportation between Asia and Europe, and European companies are seeing these new areas opening up new markets, providing easier access to the markets of East Asia and Central and South Asia.

Populations are beginning to move and an Asia of the future is emerging. Brzezinski saw aspects of this in his book – Grand Chessboard – and this has influenced US policy makers in recent times.

There is a question arising if the world will be led by a superpower or two, or are we moving to a new world. In this new world the initial phase of the United Nations (UN) will give way to a new world of nations. Where the world unites to meet the climate and health challenges, and global infrastructure moves from national to regional to global.

Some talk of multilateralism and protectionism as aspects of these huge changes of continents and regions. In reality a new world is emerging and its full characteristics may take another 75 years or more to emerge.

The technology and resources of the world are about to go through huge changes as energy transforms in response to climate change, and the service sector brings in AI, the digital world and digital currency. China's regions will lead the way to changes in the urban areas as cities become the past and metropolises with great green and agricultural areas are formed to meet the new world of up to 10 billion people (up from 7 billion).

This is the world we shall see that Mme Fu Ying has been a witness to and seen some of the turmoil that comes with change. But if we are to feed and care for the people of the world then we shall have to develop a better sense of sharing and caring, as mere profit will not be enough. From the latter part of the 19th century Europe and the USA led the industrial revolutions that transformed the world. Capitalism and Judaeo-Christianity were the core systems whose inequalities gave rise to parliamentary democracies.

The world that is coming is already stamped by the Islamic, Muslim and Buddhist religions. Their cultures and ways are influencing the world in many ways, and probably the biggest changes are sourced in a China that few saw. Today that China, like much of Asia, is appearing and influencing the world. But at its core, possibly the main source of national, regional and global change is China.

Its ways, its philosophies are driving change linked with the system of socialism that developed from Germany in the 19th century. Socialism has been linked with the centuries-old ways of China influenced by Buddha and other naturally based philosophies that characterise the way Chinese people are.

Being a Mongol by birth and developing her adult life as Chinese, Mme Fu Ying is a fine witness to the changes of modest home life through to national change and the emerging transformation of Asia. We shall all have to live in a world of many more influences than ever before. We shall protect our ways by embracing change and adapting our economies and societies to these changes. Domination by one or two religions or nations is the past.

The USA and many parts of Europe have already adapted to the new merged societies and still kept their ethnicities intact.

Mme Fu Ying's wonderful book helps us follow a Mongol girl into the world of China in Beijing to be a global representative of this new emerging nation and its impactful philosophies. Fu Ying has seen the meeting of civilisations and systems like few others, Fu Ying has witnessed this through the eyes of a Chinese minority and that makes her words the more interesting.

We should hope this book is the first of an odyssey of tales of the new world as seen from China. I know of no better story teller and witness to the huge changes of our times.

FOREWORD

It was just past noon on 4 March 2017, and the hands of the huge clock in the Press Briefing Hall of the Great Hall of the People pointed to 12:08. The press conference for the 5th session of the 12th NPC[1], which has been going on for 68 minutes, draws to a close.

As I got up to leave, many journalists crowded the area in front of the podium, shouting questions in the hope of getting a further response. I am aware that this kind of "ambush" scene would be difficult to manage. As the spokesperson for the press conference, should I take one question, the rest would expect me to take all their questions and I could easily fall into the dilemma of taking a few and missing the rest or losing control of the time limit. As there were too many people in the room, there was also the danger of creating a chaotic scene leading to a stampede. Although I could see many expectant eyes looking pleadingly at me from the crowd, I waved my hands apologetically and left quickly.

I walked through the tall and imposing corridors and out of the South Gate of the Great Hall of the People. The sun outside was shining and the sky was clear. I felt relieved and happy.

I had been a diplomat for more than 30 years, traveling extensively internationally, and had often given interviews to domestic and foreign media. However, the pressures I had and the efforts I made as the spokesperson of the NPC were new and different from what I had experienced in the past.

As General Secretary Xi Jinping said when delivering his report to the 19th National Congress of the Communist Party of China (CPC):

> "Our world is full of hope as well as of challenges. We should not give up on our dreams just because the reality around us is too complicated; we should not stop pursuing our ideals just because they seem out of reach. No country can address the many challenges facing humanity alone; no country can afford to retreat into self-isolation."

With the rapid development in information technology, the growth of new media and the strong desire of the public to acquire knowledge and information, a spokesperson faces stronger challenges. For me, the annual press conference of the plenary session of the NPC was like a rigorous examination. I had to do a lot of painstaking preparation beforehand as there was so much knowledge and information that might be needed during the press conference. The learning and memorising process was sometimes excruciating. During the press conference, I still need to be careful about the wording of every response when answering questions, making sure that I was getting my points and ideas across.

After each press conference, I would feel so relieved that, for quite a long time, I would hate to watch a video of the live broadcast.

Back in January 2013, I was elected a deputy to the 12th NPC at the Inner Mongolia Autonomous Region People's Congress, which is the region I come from. At the first meeting of the presidium of the first session of the 12th NPC, on 4 March 2013, I was selected a Deputy Secretary-General and the spokesperson of the Congress. So, by March 2017, it was my fifth time serving as spokesperson for a plenary session of the NPC.

I still remember that when, for the first time, I attended the press conference on 4 March 2013, held in the Briefing Hall of the Great

Hall of the People, the Hall, which could accommodate more than 500 people, was packed with journalists, and people were standing next to each other in the back rows and on both sides. Television cameramen and photographers were waiting for me with their equipment. Suddenly faced with such a large media array, I felt the pressure rising abruptly, and for me that kind of feeling is unforgettable.

Cameras flashed nonstop, capturing every word and gesture of mine, I was probably being photographed more than I had ever been before. How could I not feel intimidated and humbled.

Although my mouth got very dry as I spoke, I decided not to take any water, as I realised the sound of cameras clicking significantly increased as soon as I picked up my glass. For me, it was important not to be distracted, to remain calm and focused, and get my points across.

Every year, the NPC press conference is broadcast live by China Central Television (CCTV), and many other TV stations and networks relay the broadcast, with high viewing rates and a wide audience.

When I started the job in 2013, I was uneasy as I was unfamiliar with this type of press conference, but I had less fear like someone who is ignorant and fearless. Having experienced the first press conference and having seen the expectations from the public, my sense of pressure and unease rose instead of falling when preparing for the press conference the next year. I became more aware of the importance and difficulty of understanding the issues of major public interest as well as the need to increase my legislative knowledge.

By the third year, my methodology in forming ideas and expressions was much improved and the preparation had become more professional with clearer goals. I also gained more comprehensive knowledge of the work of the NPC.

Looking back over the five years, I see myself transforming from a diplomat to a legislator on domestic affairs, and experiencing a move from working on negotiations with foreign countries to learning, understanding and responding to domestic issues. My current work involving legislation and the supervision of the NPC is so different from what I experienced when involved in mediation and game-playing between countries. This transformation has not been entirely smooth. I have always been in awe of my duties and the people. With the same spirit, I have tried hard to learn and to adapt to my important new role and responsibilities, but it has been a tough learning curve.

During the five annual press conferences, I answered 126 questions put forward by 67 journalists from China and other countries and regions covering a wide range of subjects[2].

Those questions covered the most important public focus and the attention of the international community with regard to China in a crucial period of the country's development.

It was a great honour for me to be personally involved in, and to be trusted with the role of, explaining and interpreting the major issues of the time concerning the evolution of the Party, the country and the people.

Many people are interested in stories of what goes on behind the scenes at press conferences and suggested that I should write down and share the experiences.

In the book that follows, I will relate some of my work and experiences as the spokesperson of the NPC. I will describe some of the behind-the-scenes preparations and processes, which I hope are entertaining and interesting.

The stories mainly centre around my last press conference of the 5th session of the 12th NPC, held on 4 March 2017. Part I of the book focuses on the press conference itself where I explain the thinking behind preparations by deconstructing some of the questions and my answers, interspersed with reviews of press conferences of the previous four years.

Part II turns to behind-the-scenes stories which show how the press conferences were prepared for, including how I developed some of the ideas and points as a spokesperson.

Part III is about my previous experiences in my diplomatic life and my contact with the media during my tenure as Chinese ambassador to the UK.

Through these insights, I hope you will get a glimpse of how the system functions in China. I also hope that some of the experiences and lessons I recount can be of help to my peers and successors. Writing this book is also a way for me to acknowledge my gratitude and commemorate my election as deputy to the 12th NPC.

Socialism with Chinese characteristics has now entered a new era, which marks China's new self-identification for development. China is moving closer to the centre of the world stage and will eventually be able to face with a smile the spotlights that flash like the stars in the Milky Way and the world behind the camera lens.

Fu Ying, 20 Jan 2018

SECTION I
THE NPC PRESS
CONFERENCE 2017

1

WALKING INTO THE PRESS CONFERENCE

It was 10:58am on 4 March 2017 and we were in the Taiwan Hall of the Great Hall of the People.

"Are you ready? It's time, " said Mr He Shaoren as he came in. He was the Director General of the Information Bureau of the General Office of the Standing Committee of the NPC, who was the host of my press conference. He had already been to the Briefing Hall and announced some rules and requirements to the journalists who were already packed into the room.

The director from CCTV in charge of the live broadcast was standing at the door and signalled that we could enter. He controlled the time to the second.

I looked at my watch. It was two minutes before the scheduled starting time of 11:00am. I took a deep breath to compose myself and nodded to Shaoren and Han Lei, the interpreter. The three of us walked out of the Taiwan Hall towards the Briefing Hall.

LAST-MINUTE PREPARATION

Two days before, on the afternoon of 2 March, my colleagues and I came over to inspect the area and rehearse the walk. The Taiwan Hall was a good choice for waiting as it is the nearest to the Briefing Hall. We walked along the path from the Taiwan Hall to the Briefing Hall and calculated the time needed. We tested the camera and microphone for the live broadcast and, at the CCTV director's suggestion, I also decided to wear my ginger-coloured suit for that day.

A prior review of the procedures is indispensable for the success of any important event. For example, I needed to make sure that my computer could be placed on the table in the right position and that its power supply cord could be well connected.

My computer had a touch-screen and I stored all my data and materials in it. I needed to be able to access them quickly at any time during the press conference.

This time, I found that there was a new table on the podium and that the hole reserved for the computer cables was on my right hand side. This would be inconvenient, as I needed to take notes of the questions raised with my right hand and check information from the computer with my left hand. Fortunately, the staff quickly resolved the problem by immediately adjusting the connection to the left side.

On the day of the conference, some of my team members arrived early at the Taiwan Hall. As I arrived, they were busy checking the latest news at home and abroad, and appeared a bit nervous. I knew they were concerned that they might have missed something or there might be breaking news. The most awkward situation for a spokesperson was being asked about something new and not being prepared for it.

The keyword of a press conference is "news". No matter how meticulous the preparations are, there will always be unexpected situations. The 24 hours before the press conference are particularly important, as any international or domestic event may blow up into a new hot topic for the conference.

Missing any important news or information, I would likely be caught off guard during the press conference.

Therefore, my assistants not only tried to help me fully understand and prepare for the NPC session agendas, but also paid close attention to monitoring the major news outlets, the internet and social media for any new developments that could become hot topics. Especially on the eve of the press conference, we would watch very closely for any changes and new developments, making sure nothing slipped through, and we continued until literally minutes before the press conference.

I was put to the test in 2016. It was about 10:30am on 4 March and the 4th session of the 12th NPC had just ended its preparatory meeting. The minute I walked out of the auditorium, Xiao Qian, my secretary, came to me and whispered in my ear that the website of the Central Commission for Discipline Inspection had just released the news that Wang Min had just been put under disciplinary investigation, being suspected of serious violations.

Wang Min was a Vice-Chairman of the NPC's Committee on education, science, culture, and health, and a former Secretary of the Provincial Party Committee of Liaoning Province. It was about 20 minutes before the start of the press conference and I had no idea about Wang Min and what he was alleged to have done.

But I had no doubt that the journalists would also have been informed about this important news and would raise questions about it at the press conference, as anti-corruption had been of great concern to the public. Though I was prepared to respond to issues related to corruption, this specific case involving a member of the NPC Standing Committee would need a more targeted response.

Mr Yu Qing, Director of the Service Section of the Great Hall of the People, helped us find a small quiet room to work on this latest development. Xiao Qian searched on her computer for more information about anti-corruption issues from our prepared materials and I adjusted the key points to cover more specific questions on anti-corruption policies of the Congress. At the same time, my assistants gathered more data and information that I could use.

Thinking it over afterwards, I reckoned that it would have been very difficult for me to have given a good answer to the media and the public if I had heard the news only when stepping into the press conference.

With the experience of this surprise "occurrence", my team and I paid greater attention to events in the 24 hours running up to the press conferences and tried to be prepared for any unexpected development.

A spokesperson cannot speak as they wish. The response to any question needs to be evidence-based and reasonable. It requires mastering relevant policies and information, and a spokesperson cannot ad-lib a response to a question that they don't know or understand. In this information age, a spokesperson cannot take the chance that what just happened may not be known by, or be of interest to, the media and can therefore be ignored.

Even if one cannot access authoritative information or talking points due to time constraints, one should at least get to know what the facts are and give them careful consideration in order to allow enough leeway when answering the question.

2017 was not uneventful either. News came to me after 8:00pm on 3 March, the eve of the press conference, that some US warships were approaching the waters of China's Huangyan Island. While keeping in close communication with the relevant departments as they followed the US ships' movements, I started to consider how to respond to questions on this issue.

If the US ships moved close to the islands and reefs in the South China Sea, it would inevitably give rise to a sense of threat among the Chinese public, which would trigger a strong response. In which case, it would be necessary for me to have a clear response to any relevant questions. Of course, how to choose my response depended on how aggressive the US actions proved to be. I therefore spent the evening thinking and weighing up the various possible wordings.

On the morning of 4 March 2017, with about 10 minutes to go before the press conference, Meiduo, my stylist, was busy finishing my hair and make-up while I was going through the reading materials. The latest information we had received showed that the US ships were quite far away from Huangyan Island. Therefore, it did not constitute a breaking development that would require a response. But just because nothing happened this time did not mean a situation may not occur in the future.

I took note of the comment by Hu Bo, an assistant specialised in maritime military affairs, that the US activities in the South China Sea could significantly influence the situation in the region. I thought it was a good point and decided to use it when expressing my views if a journalist asked about the situation in the South China Sea.

11:00AM, 4 MARCH 2017

The press conference was routinely held on 4 March, the day before the opening of the NPC session on 5 March. At 10:00am on 4 March, a preparatory meeting of the session was held in the "auditorium" of the Great Hall of the People, chaired by Mr Zhang Dejiang, Chairman of the Standing Committee of the NPC. At the meeting, the Presidium and Secretary General of the session were elected, and the draft agenda of the session was adopted.

During the preparatory meeting, the chairman of the Standing Committee of the NPC and 13 vice-chairmen sat on the rostrum. President Xi Jinping and other leaders were seated together with other deputies in the audience area facing the rostrum.

After the preparatory meeting, the presidium members moved to the press conference hall of the Standing Committee of the NPC to attend their first meeting. They elected the executive chairman of the whole session and the acting chairman of each plenary meeting of the session, and then adopted the session's agenda. At this point in the meeting, the deputy secretary general and the current NPC session spokesperson were confirmed. The press conference was to be held afterwards.

When I gave my first press conference in 2013, I was a few minutes late arriving at the Briefing Hall. This was because I was unfamiliar with the route between the Standing Committee's press conference hall and the Briefing Hall. So, my first appearance started with an apology for being late. That was something I was never to repeat, and I would always arrive early at the Taiwan Hall in the following years.

Now at my fifth press conference on 4 March 2017, I had by this point become very familiar with the environment, and my preparations had become much smoother. At 10:59am, I walked out of the Taiwan Hall. In front of me was the open door of the Briefing Hall. I could see there was a huge crowd in the room. The passage leading towards the platform was almost blocked by journalists, leaving only a narrow corridor. As I passed through, all I could hear was the snapping shutter sounds of cameras. The room was packed and some people had to stand in the aisles and at the back.

All the camcorders, cameras and everyone's eyes were focused in my direction. As I walked in, flashes went off one after another, accompanied by the sounds of shutter snapping. Along with the bustle and noise came the stark burst of light from the camera flashes and the shouts of some journalists already eagerly asking questions. This was the fifth occasion on which I was to be the spokesperson for the NPC. Although the scene was no longer a surprise to me, my apprehension remained the same.

I smiled and walked into the Briefing Hall, stepping onto a carpeted slope that led to the platform. I was very careful every time when walking on this slope and my focus was on keeping my balance in my high-heeled shoes. Then, as I got to the centre of the table, I stood and waited for the host Mr He Shaoren and the interpreter Mr Han Lei to arrive at their places.

Looking at the audience, I saw a sea of mobile phones and almost everyone was taking photos. The flashes from the photographers' cameras in the back row became more frequent, dazzling my eyes and stimulating my nerves. In the first few seconds, my brain was almost blank.

At 11:01am, Shaoren announced the opening of the press conference. I spoke upon his invitation, greeting the attendants as well as the audience behind the camera, and then began to read out the conference's agenda. This followed a fairly standard set of opening remarks:

The 5th session of the 12th NPC will open tomorrow morning. Let me give you a brief introduction. At the preparatory meeting, the agenda of the current session was adopted and a presidium of 169 members was elected. Mr Li Jianguo was elected as Secretary General of the session and a Secretariat was established for the session. At the first meeting of the presidium, the executive chairmen and the acting chairmen were also elected. The agenda of the session and the method of voting on bills and proposals were adopted…

The press conference is a communication and interaction between the spokesperson and the journalists, and personal communication cannot be achieved without eye contact. However, the opening remarks about the session's arrangements were strictly worded. I could not memorise all of it and had to fix my eyes on the text while reading it out and could not look up. Obviously, reading a prepared text would hardly catch people' s attention, let alone arouse the public's interest.

To ease the problem, I would try to memorise some sections in the opening remarks, so that I could raise my head to establish eye contact with the attendees and people watching TV.

This time, as I read the schedule of the conference, I raised my head. Unexpectedly, I had a slip of the tongue. Instead of saying: "the opening of the session on the morning of 5 March," I actually said "on the morning of 15 March," which was the closing day. I caught a look of surprise on the journalists' faces and immediately realised that I had made a mistake. I smiled sheepishly, corrected myself and continued:

The session will open on the morning of 5 March and close on the morning of 15 March with 11 items on the agenda. In addition to the six reports, including the report on the work of the government, the draft General Provisions of Civil Law and three bills on the election of deputies to the 13th NPC will also be deliberated.

Although making errors is a human weakness, and could even be described as the beauty of humanity when compared with machines, it is still the eternal pursuit of humans to minimise or eliminate mistakes. The mistake I made was inexcusable, as I was so familiar with the content. But it did help release my tension, I calmed down and focused on the rest of the text:

"This session will be held in strict accordance with the spirit of the Eight Regulations of the Party Central Committee. This year, the Secretariat has set up a new supervisory group, which is primarily responsible for the oversight of the session's discipline and overall arrangement. The session's plenary meetings will be opened to Chinese and foreign journalists, and interviews will be arranged with some of the deputies as requested.

Over the past year, under the strong leadership of the Party Central Committee with comrade Xi Jinping at its core, the NPC and its Standing Committee have firmly established "the Four Consciousnesses"[1], and carried out the CPC Central Committee's decisions and arrangements, ensuring that the Party's propositions became the will of the state through legal procedures, responded proactively to the concerns of the masses, and persisted in scientific legislation and democratic legislation. We have improved the quality of legislation, performed the functions of supervision according to law, and made new achievements in all aspects of our work.

The current session of the NPC will comprehensively implement the spirit of the 18th National Congress of the CPC and the 3rd to 6th plenary sessions of the 18th CPC Central Committee, the spirit of General Secretary Xi Jinping's important speeches as well as his new ideas and strategies for governing the country. By conscientiously carrying out the duties entrusted in the Constitution and the law, it will be a democratic, united and pragmatic session that will mobilise the people of all ethnic groups. And it will make new contributions to achieving the "Two Centenary Goals" and realising the Chinese Dream of great national rejuvenation. Thank you.

(5 Minutes, approximately 880 Chinese characters)

WITNESSING THE DAWN OF THE CHINESE CIVIL CODE

Following the opening remarks, the Q&A session of the press conference started, and the journalists were already very eager, hoping for an opportunity to ask questions.

The journalists' questions were translated by the interpreter sitting next to me, and my answers were simultaneously interpreted by translators working in booths upstairs. In earlier years, consecutive translation was done after each answer, with over half of the press conference's time taken up by translation.

This arrangement was to benefit foreign journalists. However, in recent years, most of the foreign journalists spoke Chinese, and the demand for translation had declined. Moreover, Chinese journalists had grown to be the majority of journalists covering the conferences, and they wanted the process to be more efficient. In response to the call for change, I switched from consecutive to simultaneous interpretation at the NPC press conference in 2013.

Mr He Shaoren, as the host, was responsible for picking which journalists could raise questions. His principle for selection was to make sure that there was diversity in the journalists and their questions. Since he was helping me to keep order, I could be totally focused on answering questions.

Shaoren had been keeping in close contact with the journalists from various media groups and knew their areas of interest. This allowed him to identify the right journalist whose concern also matched the information that needed to be released at the press conference. Consequently, he would try to give the journalists the opportunity to raise the kind of issues they were interested in, also giving me the chance to release the important information about the NPC session. Shaoren would also try to make sure that the opportunity to raise questions was evenly shared among journalists from central as well as other media groups, and among foreign journalists.

At 11:06am, Shaoren gave the first opportunity to ask a question to a journalist with the *Chengdu Business Daily*, who asked about the draft *General Provisions of Civil Law*.

The journalist's question was:

The General Provisions of Civil Law will be submitted to this NPC session for deliberation. Many of the issues involved are of concern to the public, such as whether the age of people with limited capacity of civil conduct should be lowered to six years of age. What are the characteristics and significance of the draft General Provisions of Civil Law? Thank you.

The first question is usually quite important for the smooth progress of a press conference. "Well begun, half done." Moreover, the first question can serve as guidance for the questions to follow.

The deliberation of the draft *General Provisions of Civil Law* was not only an important item on the agenda but also the only item of legislation for this session. One key point of the NPC press conference was to answer questions relating to the NPC session's agenda. It was clear that Shaoren's research in the run-up to the press conference had paid off, as his selection was a journalist with a keen interest in the session's legislative issues.

The formulation of the *General Provisions of Civil Law* in China would provide a substantial basis for the civil code and guide the structural arrangement for the future compilation of various sub-sections of the civil code. Completing the civil code would significantly improve China's legal system and enrich the legislative rules and norms for the market economy and social order.

The first question raised about the *General Provisions of Civil Law* allowed me to share with the public the progress in this endeavour. Compared with the existing *General Principles of Civil Law*, it added many new elements, reflecting the new developments and demands of Chinese society. From June to December 2016, this draft had been deliberated over three rounds at the NPC Standing Committee which also solicited opinions from the general public. Now the draft was quite mature and was ready to be submitted to the NPC session. To answer this question, I not only had to give an update to the journalist, but also had to try and help broaden awareness of this important law for the whole country. I also hoped the information could reach the wider international community.

Therefore, when preparing for the press conference, the *General Provisions of Civil Law* had been one of my priorities. I normally wanted to keep my answer under three to five minutes. The difficulty was how to concisely talk about such complex and rich content in engaging and easily understood language. My team and I worked very hard and discussed this wording repeatedly in order to arrive at an ideal result. In the end, my answer to the question was as follows:

> *The draft of the General Provisions of Civil Law will be submitted to the deputies at this NPC session for deliberation. As we all know, Civil Law covers all aspects of social life. The General Provisions of Civil Law will*

regulate the basic principles and general rules of civil activities. It needs to be submitted to the plenary session for deliberation because it will be the country's basic Civil Law.

Many of us may not need to use the Criminal Law or other special laws in our lives. However, our everyday life – eating and drinking, clothing, housing and economic activities - can all be related to Civil Law.

The existing General Principles of Civil Law was formulated in 1986, and has played a significant role in safeguarding national economic development and social progress.

Of course, as we all know, great changes have taken place in Chinese society over the past 30 years, and the law needs to keep pace with the times. Therefore, in formulating the General Provisions of Civil Law, there have been many amendments and innovative elements to reflect the changes.

For example, the media is also concerned about the problems among the left-behind children in rural areas and the trend towards an ageing society. In the General Provisions of Civil Law, the guardianship system will be improved and expanded, particularly concerning the protection of the disabled and the elderly. As the form of a "legal person" has changed significantly, a new classification will be adopted. The number of categories for legal persons will be increased, and collective economic organisations, village committees in rural areas and neighbourhood committees in urban areas will also be able to take special legal persons status.

Regarding the point you raised in your question, it is still under discussion. When lowering the age of people with limited capacity for civil conduct, should we set the minimum age at 6 or 10? How can it be more conducive to the protection of minors and their healthy development? People still have different opinions. And you may also have your own. The NPC deputies will cover these and many other issues in their deliberation of the draft. I am sure they will be able to fully express their views and further improve the draft of the General Provisions of Civil Law before it is put to a vote.

The formulation of the General Provisions of Civil Law will play a leading and structural role in the future compilation of various sub-sections of the civil code. According to the current plan, the codification of the civil code will be completed by 2020, which will be of great importance in furthering our country's rule of law. Thank you.

(3 minutes, approximately 620 Chinese characters)

The *General Provisions of Civil Law* became big news for the Chinese media during the "two sessions"[2] in 2017. Many domestic media outlets used headlines such as "The law should also keep pace with the times" to report on the *General Provisions of Civil Law* that was being deliberated by the NPC deputies. Some of them analysed in great depth the perfection of the guardianship system and the expansion of the scope of guardianship and the issue of limitation of civil capacity.

As I noticed, journalists from some media outlets had interviewed experts and law scholars, asking them to interpret the significance of the *General Provisions of Civil Law* and the highlights of the draft. Such media interest played a positive role in promoting the spread and understanding of the *General Provisions of Civil Law* across Chinese society.

Civil code has long been the subject of research and has been promoted and called for by Chinese legal circles. In recent years, the media and the public have been following the process of formulating the civil code. On 23 October 2014, the 4th plenary session of the 18th CPC Central Committee adopted the *Decision on Several Major Issues on Comprehensively Promoting the Rule of Law*, which called for the formulation of the civil code. It enabled the formulation of the *General Provisions of Civil Law* to be included in the legislative work plan of the NPC Standing Committee in January 2016.

During the 4 March press conference of 2016, I was already faced with questions about the civil code.

Two days before, on the afternoon of 2 March, I joined my team to watch the live TV broadcast of the press conference of the National Committee of the Chinese People's Political Consultative Conference (CPPCC). We all noticed that many of the hot topics we had prepared to address in my press conference that were related to people's livelihood were already being asked at the CPPCC press conference. Therefore, it was reasonable to expect that the journalists attending the NPC press conference two days later would turn their attention to other matters. We consequently decided to shift our focus to issues related to legislation to be debated in the NPC session. That would require us to add new elements to my prepared items and notes.

In my discussion with the team, Huai Sheng suggested that I should pay particular attention to the development of the civil code as he believed that the media and the public were very likely to be interested in this issue. He was a member of the Legal Cases Office of the Foreign Affairs Committee and had a legal professional background. He gave me two suggestions: First, as the civil code is about private rights that involve the daily lives of the people, it should be well publicised to ensure that it attracts wide attention. That way, when the NPC Standing Committee deliberates the draft in the future and solicits public opinions, it can attract more public participation, ensuring the code reflects the people's wishes.

Second, as the civil code is an essential embodiment of the rule of law in a country, the formulation of the civil code has long been the cherished wish and pursuit of several generations of legislators in China. Since the founding of the PRC, many attempts have been made to compile it but failed, so to start again now is not easy. If it can be completed this time, it would have a considerable impact on the country's market economy and social life, and it is the unavoidable passage and an important milestone for realising the rule of law in China.

Listening to his emotional remarks, I realised that there were stories behind the codification of the civil code and that it touched the feelings of the legislators. If I could offer a good explanation, it would be of significance in increasing the public's understanding of and attention to this basic *Civil Law*. However, it was apparent that the talking points I received from the legal section fell short of this.

I discussed with my team how to formulate an answer to questions related to this issue and then tasked Huai Sheng to re-draft the main points. Due to the time limit of the press conference, he needed to keep it relatively short, ideally within 300 words. I also hoped that he could write it with passion. He was enthusiastic about the subject and readily accepted the challenge.

That night, I read more materials and comments on the subject and got to know the tortuous stories and the reasons behind China's civil code, which I will elaborate upon further in this chapter.

Early the next morning, there on my desk was the text that Huai Sheng had newly drafted, and although it was still a bit too long, it already had a moving tone. The following paragraphs are examples of this:

> *The civil code is the basic law in the field of civil affairs. Being people-oriented, it is related to the fundamental interests of every natural person and legal person[3]. The compilation of the civil code is of great significance in promoting the rule of law and advancing modern national governance. It will respond to the new challenges and problems encountered in China during its continued reform and opening up.*
>
> *The compilation of the civil code has been the wish of many generations of Chinese legislators. Since the founding of the PRC, the formulation of the civil code was launched four times, but has never been completed. Now that we have 30 years of experience in practicing the General Principles of Civil Law as well as practicing such separate civil laws as Contract Law, Property Law and Tort Liability Law, we are in a better position to move forward.*
>
> *After the civil code is compiled, it can better safeguard human dignity, better protect everyone's basic rights and lay a solid civil legal foundation for China's economic and social development.*

After reading these points, I became more confident and began to modify and compress the text, making it more conversational by adding some popular concepts. I asked legal experts to verify and check the accuracy of the wording and then submitted the key points to my colleagues within the Legislative Affairs Commission of the NPC Standing Committee for their review and approval.

By then, the new key points for an answer had become more mature. I took the time to memorise them and repeatedly practiced expressing them clearly in my own words. I also communicated with Shaoren, asking him to allow journalists interested in the civil code to ask questions.

At the press conference on 4 March 2016, when the journalist with *the Legal Evening News* asked about the civil code, I replied as follows:

Thank you for mentioning the civil code. It may not be very familiar to many people. I myself learned about it only after I started working with the NPC. For a country, the civil code is the basic law in civil affairs. Its essence is to protect private rights, that is, to allow citizens to have their problems resolved within the framework of law. That is why it is usually called "the encyclopaedia" of social life.

Compiling the civil code has been the wish of several generations of legislators in China. This is not the first time that the NPC has worked on it. It should be noted that since the founding of new China, there have been four attempts, the first time in 1954, and the last in 2002, all of which failed due to the absence of conditions needed for its completion. But you also need to know that our country has never stopped its efforts to build a civil law system. In recent years, we have formulated many individual civil laws like Contract Law, Property Law and Tort Liability Law.

In addition, the General Principles of Civil Law has been implemented for 30 years. In the decision of the 4th plenary session of the 18th CPC Central Committee, it was clearly proposed to strengthen the construction of the market law system and compile the civil code. This requirement is very clear, and I believe it also shows our Party's courage and determination to promote the rule of law comprehensively.

Now the work of compiling the civil code will start once again. This time we are determined to finish the job. In practice, there are two steps. The first is to formulate the General Provisions of Civil Law, and the second is to integrate and compile the individual civil laws. The General Provisions of Civil Law's draft for collecting public opinions has already been published, and comments are being solicited. Before this press conference, I checked and got to know that the draft Provisions is expected to be submitted to the NPC Standing Committee for deliberation in June.

This new version of the draft will also be open to the public during the Congress deliberation. We welcome your attention and suggestions. I'm confident that the completion of codification will better safeguard human dignity and better protect people's fundamental rights. It will lay a more solid civil legal foundation for the economic and social development of our country. Thank you.

(3 minutes 24 seconds, approximately 620 Chinese characters)

The main content of this answer came from the polished key points beforehand. Although it was impossible for me to memorise all of the text and keep to the sequence and sentence structure, I expressed the main points, as I was already very familiar with the core content. It did not matter if my wording was somewhat different from the prepared text. What mattered was to communicate the civil code's information and its significance to the public.

After the press conference in 2016, many news outlets reported on the civil code's codification, and a lot of netizens left comments to express their expectations. It was gratifying that senior legislators in the NPC standing committee also acknowledged my answer. I expressed passion on their behalf and made known the arduous efforts of Chinese legislators over the years. My team and I were all delighted that our work was recognised. In the small space of about 600 words, I provided all the necessary information and facts. I had also expressed enthusiasm so that people could realise the importance of the civil code for every Chinese and get to know the painstaking efforts and persistence of generations of Chinese legislators.

MY UNDERSTANDING OF THE CIVIL CODE

My study and understanding of the civil code began after I started with the NPC. I often listened to the legal experts in the NPC Standing Committee talking about it, drawing comparisons with the experiences in other countries. When it comes to the civil code, people in legal circles often refer to Napoleon, a successful general on the battlefield and a former emperor that was a controversial figure in history. Interestingly, he is most often remembered and acknowledged by later generations for the French Civil Code, which he championed more than 200 years ago.

In 1799, 10 years after the outbreak of the French Revolution, France was in the period of the First Republic. Napoleon launched the "Coup of 18 Brumaire" and became the First Consul of the Republic. The following year, he chose the candidates to form a committee, who drafted the civil code and submitted it to the legislature, which was deliberated hundreds of times. Napoleon himself participated many times in these discussions and revisions.

Finally, the first civil code in human history was adopted on 21 March 1804. With it, France completed its transformation from a feudal to a modern industrial and commercial country. To commemorate Napoleon's contribution, the French Civil Code of 1804 is also called the Napoleonic Code.

As an early bourgeois civil code, the French Civil Code of 1804 served the needs of a freely competitive economy and embodied the legislative spirit of "maximum individual freedom, minimum intervention of law." This spirit has a wide-ranging influence across the world.

Many countries, including Germany, Switzerland, Chile, Brazil and Japan, used the French Civil Code as a blueprint or for reference when compiling their own civil codes. Notably, after the second world war, when many countries realised national independence, there was a trend for building civil law systems. Civil laws serve as the record and expression of a country's social and economic life. They are also the combination of a nation's legal traditions and its belief and confidence in the rule of law. Civil laws play an important role in both the depth and breadth of a country's social and economic operations and therefore are the cornerstone of the legal system.

In modern times, the formulation or compilation of the civil code has been the fundamental project in the building of the rule of law in countries with codified laws.

The CPC and the Chinese people have long been pursuing a modern interpretation of the rule of law. After the founding of the PRC in 1949, attempts were made to formulate a civil code in 1954, 1962 and then in 1979, but failed to proceed due to the lack of proper conditions at the time, and the efforts were shelved. In 1986 the efforts restarted and instead of building a complete *civil law*, the *General Principles of Civil Law* were formulated, playing the role of a "mini-civil code."

In December 2002, a draft civil code was again submitted to the NPC Standing Committee for deliberation. However, there were still not sufficient conditions for codifying the complete *civil law* and there was a realisation we needed to shift efforts to first formulating separate individual laws that included the *Property Law* and *Tort Liability Law*. The idea was that a complete civil code would be made later after some practical experience with these individual laws and after further research on how to better codify the *civil law*.

There are reasons why the birth of the Chinese civil code has taken so many twists and turns. For example, civil code is the product of a market economy, therefore it can only be promoted after the reforms of the Chinese economic system are in place and have more or less matured.

Another reason is that the establishment of civil legal relations would require broad social consensus based on practical experience in social interactions. Only in this way can the formulated laws stand the test of time and be accepted by society. Moreover, the formulation of the civil code also needs a strong foundation of theoretical and practical preparedness.

At the 4th plenary session of the 18th CPC Central Committee, the goal of "building a socialist legal system with Chinese characteristics and a socialist country under the rule of law" was put forward, which called for "strengthening the construction of a market legal system and compilation of the civil code."

As the conditions for restarting the civil code's compilation have improved, the main task is to put together the existing civil laws and rearrange them into a proper structure. Of course, the related laws, regulations and judicial interpretations are complex and it is a big challenge to integrate them into a reasonable order. It is neither a simple compilation nor a creation of a new set of civil laws. It is also important to learn from foreign countries' useful legislative experience and reflect the needs of China's social and economic development based on China's national conditions and social reality.

During those five years working with the NPC, I witnessed the steady progress of the codification of the civil code. In March 2015, Chairman Zhang Dejiang of the NPC Standing Committee proposed in his speech at the 3rd session of the 12th NPC that we should study and compile the civil code. In April 2015, the 12th Standing Committee of the NPC adopted the adjusted five-year legislative plan, listing the compilation of the civil code as a

Category 1 project. Then in January 2016, the formulation of *General Provisions of Civil Law* was included in the legislative plan of the NPC Standing Committee. The Legislative Affairs Commission of the NPC Standing Committee established a coordination group, which comprised several ministries and agencies, and organised a special task force to carry out the codification work.

After more than a year of writing, revising and soliciting opinions, the drafting of the *General Provisions of Civil Law* was finally completed. In 2016, the NPC Standing Committee held three deliberations, publishing the draft each time on the NPC website for public comments. According to the statistics from the website, 70,227 items of opinions and suggestions were collected from 15,503 people, which helped consolidate the consensus among people from all walks of life.

According to Article 7 of China's *Legislative Law*, the NPC formulates and amends basic laws covering criminal and civil affairs, state organs and others. Accordingly, as a basic *civil law*, the *General Provisions of Civil Law* needed to be submitted to the NPC's plenary session for deliberation. This ensured that the draft was discussed more widely at the platform of the Congress, gathering social wisdom and seeking the "common denominator" in society. By doing so, the hope is to make this law as perfect as possible and effectively achieve the purpose of safeguarding people's civil rights.

On 8 March 2017, at the 2nd plenary meeting of the 5th session of the 12th NPC, Li Jianguo, Vice Chairman of the NPC Standing Committee, was entrusted by the NPC Standing Committee to explain the draft *General Provisions of Civil Law* and submit it to the deputies for deliberation.

The deputies attending the Congress deliberated on the draft at group meetings on 10 March, and the discussions were very warm, with deputies raising over 3,000 amendments. The Constitution and Law Committee of the NPC studied every suggestion and adopted them where possible before returning the revised draft to the deputies for further consideration. This workload was huge and when it was finally adopted there were 156 changes to the earlier draft.

As an example, a seemingly unimportant issue led to a heated debate. The question was: should the age for persons with limited capacity for civil conduct be maintained at 10 years of age, as stipulated in the *General Principles of Civil Law*, or should it be lowered to six in the draft *General Provisions of Civil Law*?

There was no conclusion on this issue when the NPC Standing Committee deliberated the draft. After it was submitted to the NPC deputies, there were still different views. Some deputies held that six-year-old children already have certain learning abilities and begin to receive compulsory education. Lowering the age to six was in line with China's current situation. Others argued that six-year-old children's cognitive and identification ability was still insufficient, and they did not yet have the full ability to conduct civil legal acts, so the age should still be set at 10 years of age.

Obviously, as China rapidly develops and changes, its laws and regulations should keep pace with its society's development. However, China has a large population and a vast territory, and conditions differ widely from place to place. The NPC deputies come from different places and therefore have diverse views. It is the essence of scientific legislation and democratic legislation to listen to and absorb different viewpoints. After further study, the Constitution and Law Committee suggested that the minimum age for persons with limited capacity for civil conduct be changed to eight years old, a compromise that reflected the various opinions and concerns of the deputies.

The number of articles in the *General Provisions of Civil Law* increased to 206 from 186 when it was first deliberated. This process reflected the principles of scientific and democratic legislation. As not only were the opinions of members of the NPC Standing Committee and the NPC deputies absorbed into the bill, but also the views, opinions and good suggestions from across all sections of society.

At the closing ceremony of the 5th session of the 12th NPC on 15 March 2017, the *General Provisions of Civil Law* of the PRC was adopted with a large majority of votes. After the session, President Xi Jinping signed Presidential Decree No. 66 to promulgate the law, which was to be implemented as of 1 October 2017.

In my discussions about China's political system with some

American scholars studying China, they are often dismissive of the role of the NPC. From their perspective, the NPC voting is purely a matter of formality as the NPC and its Standing Committee rarely veto any bill. From their perspective, it looks like only vetoes mean democracy.

However, the system in China works in a unique way. For example, the NPC has to go through a complicated consultation and consensus-building process before putting any bill to a vote. I often explain to foreigners how China's political system works. I would tell them how we formulate, deliberate and vote for bills. The NPC makes laws to meet the needs of the people and there is no self-interest. The legislators are willing to listen to suggestions and absorb any fair and reasonable opinions from the deputies and the general public.

Deputies are usually satisfied with the bills after repeated discussions and changes of the draft. So when they come to the voting, there is little reason not to vote for and accept the draft. This is also the case with the report on the government's work, which the Premier of the State Council delivers to the plenary meeting. The report is discussed by the NPC deputies and undergoes many revisions. The purpose of satisfying the deputies is to satisfy the people.

Of course, on some issues, the NPC deputies may have reservations and even opposition. When this is the case, they can choose to abstain or oppose in the voting. In some cases when there are too many people who disagree, that likely reflects the lack of social consensus. In such cases, the draft would be put on hold instead of hastily being pushed through for a vote. In short, in China's political system, state institutions are not antagonistic towards each other but strive for the common goal of serving the people.

MY TRANSFORMATION FROM A DIPLOMAT TO A LAWMAKER

All of my career had been in diplomacy, and like most citizens, I had limited knowledge and understanding of law. In my work as a diplomat, I had come to know some international legal instruments, which I found interesting. In my opinion, laws and mathematics have the similarities of being logical and having clear rules and boundaries. It is precisely because of this that we need to adopt a rigorous approach towards legal affairs.

From 2013 onwards, I served as chairman of the Foreign Affairs Committee of the NPC and a spokesperson during the annual NPC sessions. My new post required me to grasp some legal knowledge, meaning that I needed to become a student again. In order to adapt to my new position quickly, I asked some university professors for advice, who recommended me quite a few books on law. I also learned from the many legal experts working for the NPC. During the preparation of a press conference I would bring many issues to discuss with legal experts.

As a mature student, I realised that there was little possibility for me to acquire a vast knowledge of law and had to confine my studies within the sphere of my work, learning about relevant laws as I encountered them, and making progress slowly. In the early stage of my participation in the deliberations on legal bills in the NPC Standing Committee, I seldom spoke, as I was unfamiliar with what was being discussed. I would read the briefings and learn from other members' comments after the deliberations.

I also often read the comments from the public on legal bills posted on the internet. For example, when the NPC Standing Committee deliberated on the draft law against domestic violence, I learned a lot about the significance of this law from the debate on the internet and came to understand the difficulties that existed in establishing the boundary between state power and private rights under China's national conditions.

Another example was the draft amendment to the *Legislation Law* which was submitted to the 3rd session of the 12th NPC for deliberation in March 2015. The content relating to "statutory taxation" was one of the main areas of public attention. The draft amendment listed separately the exclusive legislative power of "taxation" and stipulated that "the basic system for the collection, suspension and management of taxes" could only be formulated by law, that is, "statutory taxation."

The amended *Legislation Law* takes "taxation" as the sixth item of Article 8. It requires that the basic taxation system, which includes the establishment of tax categories, the determination of tax rates, and tax collection management, must be formulated by law. At the time, there was a lot of discussion on this issue among the general public. I often asked Mr Hao Ruyu, a Vice Chairman of the NPC Financial and Economic Affairs Committee, for his advice on some difficult issues. He kindly explained every time and even hand-wrote two pages about the importance and significance of the principle of statutory taxation and the long path China took to move towards this goal. He was retiring and felt satisfied to see that what he and his generation of professionals had worked hard for was being achieved.

In his opinion, in the early 1980s, when the NPC authorised the State Council to formulate tax laws and regulations, it was for the sake of making more room for reform. Now with the growth of the Chinese market, it is time that taxation legislation be returned to the NPC to implement the principle of statutory taxation. He said that he had been writing and calling for this, and was happy to see it become a reality. The persistence of this senior legislator is admirable. In the NPC Standing Committee, there are many legislators like Mr Hao Ruyu, who keep to professional principles and hold a firm belief in the ideal of the rule of law.

As I gradually became familiar with the legislative work, I could also apply international vision to the legislative work. On 31 October 2016, when the NPC Standing Committee held the second deliberation on the *Law on Protection of Public Cultural Services*, I proposed to add an international perspective.

In my comment, I said that Chinese culture has a long history, and it is inclusive and always effective at absorbing the advantages of other cultures. The development of modern Chinese culture should also be open, and this law should have an "international perspective." Nowadays, all walks of Chinese life are closely connected with the outside world. More and more foreigners are working in China, and they also need to abide by Chinese laws. At the same time, China is also playing a growing role in the world and has increasingly attracted attention from the international community. Domestic legislation needs to take these factors into account.

I suggested adding into the draft "developing and strengthening international exchanges and cooperation in the field of public culture." In practice, there had already been many cases of international cooperation, as many Chinese museums and art galleries had undertaken exchanges with their foreign counterparts, and it should be affirmed in the legislation. My proposal was accepted and in Article 12 of the Law on the *Protection of Public Cultural Services*, it reads as follows: "The State encourages and supports international cooperation and exchanges in the field of public cultural services. This law was put into effect on 1 March 2017."

Participating in legislation improved my legal knowledge and understanding of how China's legislative bodies function. The Foreign Affairs Committee is one of the NPC's nine standing special committees (hereinafter referred to as the special committees). Each special committee carries out its daily work related to the legislation and supervision of its particular areas. The special committees are under the leadership of the NPC and its Standing Committee when it is not in session.

The Standing Committee is a permanent organ of the NPC which holds a plenary session in March every year. When the Congress is not in session, its Standing Committee exercises the state's supreme power. This includes interpreting the Constitution and laws, supervising the implementation of the Constitution, and formulating and amending laws, except those that must be submitted to the plenary session of the NPC. Additionally, it supervises the work of the State Council, the Supreme People's Court and the Supreme People's Procuratorate.

Usually, the NPC Standing Committee holds a bimonthly week-long meeting. The agenda includes a plenary meeting to listen to reports and group sessions for discussion. The composition of each group is diverse, and the group members will rotate every six months. This arrangement allows for a lively exchange of views and sharing of ideas.

During the NPC Standing Committee sessions, some NPC

deputies are invited to attend as non-voting participants, enabling them to join the deliberation and express their opinions on the issues under review. This arrangement allows more people with broad professional skills to take part in the deliberations which can better represent the diversity of interests in society.

The NPC Standing Committee has about 170 members who come from different fields and positions. For example, some have served as provincial Party secretary or governor, while others may have been head of a ministry or commission under the State Council. There are also generals retired from the People's Liberation Army (PLA). It has many experts from diverse fields such as law, science, education and agriculture, heads of corporations, leading figures from democratic parties, religious leaders and members from Hong Kong and Macao.

Each member of the Standing Committee has his or her own professional background and practical experience. The deliberation is often frank and warm, not without differences and debate. From their different perspectives, the members put forward their opinions and suggestions on the formulation, modification and improvement of laws. They contribute their wisdom, enlighten each other, and find the basis for consensus. The existence of different voices is conducive to absorbing and reflecting the diverse opinions of society as comprehensively as possible. These differing voices also ensure that we avoid neglecting problems or certain groups' interests.

Although we still have a lot to improve, as long as we always put people's interests first, we can continuously improve our work and bring into full play the unique advantages of the NPC system.

As my familiarity with the legislative work grew, I talked more confidently about the law and its content in press conferences and felt more comfortable using legal terms. According to my count, of the questions from 67 journalists I answered in the five press conferences in five years, 36 were related to laws, and I mentioned more than 80 laws.

This learning process gave me a sense of enrichment and a better understanding of the important role the legislature has in China's modern state governance, as I gradually transformed from a diplomat into a lawmaker. Of course, compared with those legislators who have long been working hard on the front line of legislation, I am still a freshman. Their persistence in serving the people, the country and the rule of law is something that I admire and want to learn.

SMOG IS A "MUST-ANSWER" QUESTION

During each NPC press conference in the five years from 2013 to 2017, I had to face questions about the smog and environmental pollution issue. In my meetings with representatives of the domestic media before the annual press conference, almost everybody expressed concern about the smog hanging over Chinese cities. They wanted to know the causes, i.e., what role vehicle exhaust emissions played in creating the smog. They wanted to know how to prevent and manage it, what was the impact on people's health, what the public could do to reduce the harm, and when we could get rid of it. I knew that these were the questions their audience and the public in general wanted to know.

Entering the winter of 2016, there were two long periods of heavy-smog days. The first was from 16 to 21 December. Tianjin, Hebei, Shandong, Henan and other provinces saw a wide range of heavy air pollution, and Beijing witnessed heavy-and-above air pollution. The Beijing municipal government issued a red warning of serious air pollution and adopted a series of measures, such as the odd-and-even number-plate restrictions on motor vehicles and the suspension of attendance at primary schools and kindergartens.

Such hazy weather threatened people's health, affected their way of life and depressed the mood in society. Then starting from 30 December 2016, through to the New Year holidays, an orange warning of heavy air pollution lasted for 212 hours, or nine consecutive days. It was not until 8 January 2017 that Beijing saw the first blue sky of the new year.

It was not surprising that smog management was raised again at the press conference of the NPC on 4 March 2017. The question came from a journalist with the *People's Daily*. He asked:

"Smog control is a problem that everyone has been concerned about over recent years. We know that the newly amended *Air*

Pollution Prevention and Control Law took effect as of 1 January 2016. Last year, the NPC also carried out a law enforcement inspection of the *Environmental Protection Law*. May I ask what moves the NPC will take this year on environmental protection? How will it promote solution of the problem? Thank you."

In response to the question, I began in a sentimental tone by saying:

> *"This year is my fifth press conference, and I know what questions the Chinese and foreign correspondents care about the most. The first question from a foreign journalist is usually about China's military expenditure. The must-ask question for the domestic media is about the environment. The Chinese media pays attention to the environment year by year and we respond to this problem year by year. We all work hard on it every year."*

Indeed, the Party Central Committee, the NPC and its Standing Committee, and the State Council stand with the people on this issue. As NPC spokesperson, I must respond in earnest to outstanding issues of people's concern, even if it has been raised for five consecutive years.

At the press conference in 2013, I was first asked about smog and environmental protection. At that time, I had limited knowledge and understanding of the issue, but I felt the same as everyone else. I said:

> *"Every morning, I open the curtains at home to see if there is smog. There are two masks at home, one for my daughter and one for myself."*

The reason for saying that was to acknowledge the existence of the problem and express empathy, I also wanted to express the belief that we must face up to the problem together.

It has to be admitted that China paid an enormous price in terms of environmental pollution following many years of high-speed development. However, work on the relevant legislation was never relaxed. Over 30 laws relating to environmental protection were formulated, forming a sound basic legal framework. Yet, the operability of the laws and the actual implementation fell short of public expectation.

To reflect that dissatisfaction, at the 1st session of the 12th NPC held from 5 to 16 March 2013, when voting on the composition of the NPC's Environmental Protection and Resources Conservation Committee (EPRCC), the "Yes" vote was the lowest among the nine special committees, with 850 deputies voting against it while 125 abstained, which was rare in NPC voting. The deputies clearly expressed the feelings of the general public.

Nevertheless, according to the law, since more than half of the deputies voted to agree with the composition of the EPRCC, the committee members were approved, and Mr Lu Hao was elected as chairman of the EPRCC. But it was unnerving for many of us sitting there watching the voting process, noting that as many as a third of the 2,987 deputies did not vote in favour of the committee's composition.

The committee's main task is to assist the NPC and its Standing Committee to carry out legislation and oversee the prevention and control of environmental pollution, ecological environment protection and natural resources protection. At the time, the 12th NPC had just been formed, and the members of the new EPRCC had not yet begun to perform their duties. Therefore, the "No" votes and abstentions may not have been targeted at Lu Hao and his team. It was more likely an expression of dissatisfaction with the current situation, and higher expectations and requirements. The new members of the committee understood the signal. On the morning of 17 March 2013, two days after the closing of the session, the EPRCC held its first plenary meeting to discuss how to respond to the demand of the people, making it the first of the NPC committees to start carrying out its duties.

Chairman Lu Hao addressed the meeting candidly:

"Many NPC deputies voted No or abstained in the voting on our committee, which shows they are highly concerned and have high expectations of our work. This is a spur for the new EPRCC to do a good job. Strengthening the protection of the environment and resources, and vigorously promoting ecological civilisation is a serious task for the country. Since it impacts the living conditions of people, it has become one of the hottest issues of our society."

"China has increasingly invested in environmental protection and has achieved some results in reducing and controlling the discharge of major pollutants. However, the overall deterioration has not been curbed, pollution emergencies occur frequently and incidences of environmentally triggered mass protests are increasing.

Furthermore, water shortages and pollution have not been alleviated. There are more than 80 million people in rural areas living with unsafe drinking water. Air quality has deteriorated, and the probability of smog days in some big cities is rising. In some areas, the increasing trend of soil pollution is more evident. The quality of our ecological environment is seriously degraded, and soil erosion, grassland degradation and wetland reduction are very prominent. Behind the environmental problems is the excessive consumption of resources which increases environmental pollution and significantly depletes resources.

Serious environmental pollution is posing a significant challenge and the issue has become a bottleneck that seriously affects China's sustainable development. "

On 24 May 2013, General Secretary Xi Jinping presided over the sixth collective study of the Political Bureau of the Central Committee of the CPC[4]. On this occasion, he said:

"We should have a clear understanding of the urgency and arduousness of protecting the ecological environment, harnessing environmental pollution and the importance and necessity of strengthening the cultivation of ecological civilisation. By taking responsibility for the people and future generations, and earnestly resolving to treat environmental pollution and successfully building our ecological environment, we strive to move towards a new era of socialist ecological civilisation and create a good environment for the life and work of the people. Only the strictest system and the most stringent rule of law can guarantee the cultivation of ecological civilisation."

System building and the rule of law were the direction that General Secretary Xi Jinping set for us. I noticed that Chairman Lu Hao was under tremendous pressure. Every time I met him in meetings or in the cafeteria, I saw him frowning and looking heavy-hearted, as if he had something on his mind. Over the five years, I would often bring questions to him which I had difficulty understanding with regard to environmental legislation. He would be happy to help. When I asked about progress, he rarely mentioned any achievements and preferred to talk about the seriousness of the challenges and the urgency of solving the problems. Even if there were blue skies, he would attribute it to the wind blowing away the smog.

At the press conference in March 2016, when I was asked about the smog issue, I said: "*The chairman of the EPRCC seldom smiles. I think he is under "mountainous pressure (Ya Li Shan Da [5])"* , which I genuinely believe. From its establishment, the 12th NPC and its Standing Committee had a profound understanding of the seriousness of China's environmental situation. And they made the legislation and supervision concerning environmental and resource protection their top priority. The focus was to develop a structured environmental and resource protection system based on the rule of law. We would use the saying, "like hammering a nail", be firm and persistent in terms of making and amending laws, formulating practical provisions and ensuring operability of the legal provisions.

The *Environmental Protection Law of the PRC* which, for 25 years constituted the basic law in this area, was comprehensively revised on 24 April 2014. In addition, a new law on environmental protection tax was made ’ and such laws as the *Marine Environment Protection Law* and the *Water Pollution Prevention and Control Law* were amended to fit the new needs.

Greater attention was also paid to strengthening supervision on the implementation of laws, ensuring that they were strictly applied. In doing so, the efforts in making laws and supervising the implementation of laws became mutually promoting and reinforcing, forming a virtuous circle.

In those years, the NPC Standing Committee sent a number of teams to carry out law enforcement inspections as well as to do special research on the relative laws including *Renewable Energy Law*, *Meteorological Law*, *Air Pollution Prevention and Control Law*, *Water Pollution Prevention and Control Law*, *Water Law*, and *Law on Prevention and Control of Environmental Pollution by Solid Waste*. It has established a system to consult and deliberate the State Council's annual report on environmental issues and on whether the objectives were attained. It also deliberated several work reports by various units on the development of ecological civilisation.

All in all, these efforts shaped the answers of the NPC and its Standing Committee to the public's must-answer questions.

It should be said that during its five-year term, the 12th NPC and its Standing Committee have done their part in this area at a critical stage in history.

Therefore, at the press conference on 4 March 2017, a journalist from *People's Daily* raised the question: as "smog treatment has been among the top concerns of the general public in recent years, the newly revised *Atmospheric Pollution Prevention and Control Law of the PRC* formally came into force on 1 January 2016. Last year the NPC conducted law enforcement inspection of the *Environmental Protection Law*. What efforts will the NPC make this year to treat environmental protection?"

My reply to the question continued as follows:

Indeed, managing pollution is a long-term challenge for our country. From the NPC's perspective, we should continuously improve the legal system on environmental protection and supervise the laws' effective implementation and enforcement. Last year, we carried out law enforcement inspections of the newly revised Environmental Protection Law. The problems we found included the inadequate application of responsibilities, inadequate supervision of law enforcement, and incomplete supporting laws and regulations. The NPC Standing Committee set requirements for rectification. In April this year, it will listen to the feedback report.

Over the past four years, the CPC Central Committee and the State Council have attached great importance to this issue, taken a series of robust measures and made many solid efforts. We have carried out law enforcement inspections for four consecutive years. We have also comprehensively revised the

Air Pollution Prevention and Control Law and the Environmental Protection Law.

In addition, we now have set a rule to hear the State Council's report once a year on the state of the environment and the attainment of policy goals. On the whole, we should say that many efforts have been made over recent years by both central and local governments, by enterprises and by all sectors of society, and they have been put into effect. But there is still a big gap in meeting people's expectations and the pollution has been quite severe this winter. We need to work harder and strive to achieve a better outcome.

In addition, water and soil pollution is also getting serious in some areas. The NPC Standing Committee is speeding up the pace of work on the revision of the Law on Prevention and Control of Water Pollution and the formulation of the Law on Prevention and Control of Soil Pollution, and we welcome opinions and suggestions from the public. Thank you.

(It took 3 minutes 21 seconds and 460 Chinese characters to respond to this question)

My answer for the fifth time on the smog and environment was still far from forming a "full stop" on this issue, it was merely a "semicolon". I expect that it will remain a hot topic for the next spokesperson, or even the one after next.

The people yearn for a good life, including a more beautiful environment. As long as the people's demands are not met, our efforts must continue.

SOME THOUGHTS ON ENVIRONMENTAL PROTECTION

First point:

How to look at the balance between the environment and development.

During the past 30 years of rapid development through reforms and opening up, for a long time people thought that the contradiction between the environment and development was unsolvable. Protecting the environment would restrict development and enhanced development would inevitably damage the environment. Thus, the two were mutually opposed. Development meant the growth of gross domestic product (GDP), and people could achieve happy lives only when economic development was good.

If there was a choice between the two, development was often prioritised and the environment was given little or no attention. I once visited a remote city in Northern China and saw a paper mill that had been moved and rebuilt there after becoming outdated in Southern China. The mill became a significant source of income for the city, but was causing serious river pollution. The local people were worried about the pollution but cared more about the economic benefits brought about by the paper mill.

Things have started to change in recent years. As President Xi Jinping said: "clear waters and lush mountains are invaluable assets[6]"; "The kind of mentality of caring for money more than for life, of polluting first and treating later or of destroying before constructing, should no longer be encouraged[7]."

In light of the CPC Central Committee's policy requirements and witnessing the deterioration of the ecological environment, more and more people realise that development and the environment are mutually indispensable. Protecting the environment is not only necessary for development but is also a precondition for development. Only with a well protected environment can development be sustained.

Since its 18th National Congress, the CPC has put forward a series of new ideas, new concepts and new strategies to construct ecological civilisation which was championed as an essential part of the overall plan for promoting all-round economic, political, cultural, social and ecological progress. It also put forward the five development concepts of "innovation, coordination, green development, opening up and sharing," which attached importance to a sustainable development path featuring increased production, good life and good ecology.

General Secretary Xi Jinping has issued a total of over 200 important instructions around the issue of environmental protection over the years. Premier Li Keqiang proposed in his 2014 government work report that "we should resolutely declare war on pollution as we have done on poverty."

In 2015, the CPC Central Committee and the State Council jointly publicised a document under the title of *Opinions on Accelerating the Construction of Ecological Civilisation*, which laid out a comprehensive plan to achieve its goal. It followed the planning done at the 18th CPC National Congress and the 3rd and 4th plenary sessions of the 18th CPC Central Committee.

For years the Party Central Committee and the State Council demonstrated strong determination and took firm action in resolving outstanding environmental problems.

Second point:

As consensus has grown among the public on the importance, arduousness and long-term nature of environmental management, there is also greater awareness of the need to persevere in solving the outstanding problems. The severe pollution accumulated in the past decades has turned into a chronic disease, and this takes time to overcome.

Observing the experience in the Western developed countries, it took decades, even over a hundred years, to treat pollution caused during industrialisation. When I was studying in the UK in the 1980s, I saw that the dark appearance of many churches and buildings was being gradually cleaned. They shone under the sunlight as the bright and beautifully coloured granite and sandstone was revealed. Many years later when I was in London, I noticed that the cleaning work was still going on.

As the records show, the River Thames and other significant rivers in Britain became polluted in the 19th century, a state of affairs that continued until the latter part of the 20th century. Fish and birds disappeared from the rivers, and the water quality deteriorated to the extent that in London in the 1850s, the River Thames was known as the "Great Stink". The British Parliament passed many laws, some to resolve particular local issues and others intended to manage larger and more widespread challenges, in their determination to comprehensively address and repair the environmental damage. However, it took over a hundred years to revive Britain's most famous river.

In a country as vast and economically large as ours, there are many differences and complexities that can be seen in the different areas. On top of focused efforts on some particular problems for quick results, we should also be prepared to fight a protracted struggle to achieve a comprehensive outcome. As Premier Li Keqiang once said: "To solve ecological environmental problems, action is most important, and perseverance is the key to success."

Professor Chen Jining was a member of the Standing Committee of the 12th NPC and the President of Tsinghua University. He is an expert in environmental engineering and, for some time, we were in the same deliberation group of the NPC Standing Committee. I often discussed difficult environmental issues with him and benefited from his professional knowledge and pragmatic approach. I would also share my articles with him and listen to his opinions.

He became Minister of Environmental Protection in 2015 and would readily accept invitations to attend the NPC sessions press conference every year. He had a frank attitude and was well received by the public. From his press conference one could not only learn about policies, ideas and professional knowledge, but also get an insight into the fruitful work carried out by his Ministry. He later became the mayor of Beijing in 2018.

At his press conference at the 12th NPC in 2017, Chen Jining, in the capacity of the Minister of Environmental Protection, said: "The average concentration of PM2.5 in Beijing in 2016 was 73µg /m³, down 18% from 2013; in 2016, the average concentration of PM2.5 in the Beijing-Tianjin-Hebei area, the Yangtze River Delta and Pearl River Delta was measured at 71µg/m³, 46µg/ m³ and 32µg /m³, down by 33.0%, 31.3% and 31.9% respectively, against the figures in 2013; in 2016, the average concentration of PM2.5 in 74 key cities was 50µg/m³, 30.6% lower than in 2013."

From this set of data one can see impressive improvements in addressing the smog problem that has been a common concern throughout society. I think it resulted from the joint efforts of the NPC, the State Council and all sectors of society under the leadership of the CPC Central Committee. Many citizens in Beijing, including myself, are pleased to see the increased numbers of excellent-air-quality days in Beijing and thankful that there is a gradual decrease in the frequency of heavily polluted days.

We should recognise that such progress within just a few years is remarkable. Of course, there is still a long way to go and we should not relax our efforts. It is also important to pay attention to the interests of various sectors impacted by pollution control measures. But as long as we work hard and persevere, we will be able to make progress. Finally, as I have said to every journalist that has raised the environmental issue, we need to have the confidence that we can do it!

I remember hearing from a young female reporter at discussions with domestic media in January 2017, who spoke with great emotion: "My baby was born last year. Some experts said that it would take 30 years to solve the smog problem. That's very depressing. Must our children grow up in such a bad environment?"

I told her we should have confidence. Where does the confidence come from? First, we should have confidence in our socialist system with Chinese characteristics. It has unique strengths and advantages in gathering the will power and capacity to solve tough problems under the leadership of the CPC. What the people want is the direction in which the Party and the government will direct their efforts. As long as the direction is clear, we will be able to mobilise the resources in science, technology and manpower, and effectively move into action.

Secondly, we should have confidence in the legislation, enforcement and supervision mechanism for environmental protection and society should support its operations and accountability.

Lastly, we should have confidence in the shared aspiration and will of the 1.37 billion Chinese people. We all want to see the country once again have blue skies, clear rivers, and understand that we are not only entitled to enjoy the environment, but also obliged to protect it. With our desire and actions, we will achieve a greener, healthier development and lifestyle that will benefit both China and the planet as a whole.

2

THE NATIONAL DEFENCE BUDGET, PERSONAL INFORMATION PROTECTION AND ANTI-CORRUPTION

HAS CHINA CAUSED ANY WAR OR CHAOS IN THE WORLD?

At 11:14 am on 4 March 2017, the press conference continued with a question from a CNN journalist:

"I'm with CNN. Let me ask the 'must-answer' question. As we know, China's military power has been growing in recent years. From the building of aircraft carriers and the construction and military deployments on the islands and reefs in the South China Sea, to the renewal of weapons and equipment, all have attracted the attention of countries around the world, including the United States. As the territorial disputes between China and some neighbouring countries have not yet been resolved, the growth of China's military power has made many countries wary and alert. My question is, how much will China spend on its military this year, and how much will it increase? In the case of slowing economic growth, what is the reason for the relatively high growth in military expenditure? Has it anything to do with President Trump's recent announcement of a significant increase in US military spending? Thank you."

The CNN journalist used "must-answer" to describe his question about China's national defence budget's growth rate, which brought a burst of laughter in the Briefing Room. We all knew he was referring to and making fun of my earlier remarks that "the national defence budget is the must-answer question for me raised by foreign journalists at the NPC press conference." Indeed, even before I became the NPC spokesperson, there seemed to be this tacit understanding among successive spokespersons and foreign journalists in Beijing. The number one issue that foreign journalists were concerned about was China's defence budget. It was the same every year and the first foreign journalist that got the chance to ask questions was bound to raise the issue of the growth rate of China's defence budget.

The Western media have a longstanding sense of threat and vigilance regarding China, which I felt as soon as I started preparing my first press conference back in 2013. During discussions with foreign journalists in Beijing, I found that their top concern for the NPC press conference was when they could get the budget data for China's national defence expenditure.

According to the agenda, the first item after the opening of the NPC session on the morning of 5 March 2013 was the Premier's report on the government's work. In the afternoon, the draft report on the central and local governments' budget would be submitted to the NPC deputies for deliberation. This also includes the national defence budget. As the press conference was held on the morning of 4 March, a day before the opening of the NPC session, the foreign journalists wanted to get the data in advance at the press conference.

In fact, some foreign journalists got into the routine of presenting the "China Threat". They would have drafted the article according to what was on their mind about the "threat" and waited for the defence budget figures. As soon as they got the figure at the press conference, they would quickly "fill in the blanks" and grab the headlines. This was why foreign media journalists, especially Western journalists, were so keen to have the opportunity to ask about the military budget and get the data early.

SHOULD I GIVE THE DEFENCE BUDGET DATA EARLY TO THE JOURNALISTS?

One problem was that I would be jumping the gun if I, the NPC session spokesperson, released specific budget data one day before the NPC deputies had received the draft report. After consulting some colleagues, I decided not to share the specific defence budget data at the press conference.

When I did the NPC press conference for the first time on 4 March 2013, a Reuters journalist asked a direct question: how large is China's defence spending and how big is the growth rate? In my response, I focused on China's national defence policy and defence development and avoided providing specific figures for the defence budget.

The next day, on 5 March 2013, the first session of the 12th NPC opened. That afternoon, the 2013 budget report was submitted to the NPC deputies and released to the public and media at the same time. As a result, on 6 March 2013 many international media headlines on China focused on Chinese military development. The more important information coming out of the Premier's government work report was given less coverage.

Afterwards, I tried to find out why through discussions with some foreign journalists. It seemed there was an appetite among Western readers for stories on the rise of the strength of China's defence and such reporting had a market. Much of the foreign media felt obliged to fulfil this need instead of reporting about how China dealt with domestic issues. Therefore, as soon as China's national defence budget became available, the journalists would use it to prove their points regarding the China Threat. Another reason was that even though foreign journalists could receive the government work report on 5 March, they had difficulties when it came to quickly digesting the vast amount of information in it, so it was easier to latch onto the burning issue of military spending.

News communication is a two-way game. The key is to find the balancing point between what information we want to disseminate and what the media want to report. We need to not only release sufficient information effectively but also be aware of the media and public interest, and try to make sure that what we release can interest the public and is also what they need to know.

I reconsidered and discussed with my colleagues again about when and how to release the national defence expenditure budget. We concluded that in order to avoid the intensive reporting on the defence budget by the foreign media that had occurred on the same day the government work report was delivered, it was better to provide the data earlier; however, considering the procedural restrictions, we could not provide specific data. Therefore, it would be appropriate to give an approximate figure of the national defence budget at my press conference.

From the experience of the past two press conferences, I decided to make some adjustments in 2015. In that year, the actual defence budget increased by 10.1%. At my press conference on 4 March, I gave the media the figure of "about 10%" after consultation and receiving permission. This, though not the exact budget figure, was enough to meet the foreign media's needs to acquire China's defence budget data. This would also help avoid the exposure of the data the next day overshadowing the media's attention on the Premier's government work report when the NPC formally opened on 5 March. This approach proved to be successful and has become the normal practice.

In addition, I worked on how to assist foreign journalists in reporting on the government work report. Before the opening of the NPC session, I invited foreign journalists to meet a representative from the Research Office of the State Council to explain the structure and the routine basic content of the government work report. I would also invite experts to talk about China's economic and financial situation. The Information Office of the State Council held press conferences before the NPC session, inviting officials from government departments to explain various aspects of China's economic and social development. As soon as the Premier had made his report, officials were on hand to interpret the contents of the report for the journalists. The Premier's office also started to release sheets of facts and figures together with the report to help journalists grasp the core information in the report.

These efforts facilitated and improved the media's

understanding and coverage of the NPC sessions and the Premier's government work report.

THAT QUESTION ON THE 2017 NATIONAL DEFENCE BUDGET

Before the "two sessions" in 2017, some of the international media had been speculating that China would substantially increase its defence budget. The reasoning behind this was that Donald Trump, the new President of the United States, had stressed in his speech at the end of February 2017 that the focus of the US budget in the new fiscal year was military, security and economic growth. He said he would ask the US Congress to substantially increase the defence budget by about 10% while at the same time cutting spending on non-defence areas and reducing foreign aid.

It was speculated that in order to cope with the changes in the US defence budget, China would make corresponding adjustments and increase its defence spending. How much China was going to increase it by was something people were waiting to see. This was based on the idea of pitching China and the United States against each other in terms of arms development. The reality is that China's national defence development has its own logic and path. In 2017, China's defence budget growth rate was 7%, slightly less than the 7.6% growth in 2016. This was the second year of single-digit growth for defence spending, following double-digit annual growth from 2011 to 2015, and it now accounted for 1.3% of China's GDP.

The formulation of China's defence budget is based on two main factors, first, on the need for defence development and, second, on the level of national economic development. During peacetime, China's defence budget increase has been basically in compatibility with the increase of the central government's budget and would not deviate much from it.

At the 2017 press conference, the CNN journalist's question not only touched on China's defence budget but also suggested many other possible reasons for the budget increase. For example, he referred to China's building of aircraft carriers, upgrading armaments, the South China Sea issue and territorial disputes, reflecting the Americans' concerns.

When facing a complex question, the spokesperson needs to avoid trying to respond to every detail in the question. Otherwise, you will sound defensive or as though you are lacking in confidence when the reality is that it is quite unlikely that nothing will be missed out. So it is much better to quickly zero in on the crux of the question and judge whether it is reasonable. If not, you can directly question the rationality of the question, which would make the associated questions irrelevant. Otherwise, you need to find a proper entry point which can smoothly lead your response to the prepared information.

My reply to the CNN journalist was:

The Chinese government determines the scale of annual defence expenditure according to the needs of national defence and the level of national economic growth. In 2017, the growth rate of China's defence expenditure is about 7%, accounting for about 1.3% of GDP, which is similar to previous years. I got these figures from the Ministry of Finance. You just mentioned that the US would want to increase its military spending, which is already very large. Last month I went to attend the Munich Security Conference where I learned that NATO was requesting member countries to raise their defence spending to 2% of GDP. I don't know how you would evaluate this trend, and whether you will also ask those countries why they are doing so.

When you raise concerns about China's defence budget, many people in China don't understand why. In recent decades, there have been many conflicts, even wars in the world that have resulted in huge casualties, property losses and displaced refugees. Which one of them has been caused by China? China has never done any harm to other countries. You mentioned concerns about disputes over territorial sovereignty and maritime rights, and interests around China. We advocate dialogue and peaceful settlement. At the same time, we need to have the ability to defend the country's sovereignty, rights and interests. In particular, as you have noticed, we really need to prevent external forces from getting involved in these differences. The enhancement of China's capabilities is conducive to maintaining peace and security in the region, not the contrary. Now on the disputes, the recent trend is obvious. China and some ASEAN countries have returned to the path of dialogue and negotiation, and the South

China Sea situation is tending to ease. How the situation develops in the future depends on the intentions of the United States. The activities of the United States in the South China Sea have the significance of a weather vane.

As for the South China Sea issue, I think it is misleading to talk about navigational safety in the South China Sea. In July last year, I visited the UK and talked about this issue. A legal expert in my team specially checked Lloyds of London's information in the UK, which showed that the South China Sea was not listed as a high-risk area. And there was no data showing any large international insurance company increasing its premiums for ships passing through the South China Sea. So, what is the basis for concern over the safety of navigation in the South China Sea?

We also found in a Reuters survey that some shipping companies regarded China's presence in the region as conducive to security there. So, fundamentally, the United States is worried about China catching up or surpassing it in terms of capability. I don't know if you agree with me or not on this point. In fact, China is a developing country and there is a large gap between it and the US in terms of capability. As for China's military development, it will continue, as it is required for the safeguarding of national sovereignty and security.

Whether two military powers present a threat to each other and whether they need to be on guard against each other, all depends on their strategic intentions. This is a crucial issue that needs to be seriously discussed. That is to say, are they pursuing common security or exclusive security? As President Xi Jinping has advocated, China proposes to safeguard common security, which is also the common understanding of many Asian countries. Thank you."

(4 minutes 49 seconds, approximately 940 Chinese characters)

This reply, especially the points on the growth rate of national defence expenditure and the points regarding the South China Sea issue, were widely reported at home and abroad. Let me elaborate a bit more about what I was thinking and how I constructed the answer:

Although the CNN journalist's question was critical, and even sounded offensive, I chose to calmly give general information about China's defence budget. I then mentioned the proportion of GDP that defence spending constitutes to dispel the CNN journalist's pre-set narrative. The key point in the response was about who was the real threat to the world: *"so many conflicts, even wars in the world that have resulted in huge casualties, property losses and displaced refugees. Which one of them has been caused by China?"*. This question put the United States in a questionable position. By turning my position from passive to active, I was able to credibly share my other messages.

I was quite familiar with the facts and figures about China's policies and positions regarding its neighbourhood as well as issues related to the South China Sea, and talked about such issues a lot in international forums. Therefore, as soon as I established my footing, I could easily turn to my views, supporting my points with factual data. I then concluded by returning to the concept of common security, as advocated by China.

When foreign correspondents ask questions, they tend to express doubt and criticise. I sometimes feel uncomfortable and puzzled. Why do they always try to put China on the defensive? Has China done anything harmful to the world for its own benefit?

Over the years since the Cold War, the United States and its allies have repeatedly used force, bringing irreparable damage to the countries concerned. How can they still take the moral high ground and question other countries? In discussions with my team, they all shared similar feelings of indignation. I believed that the Chinese public watching on television would feel the same. But the challenge when confronting aggressive questions from foreign journalists during such solemn occasions as the NPC press conference, is how to convince the world through reasoning while, at the same time, expressing the feelings of the Chinese people?

I would ponder such difficulties when taking a walk, imagining some subjects of debate and the possible angles of questions and then formulating my response. One of my experiences is that, in the face of a challenging question, an effective way to respond is to counter with another question, especially if the question is obviously provocative. But generally speaking, for a spokesperson to be convincing, you need to have sufficient information and knowledge about the issue you are talking about, knowing not only the facts but also the reasons behind them.

CHINA'S NATIONAL DEFENCE SPENDING

For quite a long time during the Cold War, China's national defence spending maintained a relatively high growth rate because, on the one hand, China was confronting "American imperialism" and, on the other, it was threatened by pressure from the "hegemonism" of the Soviet Union which deployed large military forces on China's borders.

Towards the end of the Cold War, China started its reform and opening up, its relationship with the major countries warmed, and its international relations generally improved. In May 1984, Deng Xiaoping made an examination of the world situation and stated: among the many problems in the world, two are most prominent; one is the issue of peace and the other is the North/South divide – meaning the issue of development.

The 13th National Congress of the CPC confirmed the view that peace and development were the "two major themes" of the world at the time. During those years, in order to focus on the needs of reform and opening up, expenditure on developing national defence gave way to the huge spending needs of economic development. The proportion of defence spending in the national budget decreased from 17.37% in 1978 to 10.63% in 1984. Consequently, national defence expenditure as a proportion of GDP fell from 4.6% in 1978 to 2.13% in 1984.

In 1978, China's national defence expenditure was 16.8 billion yuan, rising to 19.2 billion yuan in 1985, an increase of only 2.4 billion yuan in eight years, with an average annual growth rate of 1.78%. With the continuous growth of China's GDP, the proportion spent on national defence continued to decline, falling to a low of 1.01% in 1996.

Some scholars regard the years between 1986 and 1998 as the "endurance period" for the Chinese military. During this period, annual national defence expenditure was only enough to meet the military's basic needs but not enough to replace outdated defence equipment on a timely basis. In the 1990s, when visiting some military units in the provinces, I saw many of them supplementing their needs by raising pigs and growing vegetables.

In 1999, as China's economic recovery and development rapidly progressed, there was room to increase defence spending. Given the changing international situation, and the need to reinforce the protection of national security, China started increasing its defence expenditure mainly to compensate for the "shortfall" from previous years. The average annual growth rate for national defence expenditure increased to more than 10%, which was occasionally slightly higher than the GDP growth rate. But it was a compensational growth, focusing on meeting the need to improve the treatment of military personnel and update equipment.

Since the start of the 21st century, thanks to the overall growth of China's economy, national defence expenditure started to steadily increase, enabling the military to make significant progress not only in weapons and equipment upgrades but also in terms of the overall quality of personnel and the military's combat readiness. China started to achieve modernisation of its national defence and its military's main operational platforms, such as warships, airplanes and tanks, joining the ranks of the world's best. It has also grown its overseas operational capability by playing a role in UN peacekeeping, escorting international commercial shipping, overseas evacuation, and search and rescue operations.

In 2015, a major reform was launched guided by the strategic deployment and policy decision of the CPC Central Committee and its General Secretary Xi Jinping. According to the timetable of the overall reform plan, by 2020, a breakthrough was expected in the reform of China's national defence and armed forces. Continued efforts were made to reform the overall command and control system and joint operations command system. The size, structure, force composition, military policy framework as well as civil-military integration would all be optimised and improved.

In the foreseeable future, the reform will bring China's armed forces to a new level of professionalism and capability. Even so, the level of its military equipment lags far behind the Western developed countries and the gap with the United States is especially wide. The modernisation of national defence in China has a big distance to cover.

Now, the rate of increase in China's defence expenditure is

being maintained at the same level as national economic growth. As China's economy is expanding fast, although defence expenditure has been on a rising curve, its proportion of GDP has not shown much increase, keeping at about 1.5% for many years.

As China's economic growth slowed down a bit in the last few years, accordingly, its national defence expenditure rate was also adjusted. In China's 2016 draft budget report, the defence budget was 954 billion yuan, up 7.6% year on year, but down from 10.1% in 2015. Then, in 2017, China's expenditure at the central level earmarked 1,044.397 billion yuan for defence spending, an increase of 7% over 2016.

Many people outside China, especially in Western strategic circles and the media, lack an understanding of how the system in China works and are unwilling to learn. They have not developed an objective and rational view on matters related to China's defence expenditure and its military development, and yet are keen to write about them with a biased and exaggerated viewpoint.

For example, on 4 March 2015, AFP reported that China's military spending continued to increase by double digits every year, reflecting China's huge military ambitions, and that Beijing "was demonstrating its military and economic strength in a series of territorial disputes with Japan and other countries". On the same day, Reuters reported that: "The slowdown of its economic growth does not constrain the growth in China's military expenditure." It claimed that with China's increased investment in high-tech equipment, including submarines and stealth fighters, the growth in military expenditure had reached 10% this fiscal year and exceeded the economic growth rate. And it was "causing regional concerns, especially when China takes a strong position in the sovereignty disputes over the East China Sea and the South China Sea."

When they wrote these stories, there was no comparative analysis of China's overall budget arrangement and the fact that China's defence expenditure was in keeping with its general economic development. Western media adopts "a double standard" when reporting on China's military expenditure, ignoring China's circumstances and its defensive needs to protect such a vast country's sovereignty and security. This kind of reporting inevitably influences the views of the Western public.

A LOOK AT THE "CHINA THREAT THEORY"

When observing China, a familiar perspective of the Western world is concern about the "China Threat", which mainly stems from ignorance and misunderstanding, sometimes even deliberate misinterpretation. After the collapse of the Soviet Union and the upheaval in Eastern Europe, the Western world led by the United States thought it had won the Cold War and could dominate the world. However, China, under the leadership of its Communist Party, has not collapsed. Instead, it has achieved rapid economic growth and increased national strength. Its military strength has increased too and the country has grown stronger. This development made some people in the US, Japan and Europe feel uncomfortable and led to many excuses being found to criticise China, creating many versions of the "China Threat".

In recent years "China's military threat" has been a particular focus of the West when talking about China. Entering the 21st century, the development of China's military power has attracted attention from the US strategic community and media coverage has increased too. Since 2000, the Pentagon has annually submitted a report on China's military strength to the US Congress. Since 2008, the Congressional Research Service has been issuing annual reports on the impact of China's naval modernisation on the US Navy, highlighting the challenges and threats from China. The US Congress frequently holds hearings and puts forward various proposals targeting China. In spite of the growing interest, the views and positions of the Chinese people are rarely heard, or are just ignored.

Think tanks in the US produce dozens of reports on China's military development every year, hyping up various scenarios for their "China's military threat theory", ranging from space, submarine and cyber to information security threats. The most often cited concept was China's "anti-access, area-denial" threat.

The so-called "anti-access" refers to the act of China forcing US forces to operate far away from China's territory by employing anti-ship ballistic missiles, anti-ship cruise missiles, high-performance fighters, advanced mines, silent submarines, anti-satellite weapons and cyber weapons, thus impeding America's ability to access China's offshore areas in times of crisis. "Area-denial" refers to the second level of choice. If the free access of US troops cannot be prevented in wartime, China would strive to delay or reduce US troops' operational efficiency through harassment.

These concepts have been increasingly used in American observers' comments and US military reports on China. The American strategic community has exaggerated the threat to such an extent that it has become the top priority of concern. When the Obama administration implemented the strategy of "pivot to Asia" and " Asia-Pacific rebalance" in 2009, these concepts were the key words used when criticising China's national defence policy.

Since 2010, the term "maritime threat " was created to be the core element of the "China threat theory". The American media seldom mentions China's reasonable claims and views on territorial sovereignty, and maritime rights and interests. Most US politicians' speeches, official documents, congressional hearings and think-tank reports view the maritime disputes between China and its neighbours from the angle of the "China threat theory", accusing China of "maritime expansion" and "maritime coercion" in the South China Sea and the East China Sea, and blaming China for changing the status quo and disrupting regional order.

Since the Abe administration took office, Japan has not seriously faced up to the territorial dispute it has with China over the Diaoyu Islands. Instead, it has presented the territorial dispute as a threat from China to the whole of Japan. Its annual defence white paper and other official documents talked about China's "maritime expansion" and the deterioration of Japan's security environment.

When I attended a seminar in the United States, I shared the platform with the Japanese Consul General in New York. All he talked about was the "China threat", using plausible stories. When I asked him about the facts and to prove his claims, he could not provide anything. He was speaking according to the standard talking points. I was told that he was a frequent speaker at local functions.

Some assistants to US congressmen also told me that they received "plentiful" information from Japan, Vietnam and the Philippines regarding China's maritime threat.

Such a situation partly explains how the China maritime threat is influencing public opinion in the international community. The media in Europe also hold this view, suggesting that China is a threat to its neighbours.

In 2014, the wave of "China threat theory" pushed by the international media reached a new peak. The commemoration of the centenary of the first world war saw the publication of some important history books by European and American academics. Among those that caught my attention were Christopher Clark's book *The Sleepwalkers: How Europe Went to War in 1914*, and Margaret Macmillan's book *The War that Ended Peace: The Road to 1914*, which analysed the causes and course of the war from the perspective of evolution and interaction as well as the seemingly minor historical events of the decade before the war.

Interestingly enough, during the commemoration period, China was the most often mentioned country at international symposiums and by the media, and there was a strong suggestion that there was the possibility of conflict in Asia to be caused by China. Some academics even wrote articles comparing China's economic strength and rise of populism with Germany in the early 20th century, implying similarities. There were articles talking about Asia sleepwalking into war.

However, the so-called "China threat" that the Western world is so worried about is far from reflecting the reality and it shows the serious lack of understanding of China, its development and security interests. The "China threat theory" has not gone unnoticed here in China and it has stimulated the Chinese people's resentment and vigilance towards the West.

The Chinese people are aware that our continued growth is accompanied by various concerns. The unfounded "China threat theory" is an annoyance that we have to live with. It is not a rare phenomenon that when a major country rises, it inevitably faces all kinds of doubts and suspicion, let alone China, having a different political system, values and a development path which are not accepted by the Western world. What is important for us is that we need to speak up in the face of the "China threat theories", to counter and dispel the influence of negative public opinion. We need to provide a more convincing and truthful "Chinese story" to the outside world.

Among the criticisms of, and dissatisfaction with, China, some are due to misunderstanding that needs to be explained and clarified. Some are specific problems that need to be dealt with and resolved. If we do not deal with them quickly and leave them to be talked about, they may pile up into an image burden and may interfere with China's progress towards becoming a world power. We should match our words with deeds and gain an understanding of China's practical efforts in peaceful and inclusive development and in bringing shared prosperity. After all, there is nothing more compelling and convincing than the facts.

PERSONAL INFORMATION OF CITIZENS IS PROTECTED BY LAW

At 11:21 am on 4 March 2017, the press conference in the Briefing Hall of the Great Hall of the People continued.

The host called the journalist from Guangzhou's *Southern Metropolis Daily*. The question was:

"Last year, the tragedies caused by several cyber and telecommunications fraud cases aroused great concern. We conducted investigations and reported on this and found that the root cause behind it was the disclosure of personal information. The Cyber Security Law will be implemented as of 1 June this year. What role will it play in the protection of personal information? Over the years, NPC deputies have called for the enactment of a specific law on the protection of personal information. Do you have any legislative plan in this regard?"

The telecommunications fraud cases mentioned by the journalist included the sad case of Xu Yuyu, a girl from a poor family in Shandong Province who had finally gained a college place. About to start a new journey in her life, she received a scam phone call claiming to be from the college and urging her to pay the tuition fees. She found out only afterwards that she had transferred her family's hard-earned money to a fraudster. It was too big a blow for her and just as she was reporting the case, she suffered a heart attack and passed away.

The case aroused huge public anger and quickly turned into a hot topic on social media across the country. The public questioned why telecoms fraud could not be prevented and asked: "Who leaked citizens' personal information to fraudsters? Why have the fraudsters succeeded time and again?"

According to one journalist's investigation, he could buy his colleagues' hotel records, real-time location and other personal information for 700 yuan. Obviously there were serious loopholes in the personal information security system and there was no sufficient supervision or enforced legal norms for the protection of such privacy as phone calls, SMS and other personal behaviour. The media paid close attention to the newly adopted *Cyber Security Law* to be implemented on 1 June 2017, hoping it would help effectively improve the situation. They wanted to know what role it could play and how it was going to function. It was also true that some NPC deputies had called for the enactment of a personal information protection law. The media, therefore, also wanted to know whether there was any progress on it.

My answer to the question by the journalist from Guangzhou's *Southern Metropolis Daily* was as follows:

Recently there were indeed some shocking incidents of personal information leaks as reported by many in the media. With the development of the internet and the arrival of the big data era, people benefit from the convenience technology brings to our lives. But, at the same time, it also poses challenges to the protection of personal information, which is probably a global concern.

China is a country with a vast number of internet users. Given the scale of development, the challenges we face are more severe and complicated. As you just mentioned, we have reinforced rules on personal information protection in a number of laws. For example, the NPC Standing Committee adopted the decision on measures for strengthening cyber information protection in 2012, and the Amendment (ix) of the Criminal Law in 2015 has provisions on the protection of personal information. Last year, we formulated the Cyber Security Law. The basic rules of personal information protection have been set, which explicitly require that network operators cannot collect personal information that has nothing to do with the services they provide. In addition, personal information should not be transferred to other people without the permission of the relevant person.

In the draft of the General Provisions of Civil Law that we will soon deliberate, it clearly stipulates that a natural person's personal information shall be protected by law. The E-commerce Law, under consideration, also includes such provisions as protecting the personal information of consumers. This year, we are going to carry out a law enforcement inspection on the Cyber Security Law. One of the things we focus on is a particular concern in society about illegally providing personal information to others and cyber fraud. Through law enforcement inspections, we should be able to promote stricter execution of laws. Now we see the rapid growth of new technologies and new business models, which inevitably pose new challenges to legislation. We should keep on improving our legal system and keep up with the times. Thank you.

(3 minutes 20 seconds, about 525 Chinese characters)

SIMPLIFYING THE COMPLEX

Understanding a complex issue often requires deconstructing it into simpler elements.

What is an ideal press conference? People could be easily misled by the name "press conference" and see it as one-way communication – a spokesperson issues a prepared press release or information to the public. A successful press conference that meets people's expectations must be a two-way interaction. Journalists should raise questions that the public want to know about, and the spokesperson should give answers that are not only authoritative but also convincing. In order to achieve this objective, both the journalists and the spokesperson must make good preparations.

My experience is that the preparation of a spokesperson should include at least three steps: First, to communicate with the media in advance or read the latest reporting in order to learn what the

55

media and public are most concerned about; Second, to research the matter and learn about the policies concerned; Third, to construct key points of response based on sufficient information and materials collected on the issue in order to release the information effectively.

When I prepared for a NPC press conference, I mainly looked for the following questions: What were the hot issues of public concern and media pursuit? What were the facts about the relevant issues? What were the solutions to the problem? What were the policies that had been formulated and what kind of legislative steps had been taken? And how were the relevant laws reinforced?

Therefore, I needed to keep track of and pay attention to major social events. Entering 2017, personal information protection became a hot issue in society and I readily included it into my list of key issues to work on. For me, when facing a question, the entry point and angle of narrative should always be the position of the NPC and its Standing Committee. I needed to construct my response to the public's concerns around what we had done, what we were doing and what more we were going to do, and strive to boost public confidence. Of course, I should not avoid admitting that problems still exist.

I thought, should journalists raise questions about personal information protection at my press conference, what they wanted to know would be how the NPC viewed the matter, what it had done, and what it intended to do in future. I, therefore, chose to focus on introducing the NPC's legislative activities. The first was the *Decision of the NPC Standing Committee on Strengthening Information Protection on Networks* (hereafter referred to as "The Decision"), which was adopted on 28 December 2012. Article 1 of "The Decision" stipulates: "the State shall protect electronic information that can identify the personal identity of citizens and involves their personal privacy. No organisation or individual may steal or otherwise illegally obtain citizens' personal electronic information, or sell or illegally provide citizens' personal electronic information to others." I chose to talk about "The Decision" because it had already been issued by the highest-ranking legal institution. "The Decision" demonstrated that the NPC and its Standing Committee had for the first time specifically regulated information protection. It not only demonstrated the importance attached to personal information protection, but also provided a legal basis for the formulation and revision of other laws and regulations.

To reinforce the point, I also wanted to introduce two more amended laws that were passed in 2015 and 2016 respectively, namely the *Criminal Law* amendment (ix) and the *Cyber Security Law*. The changes relating to personal information protection in the *Criminal Law* amendment (ix) are mainly reflected in Article 253: "Whoever, in violation of the relevant provisions of the State, sells or provides personal information of citizens to others, if the circumstances are serious, shall be sentenced to fixed-term imprisonment of not more than three years of criminal detention and shall also, or shall only, be fined; if the circumstances are especially serious, they shall be sentenced to fixed-term imprisonment of not less than three years, but not more than seven years, and shall also be fined. Whoever, in violation of the relevant State regulations, sells or provides personal information of citizens obtained in the course of performing their duties or providing services to others shall be given a heavier punishment in accordance with the provisions of the preceding paragraph. Whoever steals or illegally obtains citizens' personal information by other means shall be punished in accordance with the provisions of the first paragraph. Where a unit commits the crimes mentioned in the preceding three paragraphs, it shall be fined. The persons who are directly in charge and the other persons who are directly responsible for the crimes shall be punished in accordance with the provisions of the preceding three paragraphs."

Compared with the old articles before the amendment, the rules used to be only targeted at special subjects such as "the staff of state organs or financial, telecommunications, transportation, education, medical and other units." The amendment (ix) of the *Criminal Law* extended it to cover wider participants and units. In other words, everyone is is subject to the law and the maximum penalty was raised from three to seven years imprisonment, creating a more powerful deterrent.

The *Cyber Security Law* passed in November 2016 contains further provisions on the protection of personal information. For example, network operators are now required to establish and improve the user information protection system. They should clarify the principles, rules, purposes, methods and scope of the information they collected and use. Operators must not collect personal information unrelated to the services they provide. They are also not allowed to disclose, tamper with or damage the personal information they have collected nor provide personal information to others without the consent of the persons from which the information is collected.

According to its 2017 work plan, the NPC Standing Committee was to carry out a review of the *Cyber Security Law* and one of its key subjects was about the disclosure of personal information and network fraud. So I put this information into my prepared notes. This subject was also included in the *General Provisions of the Civil Law* being formulated. Article 114 of the draft *General Provisions of the Civil Law* states: "the personal information of natural persons is protected by law. Any organisation or individual that needs to obtain another's personal information shall ensure the information's security according to law. They shall not illegally collect, use, process or transmit personal information, shall not illegally trade, provide or disclose personal information." It was of great significance that the personal information protection clause was written into the *General Provisions of the Civil Law*. Vice-Chairman Li Jianguo of the NPC Standing Committee specifically noted this point in his explanation of the draft: "in this information age, the protection of personal information is particularly important, and the draft has made targeted provisions on it."

All of this information is what I needed to relay to the public when responding to questions regarding personal information protection issues. Clearly, it was not quite possible to put all these legal materials into four or five hundred easily understandable words. As I had no idea how the journalists were going to frame their questions, I needed to build some core information and then elaborate around it according to how the journalists' questions were framed.

Xiao Zuo in my team was a postdoctoral student of law. He had been conducting solid research into this issue and had collected lots of materials. I benefited from his contribution in our discussions. And we worked together to try to simplify the complex legal information, not without disagreement. I preferred to express legal terms in a kind of language that was as simple as possible, avoiding too much jargon. In this way I could memorise it more easily and it would also be easier for people watching TV to understand. Of course, should the questions concern some specific legal provisions, I would have to check from the computer.

Internationally, there are basically two trains of thought relating to legislation on personal information protection: One, which is mainly prevalent in Europe, advocates special legislation on the matter and the formulation of separate personal information protection law. The European Union adopted the General Data Protection Regulations (GDPR) in 2016 which is regarded as a landmark law. The other is represented by the US proposing decentralised legislation with specific provisions contained in different laws. The two ideas have their respective merits, and China's legislative thinking is nearer to the decentralised model of the US.

Therefore, in my response to the journalists, I said that "we are focusing on, and strengthening the protection of, personal information in a number of laws." Whether or not our country would create special legislation and further improve the legal protection of personal information, there was no clear consensus yet at that stage, and further observation, research and discussion were needed. When I responded to the question, I took an open approach: "we see fast growth of new technologies and new business models, which inevitably pose new challenges to the legislation. We should keep on improving our legal system and keep up with the times."

Currently, we see the flourishing of new technologies such as big data and artificial intelligence. New business models are emerging constantly. New developments will demand higher requirements for legislation. The third and fourth plenary sessions of the 18th CPC Central Committee all mentioned "the key is to improve the quality of legislation." The NPC Standing Committee has also emphasised the need to improve the quality of legislation, highlight legislative priorities, speed up legislation, and improve legislative mechanisms and their effectiveness. Over five years of working with the NPC, I have gained a keen insight into the complexity of the legislative work and the need for high professionalism. While striving to be proactive, we also need to be prudent and rational in order to strike the right balance among the different interests and values that reflect the current social realities.

RESPONDING TO ECONOMIC CONCERNS

Among the many areas of public concern, economic issues have always received much attention, especially so during the five-year term of the 12th NPC; 2016 was the first year of the 13th Five Year Plan for China's national economic and social development, and the decisive stage in comprehensively achieving the target of building a "Xiaokang society (moderately prosperous society)". Toward the end of 2016, the trend of economic progress was clear. According to data from the National Bureau of Statistics, the efficiency of industrial enterprises had improved, the high-tech and high-end equipment manufacturing industries had grown rapidly, the new business forms and new models led by the internet economy were growing strong, and the supply-side reform had made positive headway.

However, 2016 was hardly a smooth year. Although economic growth was better than expected, the growth rate for the first three quarters of the year was only 6.7%, the lowest in nearly two decades. The US dollar exchange rate against the Rmb climbed from about 6.4 at the beginning of the year to almost 6.9, accompanied by noticeable capital outflows. The burden on businesses was greater with the economic downturn. There were discussions on whether the tax burden on businesses was too heavy and the protection for workers had become excessive. Internationally, the emergence of trade protectionism and de-globalisation had also added uncertainty to the world economy.

In this context, the public was more aware and had greater expectations of the NPC and its Standing Committee with regard to creating and amending legislation relating to the economic issues. The media also hoped that the "two sessions" could respond to such concerns.

Entering 2017, the public's concerns about the economy focused on six outstanding issues: 1. Revision of the *Securities Law* and the progress in reforming the stock issuance registration system; 2. Implementation of the *Law on the Promotion of Small and Medium-sized Enterprises*; 3. The issue of the so-called "death tax rate[1]"; 4. *Labour Contract Law* and the employment costs of enterprises; 5. Individual income tax and income distribution; 6. Real estate tax legislation.

For spokespersons, the most difficult thing is to talk about something they do not understand or have sufficient knowledge of. When I first started with the work, Chairman Zhang Dejiang of the NPC asked me about my preparations for my first press conference. After listening to me intently, he commented frankly, "you are familiar with international affairs, but may not be so familiar with economic issues. You should spend more time working on them."

Indeed, the economy was not familiar territory for me and I needed to work harder on it.

However, even as the press conference drew close, I was still not quite comfortable with subjects in this area. I felt I did not quite understand the existing problems, did not grasp the key points and was not abreast of the latest developments. For example, regarding the debate on the enterprise burden, was China's enterprise tax excessive? Experts had different views, while the government departments had their own. Why were there so many differences? What were the reasons behind them?

Another issue was the *Securities Law*; the revised draft of this law was deliberated for the first time in April 2015 and had been shelved since. If the second deliberation was not conducted in 2017, it would become invalid. Should it need to be revised in future, it had to be resubmitted. What was the plan for this? In December 2015, the NPC Standing Committee authorised reform of the stock issuance registration system and set a two-year limit. Could the State Council's relevant department make its interim report to the NPC's Standing Committee in 2017? These questions concern the advance of China's capital markets and how the reform was going to proceed was of great public interest.

Another closely watched development was legislative progress on the real estate tax, which is a publicly sensitive issue. In its 2017 legislative plan, the NPC Standing Committee included it in the list of preparatory and research projects.

How to respond to these questions in the press conference needed careful consideration.

I realised that it was necessary to seek expert advice and organised a small-scale symposium, inviting people from the Legal and Budget Working Committees of the NPC, the Ministry of Finance and the State Administration of Taxation, to have in-depth discussions. They explained in detail the origins and development of the various issues, the difficulties they had encountered, and the efforts made to solve the problems. Based on what I learnt at the meeting, I researched and read many reports and articles to understand the issues better. I also met leaders in charge of those affairs. The picture gradually became clearer, and I gained confidence in my ability to respond to questions about these issues and had a better idea of the information we needed to release. Since I could not predict exactly what economic issues the journalists might raise, my team and I decided to package similar concerns into one response. And when any particular issue was raised, I could release the information on other issues together at the same time. For example, should the concern of small and medium-sized enterprises (SMEs) be raised, I could talk about it in combination with the issue regarding the burden on enterprises. The questions concerning Personal Income Tax could be addressed through the angle of reform.

At the NPC press conference in 2017, the economic issue was again one of the hot topics and among all the questions, three were related to economic issues. The first was a question from the Xinhua News Agency:

"Tax and fee reductions have attracted wide interest. We have noticed that the Party Central Committee and the State Council have taken strong measures to reduce tax and fees. However, enterprises are only feeling the pinch, not much benefit. What's your comment about this conflicting view? We have also found that high fees are an important reason for the heavy burden on enterprises. In 2017, how will the NPC supervise the government departments to be more transparent about their list of fees, abolish unreasonable fees and cut administrative expenses?"

To which I responded:

The issue you raise has been a hot topic of discussion recently throughout society, especially among the business community. I remember that Wang Guoqing, spokesman of the CPPCC, gave a fairly professional explanation on this issue at his press conference the day before yesterday. When people debate about whether the problem lies with taxes or fees, most think that fees are more of a problem.

I think this discussion in itself is helpful for finding a path to solve the problem. In recent years, China's economic development has experienced downward pressure and its international environment has also become difficult. Therefore, enterprises have become more sensitive to taxes and fees, and it is natural that there are more concerns in this regard. Overall, easing the burden on enterprises has a lot to do with revitalising the economy and is a key problem to be addressed in the current reform.

I have seen reports that the recent meeting of the Central Leading Group on Finance and Economics has made it clear that efforts will be made to make sure that the burden on enterprises is eased. In 2016, in order to give way to reform, the NPC Standing Committee packaged a number of laws and amended them together on three occasions. The purpose was to decentralise or remove a series of administrative approval and recognition procedures, and some qualification recognition requirements. It also revised the Law on the Promotion of Small and Medium-sized Enterprises. All these efforts were aimed at creating conditions for reducing the burden on enterprises. In 2017, the NPC Standing Committee will carry out special research on regulating non-tax revenue in order to make sure that the non-tax revenue is managed according to regulations and the law. It will also tighten examination and supervision of the government's full budget and final accounts. China's tax system needs to be constantly improved. According to the current plan, statutory taxation will be achieved in 2020. So the overall goal is the same, to provide a good environment for the healthy development of enterprises. Thank you.

(2 minutes 25 seconds, about 490 Chinese characters)

The first and second paragraphs of the answer responded to the question, expressing my approach and stance. The third was about relevant legislation by the NPC, which was also the essential information I wanted to provide to the public.

The second question on economic issues was raised by a journalist with *the Economic Daily:*

"Data shows that the number of stock market shareholders in China has exceeded 100 million. How will the interests of small and retail investors be protected? The laws need to be revised. We know that as early as at the beginning of 2015, the revision of the *Securities Law* was launched and the goal was to apply stronger regulation to the stock market. However, after suffering a stock market crash that year, the revision of the law seems to have stalled. I'd like to ask whether amendment of the *Securities Law* will be included in this year's legislative plan and what are the specific arrangements and considerations?"

My answer was as follows:

You have a good memory. The Securities Law's revised draft was submitted to the NPC Standing Committee in April 2015, for its first deliberation. Then at the end of 2015, the NPC Standing Committee authorised the State Council to carry out the reform of the stock issuance registration system. It has now been nearly two years since its first deliberation and, according to the current arrangement, the draft should have been worked on again and be submitted to the NPC Standing Committee for deliberation again in April this year.

The revision of the Securities Law is part of the top-level design of our country's capital market legal system, so it involves complex issues that also include the protection of investors' rights and interests. In particular, the abnormal fluctuation of the stock market in 2015, that we all remember, has exposed some new problems. Therefore, lessons need to be learnt from the experience and re-evaluation is required. The Law Working Committee of the NPC Standing Committee listened to the opinions of different parties and conducted a new study together with the relevant government departments and has now completed revising the draft of the Securities Law. It should be submitted for deliberation in April.

(1 minute 41 seconds, about 290 Chinese characters)

The core information for this response came from the China Securities Regulatory Commission (CSRC) and colleagues from the Law Working Committee of the NPC Standing Committee provided me with information on progress concerning work on revising the *Securities Law*. For these kinds of very specific issues, it is essential to do research and prepare in advance. Ad-lib responses risk making mistakes. Of course, a spokesperson is not a know-it-all, if you encounter something you are not prepared for, it is quite alright to admit that you just don't know.

The third question on economic matters was raised by a journalist with the *Legal Daily*:

"We have noticed that since last year the increase in the price of housing has become a particularly sensitive issue. Many people believe that the introduction of a real estate tax may help control house prices. And we have also noticed that the introduction of the *Real Estate Tax Law* has been mentioned several times. The question I want to ask is, will the *Real Estate Tax Law* be included in the NPC agenda for 2017? How far are we from the actual promulgation of the *Real Estate Tax Law*? "

I answered as follows:

This has been a hot issue recently. A few days ago, I looked up some authoritative information about it. First of all, this task was put forward by the Third Plenary Session of the 18th CPC Central Committee which called for speeding up real estate tax legislation as well as timely reform in this area. So, the current NPC Standing Committee has included the Real Estate Tax Law in its five-year legislative plan. Of course, this law involves wide interests and there are bound to be lots of discussions. According to my knowledge, there is no arrangement to submit a draft real estate tax law to the Standing Committee for deliberation this year.

(51 seconds, about 175 Chinese characters)

NOTHING OFF LIMITS FOR ANTI-CORRUPTION

At 11:29 am on 4 March 2017, the press conference continued.

A journalist from the Central People's Broadcasting Station asked:

"At the end of last year, the NPC Standing Committee adopted the decision to carry out pilot reform of the state supervision system in Beijing, Shanxi and Zhejiang Province. Now in some pilot areas new anti-corruption organisations, the Supervision Committees, have been set up. What I want to ask is, how will the NPC Standing Committee play its role in ensuring that the Supervision Committee exercises its power in accordance with the law and regulations? In addition, the reform of the state supervision system is a major political reform that has an overall impact. In order to carry it out smoothly, will the NPC and its Standing Committee consider amending the *Constitution*?"

This issue is related to anti-corruption and the reform of the state supervision system. During my five years as the spokesperson for the 12th NPC, questions on anti-corruption were raised in every press conference not only by domestic but also by foreign journalists who were both very interested in this topic, though paying attention to different aspects of the issue.

In recent years, strong efforts were made to achieve significant progress in anti-corruption work every year, building up an overwhelming momentum in the country. As for the 12th NPC and its standing committee, the key emphasis was on building up an anti-corruption system. Now the unveiling of the pilot reform of the state supervision system represented a new peak in the system-building efforts in the five-year anti-corruption drive led by the Party

Central Committee. In 2017, the focus on anti-corruption turned to reforming the state supervision system.

On 7 November 2016, Xinhua News Agency released the news that the General Office of the CPC Central Committee had recently issued *The Plan for Pilot Reform of the State Supervision System in Beijing, Shanxi and Zhejiang* (hereinafter referred to as "The Plan"). It included setting up supervision committees and building the mechanism and systems on a trial basis, to accumulate experience before rolling it out countrywide. According to "The Plan", the objective of reforming the state supervision system was to establish a state anti-corruption working organ under the unified leadership of the Party, renovating the organisations and institutions, integrating anti-corruption resources, expanding and enhancing the scope of supervision over all public officials who exercise power, and establishing a centralised, authoritative and efficient supervision system. The objective is to build an effective system in which public officials dare not, cannot and do not wish to become corrupt.

According to "The Plan", the Provincial (Municipal) People's Congresses in Beijing, Shanxi and Zhejiang, would form supervisory committees, which would serve as a special body to exercise the state's supervisory functions. The Party's Discipline Inspection Committee would be working as one with the Supervision Committee. The Supervision Committee's organisational structure would be reinforced and its functional responsibilities be clearly defined. It should also coordinate with the judicial bodies so that the supervisory committee itself was also subject to supervision and restrictions.

I had no doubt that this major reform would attract media attention. This development was so important that it not only concerned the anti-corruption drive but also signified a major reform of the country's political system. In the words of "The Plan", this was "a major political reform with an overall impact" and "a top-level design of the state supervision system".

On 19 December 2016, the 12th NPC Standing Committee convened its 25th meeting. One of the agenda items was to deliberate its decision to carry out pilot projects for the state supervision system reform in Beijing, Shanxi and Zhejiang (hereinafter referred to as "The Decision"). It was adopted on 25 December, which released more information to the public. It can be summarised in the following four points:

The first was to transfer and integrate the relevant official functions. Supervisory committees were to be set up in Beijing, Shanxi and Zhejiang, including at the governmental levels of counties, cities and municipal districts to exercise supervisory functions and power. The existing relevant local government functional bodies like the supervision departments (bureaus), corruption prevention bureaus, the people's procuratorate organs; the bodies dealing with corruption and bribery, dereliction of duty and prevention of job-related crimes, were all to be integrated into the Supervision Committee.

The second was to define the relationship between the People's Congress and the Supervision Committee in the pilot areas. "The Decision" stated that the pilot areas' supervision committees were to be formed through elections by the People's Congress at the same level. The chairman of the Supervision Committee should be elected by the pilot area's People's Congress at the same level. The Supervision Committee was to be responsible to the People's Congress and its Standing Committee at the same level as well as the higher-level Supervision Committee.

The third was to determine the functions and power of the Supervision Committee. In the pilot areas, the Supervision Committee should, in accordance with its administrative authority, supervise all public servants exercising government power in the region according to law. It should perform the duties of supervision, investigation and disposal. To perform the above functions, the Supervision Committee could take such measures as talking, interrogating and inquiring, as well as freezing, transferring, sealing up assets, searching, inspecting, appraising and detaining.

The fourth was to temporarily adjust or suspend some relevant laws in Beijing, Shanxi and Zhejiang. Early in 2017, when I had discussions with the media, I noticed that the journalists' attention on anti-corruption was focused on the reform of the supervision system. Their main interest could be summarised into the following questions: What was the overall structure of the State Supervision

Committee? What was the roadmap and timetable? How would the Supervision Committee exercise its functions and powers in the future? How should one view the validity and legitimacy of the decision of the NPC Standing Committee on the pilot project? What was the relationship between the NPC and the Supervision Committee? Would the People's Congress supervise the Supervision Committee and, if so, how? How to exercise the lien power? What was the difference between the new arrangement and the currently practiced "two specified rules" and "two designated points" that people are familiar with? Should there be amendments to the *Constitution* when reforming the state supervision system? If necessary, is there a timetable for amending the *Constitution*?

These questions could be roughly put into two categories: one is about the supervision committee itself, how it will be organised through reform and how it will function. The second is about its role and the relevant reform in the larger context of modern national governance and further political system reform. During my off-the-record discussions with journalists, they raised many questions to which I had no answer as the reform was just starting.

My team and I were impressed by the journalists' ability to raise such perceptive and forward-looking questions. It demonstrated the great interest among the media and the general public about the reform. If something was unimportant or irrelevant, no one would rack their brains to scrutinise it, let alone ask questions. Moreover, most of the tough questions came from the domestic media, which reflected the heightened public awareness of the rule of law. In the past, in the face of major reform, people mainly cared about the result. Now, in addition to expecting a good result, they were also becoming interested in such issues as the legitimacy of the procedures and whether there was effective supervision. From the legal point of view, one could say that society was increasingly interested about procedural and formal justice in addition to caring about substantive justice.

The 18th National Congress of the CPC stated in its report that "the Party must act under the *Constitution* and the law. No organisation or individual shall have the privilege to go above the *Constitution* and the law." The third and fourth plenary sessions of the 18th CPC Central Committee also called for safeguarding the authority of the *Constitution* and law, strengthening the implementation of the *Constitution*, and stipulating that major reforms should be guided by the law. When the media was asking whether the reform of the supervision system would involve amending the *Constitution*, it showed that they "take the *Constitution* seriously".

We all agreed that reform of the state supervision system was a "good thing." But some people still questioned whether the reform was in accordance with the *Constitution* or whether we needed to amend the *Constitution* to give this reform more legitimacy. This was an indication of rising public consciousness about the rule of law. As General Secretary Xi Jinping said at the conference to mark the 30th anniversary of the promulgation and implementation of the current *Constitution*, "the foundation of the *Constitution* lies in the heartfelt support of the people, and the great strength of the *Constitution* lies in the genuine faith people have in it." To safeguard the authority of the *Constitution* and its implementation takes the effort of not only the Party, government, media and social organisations but of every citizen.

In light of the above, my team and I undertook serious research on the pilot reform of the supervision system and held many discussions with the government institutions concerned. In preparing the key points related to this issue, I tried to cover all the aspects of the issue and explain the "matter" in plain and simple language so as to reinforce the political signals conveyed by "The Plan" and "The Decision".

At my press conference, the Central People's Broadcasting Station's journalist raised a question on this subject, mentioning not only reform of the supervision system but also possible amendments to the *Constitution*. I answered it as follows:

> *The reform of the state supervision system is a major step in the system building for anti-corruption under the leadership of the CPC Central Committee with Comrade Xi Jinping at its core. It is also a political system reform, which will have an overall impact on the country.*
>
> *According to the rule, all major reforms should be based on the law. The*

NPC Standing Committee endorsed the decision at the end of last year, on the pilot reform of the state supervision system in Beijing, Shanxi and Zhejiang. To facilitate the reform, temporary adjustments have been made regarding the application of the relevant laws, allowing the three places to test reform of their government operational system, institutions and mechanisms.

Now that the pilot work has been rolled out comprehensively, their experience should be able to provide valuable knowledge when the reform is promoted countrywide.

Work has begun to amend the Administrative Supervision Law which will be turned into the State Supervision Law. Its draft should be submitted to the NPC Standing Committee for deliberation within this year. This is a major step in developing anti-corruption legislation, which will further promote legal thinking and legal methods, and ensure that state supervision and punishment for corruption follow the rule of law.

You have asked whether it is necessary to amend the Constitution. Amending the Constitution will be a major event for the country. It should be carried out under the CPC Central Committee's leadership, and should follow the procedures stipulated in the Constitution. We will release the relevant information to the public should there be such a development. Thank you.

(1 minute 50 seconds, about 340 Chinese characters)

RULE OF LAW AND SYSTEM CONSTRUCTION

This was not a long answer, but it took my team and I a lot of work. To prepare to answer questions concerning this issue, we made a draft of the key points and then kept on changing it. The first draft was written by Xiao Zuo, who was familiar with the subject and had been following the discussions in academic circles. He wrote the draft in professional language with legal jargon. However, at a press conference the language used needed to be as straightforward and concise as possible. His draft was too long and too literal. I asked him to change the legal jargon into simple language and have it cut down to around 100 words, without compromising the key content and information. It was a frustrating and sometimes even painful process for him.

But, thanks to such repeated discussions and modifications, we were able to achieve the goal. For every key point in the text, we repeated this back-and-forth process of modification. In this way, we were finally able to come up with the most concise response on every issue of public concern.

When I responded to the question on the reform of the supervision system, it only took me less than two minutes to deliver the key points. The original text had approximately 300 Chinese characters, containing five sentences, and each conveyed a relatively independent message.

The keywords in the first sentence were "system building" and "political system reform", which represented the most important thing I have learned when working with the NPC. Anti-corruption has been an important drive since the 18th CPC National Congress, in the interest of the country and people. But what role should the NPC and its Standing Committee play as the highest legislature? My understanding was that its task was to build a legal environment that would ensure clean and honest government. What the NPC and its Standing Committee could and should do was to create a permanent anti-corruption solution. When I talked about anti-corruption at press conferences, the Chinese term "system building" was a key phrase in all my answers to the relevant questions.

The "political system reform" embodied a higher purpose for system building to be achieved through the setting up of the state supervision system and the battle against corruption. That is to say that we can achieve a bigger goal, mainly by deepening all-round reforms, implementing all-round rule of law and promoting the modernisation of the state governance system and governance capabilities. In this sense, reform of the state supervision system began with anti-corruption but will go beyond it.

In the second sentence, the keyword was the principle of "to be based on the law," as proposed by General Secretary Xi Jinping on 28 February 2014, at the second meeting of the Central Leading Group for Comprehensively Deepening Reforms. They were later written into the Decision *on Several Major Issues Concerning Comprehensive Promotion of the Rule of Law*, adopted at the fourth plenary session of the 18th CPC Central Committee. This principle defines the role and function of the NPC and its Standing

Committee in promoting reform of the legal system. By adopting the decision to carry out the pilot work of state supervision system reform, the NPC Standing Committee provided a legal mandate for major political system reform.

The third sentence emphasised the significance of "the pilot project". There was also a subtext here, that was, that some questions had no answer yet and would have to wait to see what can be found through reform and what lessons can be learnt. That was exactly why we needed a pilot project. No matter how good the design and concept were, they needed to be tested in the real world. The purpose of the pilot was to accumulate experience that would pave the way for reform countrywide.

In the fourth sentence, the key message was that, to combat corruption, we must apply legal thinking and legal methods. It came from the speech by General Secretary Xi Jinping at the second plenary session of the 18th CPC Central Commission for Discipline Inspection: "We must be good at adopting legal thinking and legal methods in combating corruption." When answering questions about anti-corruption at the NPC press conferences, I often talked about anti-corruption legislation. For example, I mentioned many laws, including the *Criminal Law*, the *Criminal Procedure Law*, the *Civil Service Law*, the *Anti-Money Laundering Law*, the *Government Procurement Law*, the *Bidding Law, and* the *Budget Law*. The deliberations on the draft of *the State Supervision Law* in 2017 provided the most powerful impetus for the anti-corruption legislation.

The fifth sentence was about whether there would be constitutional amendments and a possible timetable, which were also what the media and the public wanted to know. Article 64 of the Chinese *Constitution* stipulates: "amendments to the *Constitution* must be proposed by the NPC Standing Committee or by one-fifth or more of NPC deputies and be adopted by a vote of at least two-thirds of NPC deputies." Since the *Constitution* was promulgated in 1982, it was amended on four occasions, in 1988, 1993, 1999 and 2004 respectively, with 31 amendments. The Central Committee of the CPC made the proposal for amendment to the Standing Committee of the NPC which, under the provisions of Article 64 of the *Constitution*, would then put forward a draft amendment and submit it to the NPC for deliberation.

To carry out the state supervision system reform and create a new state institution such as the State Supervision Committee from scratch was a complicated process. As the formulation and amendment of the State *Supervision Law* and a series of subsequent laws required a constitutional basis, the amendment of the *Constitution* was obviously a necessary step. According to the legislative process, it was expected that the amendment of the *Constitution* would be initiated at the first session of the 13th NPC in 2018. As one could see, amending the *Constitution* needed to follow strict procedures and was a major and serious matter in the country's political life.

However, before the press conference in March 2017, I did not have a releasable timetable for that matter. Therefore, after consulting with the relevant departments, I thought, if asked, I would just say: "I don't have the exact information," or "I have no information to announce at present." Such a statement would be honest, and people would accept it given the circumstances, but it would sound a bit indifferent. Noticing my hesitation, Chairman Zhang Dejiang suggested: "In this case, why don't you say that you will share the information when you have it?"

This was good advice. So when responding to this question, I said "we will release the information about this aspect to the public as soon as it is available." Although there was no difference in substance between these two expressions, the latter sounded much better, as it carried a positive tone.

As a press conference has time constraints, it is not always possible for a spokesperson to take all the questions and respond to all the concerns. Furthermore, a spokesperson cannot know everything and therefore there are often questions for which there is no conclusive answer. Therefore, the spokesperson needs to make wise choices, speaking more when you know the subject well, and less or not at all when you don't. When confronting questions about something you have little or no knowledge of, it is better to admit it or skirt around it. It is important to take an honest approach and speak only when you have something to say, making sure that every answer has substance and your core message is clear and easily understood.

THE ROLE OF THE PEOPLE'S CONGRESSES IN ANTI-CORRUPTION AND ANTI-CORRUPTION IN THE PEOPLE'S CONGRESSES

At my five press conferences between 2013 and 2017, I came across six questions on anti-corruption. They could be divided into two categories. The first was "anti-corruption and the role of the people's congress", which was about what the NPC and its Standing Committee had been doing in the fight against corruption, especially through legal means and institutional design. The other was "anti-corruption in the people's congresses". The media and the public wanted to know how the people's congresses had faced the corruption problems found within, such as the Hengyang case, the Wang Min case and the Liaoning bribery case.

The two types of issues were related. The anti-corruption activities by the NPC were an integral part of the Party and State's overall anti-corruption drive to ensure a clean government. The NPC and its Standing Committee, together with the Central Commission for Discipline Inspection, the State Council, the Supreme People's Court and the Supreme People's Procuratorate, all had their respective responsibilities and roles. Moreover, as the saying goes: "one must be strong to forge iron." Only by ensuring that the NPC itself is a clean and honest body can it play an important role in creating legislation and supervising the fight against corruption.

On 15 November 2012, Comrade Xi Jinping, who was elected General Secretary of the CPC Central Committee at the first plenary session of the 18th Central Committee of the CPC, stressed when meeting Chinese and foreign journalists: "Under the new situation, our Party is faced with many severe challenges, and there are many problems to be solved in the Party. In particular, corruption, being distanced from the masses, formalism and bureaucratism among some party members and cadres must be addressed with great efforts. The whole Party must be on the alert.

It takes a good blacksmith to make good steel." It was a powerful speech and sounded a clarion call. The metaphor of the blacksmith is quite down to earth and quickly became popular on the internet.

After starting with the NPC in 2013, I held my first press conference on 4 March, at which a journalist from Xinhua News Agency asked me directly:

> "What are the plans of the NPC and its Standing Committee for anti-corruption legislation, and what new measures will be taken to promote the construction of an anti-corruption system?"

In my answer, I started by saying that the national legislation against corruption was a comprehensive and systematic project, and talked about the efforts of the NPC and its Standing Committee in the development of the legal system. I then emphasised that legal thinking and legal methods must be applied in combating corruption, acknowledging the need to revise and improve relevant laws in a timely manner, the importance of improving supervision of the implementation of laws, and the requirement of state organs to exercise their power according to statutory authority and procedures.

In the press conferences over the following years, "system and law" had always been my emphasis when responding to questions on this issue.

At my press conference in 2014, a journalist from Singapore's *Straits Times* started his question by referring to the Hengyang election sabotage case and then asked about China's anti-corruption efforts. The focus of his question was what actions could be expected from China's NPC and its Standing Committee to improve electoral integrity.

At that time, the basic facts of the Hengyang election sabotage case were already clear: from 28 December 2012 to 3 January 2013, Hengyang City in Hunan Province held the first session of its 14th people's congress. There were 527 deputies attending the meeting (two deputies were absent), and they elected 76 deputies to the provincial people's congress from among 93 candidates. During this process, there were serious acts of bribery in violation of discipline and law that undermined the election process. The result of an investigation showed that 56 elected deputies to the provincial people's congress had spent money to buy votes. The total amount involved was over 110 million yuan, with 518 deputies to the people's congress of Hengyang City and 68 staff members found to have received money and goods. The election of deputies is the foundation of the people's congress system. The Hengyang bribery case which had been uncovered served as a profound lesson.

My answer highlighted "system building", and I emphasised the importance of safeguarding the election system of the people's congresses. I cited the need to abide by the *Law for Election of the NPC and Local People's Congresses* and the *Law on Deputies to the NPC and Local People's Congresses*. Fairness and honesty are the basic requirements of any election system, as only in this way can the most suitable candidates be selected. The Hengyang election sabotage case, which involved giving and receiving money, was an infringement of the laws and election system. How could we expect the deputies who were not legitimately elected to be in a position to represent the people?

Furthermore, the Hengyang election sabotage case was a violation of the political system. The people's congress system is an important component of the socialist system with Chinese characteristics, and the fundamental political system underpinning China's state governance. Article 2 of the Constitution stipulates: "all power in the PRC belongs to the people. The organs through which the people exercise state power are the NPC and the local people's congresses at all levels." The success of the anti-corruption and system-building effort, as well as overall state governance, all depend on the people's congresses to perform their duties honestly and in accordance with the law. The effective operation of the people's congresses depends on their deputies. If something improper occurs during the election of deputies, there could be a knock-on effect on the operation of the people's congress system, and our political system as a whole. Therefore, we did not hesitate to disclose the scandal to the public and demonstrated a "zero tolerance" policy on such behaviour as bribery to secure votes and sabotaging elections.

Usually, in a press conference, journalists rarely repeated a question that had already been asked. However, at the March 2015 press conference, the anti-corruption issue was raised twice.

The first question came from the *Southern Metropolis Daily*, in which the 2014 Hengyang election sabotage was again mentioned:

"So far, 39 deputies to the 12th NPC have resigned or been removed because they are suspected of violating the law and discipline. This number is more than the total over the last five years. Does this mean that you did not have a good sense of oversight when it came to the election of the deputies, or is the electoral system itself flawed?"

The question was quite sharp. Indeed, did the resignation and removal of so many deputies mean that something was wrong with the system itself? My answer had three main points.

The first point was to emphasise that being a deputy to the People's Congress carries no prerogative, but carries an important mission and responsibility. We must investigate and deal with anybody who violated the law and discipline, and be firm every time it occurred.

The second point I made was about the relationship between 3,000 and 39. There were nearly 3,000 deputies to the 12th NPC. Now, 39 of them had resigned or been removed. Although this was disappointing, we should not deny the credibility of the whole electoral system of the NPC just because of the mistakes of 39 people. On the contrary, the proper handling of the bribery cases reflected the determination and strength of the NPC in fighting corruption.

My third point focused on the forthcoming elections. In 2015, the county and township-level people's congress elections were to be held, and it was important to send a clear anti-corruption message. China's people's congress system has five levels, and the total number of deputies across all of the people's congresses is approximately 2.67 million, with roughly 90% of them belonging to the grassroots people's congresses at county and township levels. The quality and performance of these grassroot deputies have a fundamental influence on the health and efficiency of the people's congress system. It is, therefore, important to use the opportunity of the press conference to reinforce the anti-corruption point and ensure that the upcoming elections would be conducted cleanly and honestly.

After the journalist with the *Southern Metropolis Daily*, a correspondent from Singapore's *Lianhe Zaobao* pressed the point by asking: "How are you going to further promote the improvement of the system so that your anti-corruption effort can be transformed from addressing the symptoms to addressing the root cause?" I replied to him:

In order to address the issue more fundamentally, the NPC and its Standing Committee would strengthen anti-corruption legislation and build a legal environment that would tolerate no corruption.

I then gave two examples, saying that in 2014, the NPC Standing Committee revised the *Budget Law*, explicitly requiring that all government revenues be included in the full calibre budget, thus further tightening restrictions on administrative power. And in the draft Amendment (ix) of the *Criminal Law*, the punishment for corruption and bribery was also increased.

I also mentioned international cooperation on anti-corruption and the importance of building an international anti-corruption cooperation network. I said that China, as a party to the United Nations Convention Against Corruption, advocated the promotion of international cooperation against corruption within the frameworks of APEC and the G20. In addition, China was also formulating an *International Criminal Judicial Assistance Law* to regulate and strengthen criminal judicial cooperation with foreign countries. The hope was that, through full use of international laws and international mechanisms, we can make sure that corrupt individuals, no matter where they might flee, would be brought to justice and face legal punishment.

At my press conference in 2016, the anti-corruption issue was again raised. As I mentioned earlier in this book, about 20 minutes before the start of the press conference, I was informed that Wang

Min, a former vice chairman of the NPC Committee of Education, Science, Culture and Public Health, was under investigation for suspected violation of discipline. This news gave rise to the attention of the journalists at the press conference on the anti-corruption effort inside the NPC. Mentioning the news of the Wang Min investigation, a journalist with the Xinhua News Agency raised a question about anti-corruption and the focus was on the progress in system building.

My answer started with the investigation of Wang Min. I said: "anti-corruption is a very important element in modern state governance, and we have achieved remarkable results in the fight against corruption over the past three years. The anti-corruption drive has gained strong support from the general public."

At that moment, I knew no more than the journalists about what was happening regarding the investigation of Wang Min. According to subsequent news reports, Wang Min was taken away on the morning of 4 March 2016 from the hotel where he was staying with the Liaoning Province delegation just after he had finished breakfast and was waiting to go and attend a preparatory meeting at the Great Hall of the People.

That morning, as I was coming out of a preparatory meeting for the 12th NPC, I heard the news that Wang Min was being investigated. I immediately started thinking about how to respond to possible questions at the press conference. The first thought that came to my mind was, "no one is an exception in anti-corruption." So, when the Xinhua News Agency journalist asked the question, I used that phrase and stressed that this also applied to the deputies to the NPC and the people's congress at all levels. If any deputy to a people's congress is suspected of violating discipline and breaking the law, they should face disciplinary investigation and, if necessary, be brought to criminal trial.

When waiting in the lounge, I looked into the materials I had saved before about anti-corruption within the NPC. I noted that between 2013 when the current NPC started until 2015, 43 NPC deputies had resigned and 27 had been recalled. Many of them were removed by the congress where they were elected or voluntarily submitted their resignation because of a violation, or suspected violation, of discipline and law. The *Constitution* and the law grant various rights to the deputies while stipulating that they must also be model citizens abiding by the *Constitution* and the law.

In the press conference, I continued:

During 2015, the NPC and its Standing Committee has actively played its role in rooting out corruption and has accelerated state anti-corruption legislation as proposed by the CPC Central Committee. In making or revising laws, we have mainly reinforced anti-corruption provisions in order to build a sound legal system for anti-corruption in China. For example, Amendment (ix) of the Criminal Law, adopted in 2015, strengthened the anti-corruption provisions by introducing life imprisonment and improving the standards for convictions and sentencing.

In my reply, I also mentioned that amending the *Administrative Supervision Law* was also under consideration.

On 12 January 2016, General Secretary Xi Jinping delivered an important speech at the sixth session of the 17th Central Commission for Discipline Inspection. On 20 January, I invited some officials from the Central Commission for Discipline Inspection to join my team for a discussion. The interaction was lively. I consulted them on some hot issues and cases, and we talked about revising *the Administrative Supervision Law*. The amendment of this law was directly linked with the anti-corruption legislation, and a later decision to change *the Administrative Supervision Law* into *the State Supervision Law* would further advance the system building.

A few months after the NPC press conference in 2016, another serious case of election tampering surfaced and attracted public attention. It was in Liaoning Province involving canvassing and bribery which happened in the same period as the Hengyang case in 2012-2013 during the new term elections. This time, the people involved were more senior, and the transgressions were shockingly serious. The case investigation revealed the following: In January 2013 when electing NPC deputies at the first session of the 12th Liaoning Provincial People's Congress, 45 newly elected NPC deputies used bribery when canvassing for votes from among 523 Liaoning provincial congress deputies. Of the 62 members of its

Standing Committee, 38 were involved in the fraud and were therefore disqualified as deputies and removed from their positions in the Provincial Standing Committee. Since these people accounted for half of the Standing Committee, it could not meet the quorum and therefore could no longer perform its duties.

On 13 September 2016, the Standing Committee of the NPC held the 23rd meeting specially to address this issue and deliberated on a report by the deputy qualification review committee. The report concluded that the 45 deputies to the 12th NPC elected by Liaoning Provincial People's Congress were invalid. Then, to address the problem, a creative and unprecedented arrangement was made by the NPC Standing Committee which took the decision to set up an interim body to perform some of the statutory duties of the standing committee of the Liaoning Provincial People's Congress in preparation for its seventh session.

On 13 September 2016, Vice Chairman Li Jianguo put forward this draft decision for deliberation by the Standing Committee of the NPC. When introducing the draft, he admitted that this was unprecedented: "We have never seen such an occurrence with a provincial people's congress since the founding of the PRC."

When commenting on this issue, Chairman Zhang Dejiang used such phrases as "for the first time", "very serious" and "challenging", emphatically describing the Liaoning canvassing and bribery case. He said, "This is the first case of such seriousness at the provincial level that has been discovered and dealt with since the founding of the PRC. It is a major case involving serious violation of Party discipline and state laws, serious violation of political discipline and rules, serious violation of organisational discipline and regulations for term change, and serious infringement of the electoral system of the people's congresses. It is a challenge to the people's congress system, to socialist democracy, and to state law and Party discipline. It has touched the bottom-line of the socialist system with Chinese characteristics, and the bottom-line of the CPC as the ruling party." He stated that while conducting a serious investigation and determining due handling, we must learn lessons from it and prevent any similar recurrence.

The NPC's serious approach in handling the Hengyang election sabotage case and the Liaoning canvassing and bribery case, demonstrated its "zero tolerance" attitude towards corruption within its system, as well as its determination not to tolerate or indulge internal corruption, and to make sure that every case would be investigated and dealt with according to law.

During my years with the NPC, I witnessed and participated in the efforts by the NPC and its Standing Committee to tighten discipline by way of practicing rule of law, and the expression we used was "tighten the cage of rules." In due course, this would help create an institutional environment in which officials dare not, cannot and do not want to be corrupt. Starting the reform of the state supervision system was the high point of this process. Of course, anti-corruption is an ongoing campaign, and the reform of the state supervision system was just the beginning of another journey. Personally, it was a memorable experience for me to witness and record.

3

THE PROTECTION OF WOMEN AND CHILDREN AND CHINA'S INTERNATIONAL ROLE

BRILLIANT IDEAL AND HARSH REALITY

At 11:45am on 4 March 2017, I was half way through with the NPC press conference.

The moderator, He Shaoren, called for the next question. A journalist with the *China Youth Daily* raised the eighth question:

> "I would like to ask a question on behalf of some young mothers. The adoption of the two-child policy is widely welcome. However, our investigation shows that while many families enjoy sweet happiness with their second child, the mothers often encounter such difficulties as discrimination in employment and conflicts between maternity leave and career promotion. So, what's your view on the protection of women's rights and interests, especially mothers with more than one child?"

This question touched my heart. As a woman, I have kept a close eye on issues concerning women's rights and interests over the years. In the late 1980s, I was working as an interpreter at the Ministry of Foreign Affairs and sometimes appeared on public occasions. I often received letters from women in difficulty who hoped that I could help them forward or solve their complaints as I was seen interpreting or translating for national leaders. The letters were mostly about cases of domestic violence, discrimination in employment or other unfair treatment. I would usually follow the procedure and transfer the letters to the relevant authorities. I myself also learned a lot about social problems and realised that women were the weaker group in society and were more likely to run into difficulties. During my career, I have often held dialogues with female colleagues and have stood up for protecting women's rights and interests.

There are international similarities in women's social experience. For instance, whether in China or other countries, professional women face the same difficulty of trying to find the right balance between family and career. This is also the question I get asked most frequently. During my term as the Chinese Ambassador to the UK, the Foreign & Commonwealth Office organised a symposium on 8 March, International Women's Day 2009, and invited me and two other female ambassadors in London to talk with British female diplomats. They were mostly interested to know how female ambassadors balanced family and career. When the ambassadors talked about their life experience, we had many similar stories. Later, when visiting Singapore, I was invited to speak on the international situation to their diplomats. During the Q&A session, a young female Singaporean diplomat asked: What are the advantages and difficulties you encounter at work as a female? How do you balance family and career? It can be concluded that these are the same challenges for professional women across the world.

From my own experience, it is very hard to strike a balance between family and career in terms of time management. Women have 24 hours in a day, no more than men. It is almost impossible for a professional woman, especially as she strives for career advancement, to take sufficient care of both work and family. For instance, you cannot tell kids bedtime stories if you are working overtime late at night. This is not something you can multitask, but a tough choice many women have to face in their career and in their life. However, there are other ways to make up for it. As long as you love your family and truly care about them, your family can always feel the love and care. Family members can also help you share responsibilities. In my case, although I was not able to spend as much time as I wanted with my daughter, she could feel the deep care I had for her. I paid keen attention to her studies, choice of major, and the nurturing of her character, and I never missed the big days in her life.

For instance, on the day of my daughter's national college entrance examination, I was in the middle of a bilateral negotiation with Shivshankar Menon, India's ambassador to China at that time. Both events were important. That morning, after dropping my daughter at the exam hall together with my husband, I rushed back to the office for the negotiations. Around noon, I requested a two-hour recess, which was unusual. When I explained that I would be having lunch with my daughter following her big exam, Mr Menon showed great understanding and readily agreed. That was a successful balance, but the chances of making such an arrangement were slim. During the years I worked overseas, my family and I had more time apart than together. We made a deal — whenever our daughter was on holiday, she would join me in the embassy, enabling the family to live, travel and spend time together. It made up, to some extent, for our separation but, more importantly, we got to find out more about each other, and as a parent I could keep track of my daughter as she was growing up.

In early 2017, topics of public concern included whether employment and promotion discrimination, which have long troubled female workers, would worsen following the adoption of the two-child policy. I understood that the Chinese journalists wanted to know what the NPC and its Standing Committee would do to secure better conditions for women in their lives and careers.

Before the press conference, my team also had a heated discussion on this issue. Some defended women, saying that modern women had to manage their heavy workload while caring for their families, which was already a big challenge. It was unfair for them to face further pressure from gender discrimination in jobs. Others expressed sympathy for employers who were reluctant to hire women, as the missed hours during one pregnancy and maternity leave was already costly, a second pregnancy would only double the pressure on the business's performance. Some stated that as women's wellbeing concerned social stability and national development, the government should introduce policies to support them, rather than just urging employers to cope.

China has many laws that require the protection of women's right to employment and forbid gender discrimination. For instance, Article 13 of the *Labour Law of the PRC*, which took effect on 1 January 1995, specifies that: "Women shall enjoy equal employment rights to men in employment. Gender shall not be used as a pretext for excluding women from employment during recruitment of workers unless the types of work or posts for which workers are being recruited are not suitable for women, according to State regulations. Nor shall the standards of recruitment be raised when it comes to women. " And in the *Law of the PRC on the Protection of Women's Rights and Interests*, which took effect on 1 December 2005, the whole of Chapter IV deals with the protection of women's rights and interests relating to work and social security. But unless the government and society put in place incentives or compensation mechanisms, there will always be employers who find ways to circumvent these regulations.

A press conference cannot solve problems that are unresolved in society, so I should not brag or make empty promises but, equally, I must not unsympathetically restate the sober reality. During discussions with my team, we agreed that if this kind of topic was raised, I could propose some suggestions for improvement besides quoting relevant policies and laws. For instance, I could suggest supporting the existing laws with more specific policies and facilities. I could also call for employers and institutions to set up nurseries or childcare centres, so that female employees could take care of their children during breaks, thereby increasing working efficiency. Society as a whole should learn to care more about women.

A friend told me his experience on a recruitment occasion. There was a woman with reasonably good qualifications. Initially, his preference was to hire her. But as his unit was not big, he worried that she might not be able to work full-time when she wanted to start a family, so he ended up recruiting a young man instead. I asked him how he would feel if this kind of situation happened to one of his own family members. He admitted that it would be awful. I think we cannot ignore the contradiction between reality and the ideal. As the saying goes: "The ideal may be 'full-grown', but the reality is 'skinny'."

In response to the question from the *China Youth Daily*, I thought of this story. I needed to admit that the issue existed and plead for equal treatment of women. So, I answered:

It has been a year since the adoption of "the universal two-child policy". The results are generally good, and the whole society welcomes and supports this policy. Nevertheless, certain new problems have emerged, such as employment discrimination against women, as you mentioned. It has been a longstanding problem, and in today's job market, more young women find themselves being treated unfairly. The issue is more prominent now and more frequently raised since "the universal two-child policy" was adopted.

For women, employment is important for pursuing personal value and supporting the family. Their participation is also important for society's development. We often say that "women hold up half the sky." But as brilliant as this reasoning is, the reality may be "skinny". Speaking of this issue, I would like to share with you a typical example. A friend told me that he had just finished recruitment for his unit and had turned down a young woman with strong qualifications. He said his unit had only a handful of posts, and if he had employed a female employee of childbearing age, and she was to have two children, business performance would be adversely affected. However, he also admitted that if his wife or daughter were to face such discrimination, he would feel awful and distressed.

Social life in itself is full of contradictions like this. As I see it, we need to change society's way of thinking, truly respect women's rights to employment and recognise that the development of women and children matters for the country's future. Furthermore, it is very important that supporting policy measures and services must keep pace with the implementation of "the universal two-child policy". For example, the facilities for caring for new mothers and their babies are currently quite insufficient. Therefore, we need to make quick adjustments to meet the needs both with government resources and with market resources. In terms of national laws and regulations, discrimination in employment should be forbidden and our policy attaches great importance to the protection of women and children's rights and interests. Thank you.

(3 minutes 23 seconds, about 630 Chinese characters)

When preparing for press conferences, my team and I studied and discussed many social issues, including school bullying, private education, transgenic technologies and food safety. I was prepared for answering such questions. Although many of the prepared issues were not raised at the press conference, it was a good learning process for me. The knowledge I had accumulated about the issues and my better understanding of the policies and laws all came together to create a concrete basis that enabled me to tell the story of China in the future.

WITNESSING INTRODUCTION OF THE *ANTI-DOMESTIC VIOLENCE LAW*

In Chinese society, domestic violence was a hidden pain that existed not only in urban areas but was more severe in rural areas. Nevertheless, the traditional thinking of "keeping a family problems private" had deep social roots, as the saying goes — families should not air their dirty linen in public. What was more worrying was that if the female victim of domestic violence made the family conflict known by others, she was very likely to be divorced. And in the case of rural women who lacked economic independence, life would be much harder for them. Therefore, the question of whether we should legislate against domestic violence has been a point of debate for a long time. Most women suffering from domestic violence resorted to social support groups, such as the Women's Federation and the Women's Home. Some provinces or municipalities had already enacted local regulations against domestic violence, yet without a specialised law, help extended to the victims was limited. Since the 1990s, a group of Chinese experts, scholars and social support groups had been studying this issue and were committed to promoting the promulgation of a special anti-domestic violence law.

In recent years, public opinion also grew for such legislation to be enacted.

Happiness in the family is the foundation of a harmonious and stable society. The NPC Standing Committee has followed this issue and conducted research. Since the first year of its five-year term, the 12th NPC Standing Committee had been considering enacting a special law on domestic violence, included it as a preparatory subject into its 2013 legislative agenda, and conducted several investigations across the country. These developments attracted much public attention and I was asked three times about the legislation on domestic violence at press conferences.

In 2015, the 12th NPC Standing Committee included the *Anti-Domestic Violence Law* into its annual legislative agenda. The State Council led the drafting of the law, and the All-China Women's Federation contributed a lot to the process. A draft was initially deliberated on at the 16th meeting of the NPC Standing Committee in August 2015 and was then distributed to all relevant authorities before being fully released online to solicit the public's opinion. The draft was revised and then deliberated on for the second time and approved at the 18th meeting of the NPC Standing Committee held in December 2015. The most difficult thing in drafting the law was to properly determine under what circumstances, at which time and using what means can public authorities intervene in family affairs. In a country with deep-rooted traditional ideas like China, family matters are highly personal. There is an old saying, "even upright officials cannot settle family disputes." However, if a vulnerable person continues to suffer from domestic violence, the government must act to protect the rights of the victim. The challenge for the legislation was how to strike the right balance between family privacy and public interference. When public opinions were solicited online, I noted many good suggestions and interesting opinions and clearly the public was looking forward to such a law. Actually, the discussion and preparation of the *Anti-Domestic Violence Law* was in itself beneficial in increasing public awareness of the issue of domestic violence and encouraging the good social conduct of "managing family affairs virtuously."

The *Anti-Domestic Violence Law* took effect on 1 March 2016. On

that very day, there was a first case handled according to this law —
Beijing Fangshan District People's Court reached a verdict to issue a
personal protection order to a 61-year-old woman who had
complained about being abused by her husband for 30 years. Seeing
this law providing legal protection to a long-suffering victim of
domestic violence, I was deeply moved.

Whether women's rights can be safeguarded is an important
indicator as to how far a society has progressed. Data shows that the
labour force participation rate of Chinese women is rather high,
even exceeding the world average. According to the *China Labour
Market Development Report 2016*, compiled by the Labour Market
Research Centre of Beijing Normal University, the labour force
participation rate of Chinese women stood at around 64%, higher
than the world average of 50.3%.[1] According to the *Charting
International Labour Comparisons (2012 edition)*, released on the official
website of the US Department of Labour, the labour force
participation rate of Chinese women was 68%, higher than the rates
in other major economies (59% in the US, 52% in Germany, 51%
in France, 48% in Japan and 29% in India)[2]. It can, therefore, be
inferred that the Chinese government has adopted appropriate and
effective policies to protect and encourage female employment. The
rapid development of China's economy would not be possible
without the contribution of these working women.

In the early days of the CPC, the women's liberation movement
was part of the New Democratic Revolution. At that time, many
revolutionary leaders wrote to advocate gender equality. After the
founding of the PRC, the Party and the central government
attached great importance to protecting the rights, interests and
social status of women in terms of policy and law. The *Charter of the
CPPCC* approved by the First Plenary Session of the CPPCC in
September 1949 established the policy of gender equality and
protection for women. The General Principles stated that "The
PRC shall abolish the feudal system which holds women in bondage.
Women shall enjoy equal rights with men in political, economic,
cultural, educational and social life."

In the 1950s, the rights and social status of Chinese women were
improved dramatically. One incident triggered further policy

changes in favour of women's status. In December 1953, the central government issued *Decisions on Developing Agricultural Production Cooperatives* and set targets for the production of the cooperatives[3], which stimulated a wave of agricultural production countrywide. In 1954, in Puzi Village in Guizhou Province, an agricultural production cooperative was set up which formulated the rule that a man could gain seven work points for a day's labour, while a woman received only 2.5 points. This sparked a controversy about whether men and women should receive equal pay for equal work. Having listened to the debate among the villagers, the Party Committee of Puzi Village cooperative finally supported the women's view and agreed to equal pay for men and women, meaning that there would be no gender distinction in recording work points. It proved very successful in motivating women to join the labour force.

In 1954, there were already female delegates at the first plenary session of the first NPC held on 15 September, when the *Constitution of the PRC* was passed. Article 85 of the *Constitution* stipulated that "Citizens of the PRC are equal before the law." Article 86 specified that "Citizens of the PRC who have reached the age of 18 have the right to vote and stand for election, regardless of their nationality, race, gender, occupation, social origin, religious beliefs, education, property status or length of residence… women have equal rights with men to vote and stand for election." And Article 96 stated that "Women in the PRC enjoy equal rights with men in all spheres of political, economic, cultural and social, and domestic life. The state protects marriage, the family, and the mother and child." The contents of all these provisions was included or implemented in the current *Constitution*. There are also newly added contents: "The state protects the rights and interests of women, applies the principle of equal pay for equal work to men and women alike, and trains and selects cadres from among women." This later addition embodies the continuity and progress in China's legal thinking and policy ideas with regard to safeguarding the rights and interests of women.

Puzi Village pioneered the practice of equal pay and its story was carried in the publication of the Guizhou Democratic Women's Federation in 1955, under the title of *Implementing Equal Pay for Men and Women in Cooperatives*. Mao Zedong read the story and wrote an instruction on it: "Recommend all counties and cooperatives do the same." That was also what prompted him to raise the idea that "women hold up half the sky," which greatly motivated Chinese women. This phrase was later widely spread throughout the world.

As China develops, there are higher public expectations for the protection of women's rights and interests. Therefore, there is more attention given to problems in this area and greater urgency for solutions. This is also an internationally shared concern. I once discussed these women's issues with Christine Lagarde, then Managing Director of the International Monetary Fund (IMF). She was very interested in China's *Anti-Domestic Violence Law* and shared her views on domestic violence which was also a conundrum hidden deep in French society. As she saw it, human society must fight relentlessly against this social problem.

PAY ATTENTION TO ISSUES OF "LEFT-BEHIND CHILDREN"

"Left-behind children" is a unique phenomenon that appeared at a time when China's society was changing by leaps and bounds. Over the past four decades, remarkable achievements have been made in urban development. Foreigners who come to China are most impressed by the skyscrapers that have sprung up in Chinese metropolises, the wide streets, long bridges and high-speed railways. All of these achievements would have been impossible without rural migrant workers, who in 2016 totalled 280 million. Unfortunately, the growing cities had difficulties meeting all the increasing demands for education, healthcare and other public services. Inevitably, most of the rural migrant workers chose to leave their young children at home with their grandparents or even alone. I once visited a primary school in rural Guizhou. The textbooks the children used there were basically the same as those of urban schools, and the school buildings were not bad either. But looking at those children made me a bit sad — young as they were, they looked serious and much more mature for their age. I supposed, growing up without parents around, they must have encountered more difficulties than the others.

These kinds of challenges that concern people's wellbeing tend to emerge when a country is rapidly developing and, unfortunately, take time to resolve. However, some of the special issues must be addressed on a timely basis. In China, there are other kinds of workers whose jobs also take them away from their families. Now, as our economy has improved, Chinese society is more aware and willing to face such issues, and there are also more resources to drive and support solutions. There is reason to hope that these kinds of difficulties will be resolved soon. In terms of legislation, the NPC and its Standing Committee are working hard to keep up with the progress in society.

In 2015, a number of serious cases occurred involving the harming of left-behind children, which gave rise to strong public concern and grief. Some people even accused the parents of being "irresponsible". Legislators of the NPC and its Standing Committee followed the development closely and started considering how to make sure, through legislation and law enforcement, that parents and guardians shouldered their responsibilities. When I was preparing for the press conference in 2016, public concern on this matter was quite high. As I anticipated questions on the issue, I studied the relevant laws and policies and prepared for an answer.

I wanted to make two points. First, to prevent such horrible incidents, I would highlight the point that the local governments and social organisations needed to be fully cognisant of what was going on in their region and perform their duties, including the supervision of the guardians. The other point was that neither local governments nor social organisations could assume the responsibilities of a family. According to the *General Principles of the Civil Law*, parents have the obligations as guardians. If parents fail to perform such obligations for a long period and unacceptable incidents happen, by law, they will also be held accountable.

When I started discussing this with my team and presented them with my two points, my secretary Xiao Qian, a young mother herself, disagreed. She candidly said: "I don't think this is the right thing to say! No parents want to leave their children behind. Now the country is growing fast, many parents have made the difficult choice of working in faraway places and they want to earn more so that their children can live better lives."

Her words were touching. Indeed, my comments sounded cold and hurtful toward those parents who are trying to earn a living far from home. To be more caring and empathetic, my team suggested the following points: first, no parent wanted to leave their children behind, and yet it was a reality in China that there were a great number of migrant workers; second, as urbanisation was expanding, we needed to accelerate the improvement of social services and insurance facilities.

WHAT ROLE WILL CHINA PLAY IN THE WORLD?

At 12:04pm on 4 March 2017, the press conference had lasted for 64 minutes and was almost at an end.

At any press conference, only a limited number of journalists have the chance to raise a question. Normally, my NPC press conferences last for approximately 60 minutes. After the starting words of the moderator and my opening remarks, I had enough time to take between 10 to 15 questions, provided I could answer each question in around three minutes. So, for the more than 500 journalists present, they only had about a 3% chance of asking a question. The moderator, for their part, needed to try to make sure that as many types of media as possible had a chance to ask a question. Apart from allowing the major state media organisations to have their turn, the moderator also had to pay attention to city-level media outlets that had large readerships and viewerships. There is also the professional media whose circulation might not be big, but their journalists usually had good knowledge of the issues closely related to the functions of the NPC, and were therefore more likely to be picked. International journalists had a growing interest in covering the "two sessions" and they also received special attention as they could help me to talk directly to the international community.

At this moment, the moderator announced that we were going to have one last question. Many hands were up. The lucky one was Rita Fatiguso, a Beijing-based correspondent with the Italian newspaper *Il Sole 24 Ore*. She stood up, took over the microphone, and asked in English:

> "How is China improving its role as a global citizen? Moreover, how can China contribute to global governance?"

I noticed earlier that she had raised her hand several times throughout the conference. I had known her for a few years. Every time I held a dialogue or symposiums with foreign journalists based in Beijing, she would come. She did not speak Chinese, nor did she know China well. Her questions were always hard to answer — not that they were asked out of prejudice or in a deliberate attempt at embarrassment, but because her questions were general and her concerns were mostly very basic. For example, in our small group talks, she would ask: "What are the respective responsibilities of the NPC and local governments in terms of environmental protection? How are the measures implemented?" It took me lots of time to answer a question like this. I had to start with the NPC system and government functions, then move on to the process of environmental protection legislation. Then I talked about the supervision of the NPC and its Standing Committee on the State Council, the Supreme People's Court and the Supreme People's Procuratorate. Only then could I finally describe the respective responsibilities of the central and local governments. So, every time I met her, I had to respond at length to her simple yet complex questions. At such fast-paced congress press conferences, especially considering different perspectives of the Chinese people and the international community, I usually found it hard to respond to such questions.

For foreign journalists, it was not easy to understand China's political system and how its government functioned. They could not find sufficient materials in foreign languages to suit their needs, let alone interview Chinese officials. Therefore, although many foreign journalists had been based in China for years, they still had limited knowledge about the country. They were often tasked to ask negative questions by the editors at their headquarters, and some of them came with their own bias, which clearly had an effect on their reporting. But I noticed that the international community was giving greater credit and attention to China's achievements. And with the generational change among the Beijing-based foreign media in recent years, the newly arrived foreign journalists had been more active and their coverage of Chinese stories was more objective and comprehensive. This also meant that we needed to be proactive in providing information and stories to them so that their reporting would have more overlaps with the ideas and information we wanted to promote to the world.

Rita was sincere. She wanted to introduce China to her Italian readers. On the eve of the Spring Festival of 2017, I attended the New Year reception for international journalists based in Beijing which was held by the State Council Information Office (SCIO). She approached me and introduced several newly arrived Italian journalists. Full of curiosity about China, they asked many questions and expressed high hopes for attending China's "two sessions."

I was happy that, at last, she had a chance to raise a question at my press conference. But deep down in my heart, I was a little nervous. Not surprisingly, Rita once again asked one of her simple yet complicated questions: "China is accelerating its role as a world citizen. How can China contribute to global governance?" How is China improving its role as a global citizen? And furthermore, how can China contribute to global governance?"

Her questions had multiple layers of meaning. How to define "global citizen" and its improvement? Who was the standard-setter? What was her implication of "contributing to global governance?" She was asking in a usual Western way with a value judgment in it. A press conference was not an academic seminar, and I did not have the time to debate value judgments, nor could I possibly peel the question's layers off and evaluate them one by one. The essence of her question was about what kind of role China was going to play in the world. When confronting a broad question with complex meaning, it was better to approach it by repackaging it. So I needed to reinterpret the question and address her core concerns, while not appearing to dodge the question.

I started my response:

"This is a really big question, and I cannot tackle it thoroughly in a word or two. According to my understanding, you want to know China's view on the international order and the role China will play in the world after becoming a major country at the world level."

I summarised Rita's question in my own words and channelled her question onto a path I am more familiar with, thus allowing me to respond more easily and succinctly.

Rita put on her simultaneous interpretation headset, looked at me and nodded in confirmation.

I continued with my response:

"I think that first, China needs to run its own affairs well. In the next two weeks, you will have a chance to closely observe the "two sessions" and witness how the CPC and the Chinese government are working hard to improve people's wellbeing. We still have lots of obstacles on the road towards realising the Two Centennial Goals. We will devote ourselves to tackling the challenges in an earnest manner. And in doing so, the focus will be on running our own affairs well, while further opening up to the world and drawing on international experience.

Of course, for a country as large as China, the world has expectations, and China also needs to play a bigger role. China values the international system and the international order with the United Nations at its centre. China, as a founder, beneficiary and contributor to the international order, is also willing to act as a reformer. But how to reform? We maintain that international affairs should be discussed and decided by all countries concerned. Last January, President Xi Jinping delivered important remarks in Davos and Geneva, and proposed China's ideas and solutions to some major international issues. The remarks drew wide attention, as you have probably noticed.

Additionally, China is advancing the BRI. This May, we will hold the Belt and Road Forum for International Cooperation. Under China's initiative, the Asian Infrastructure Investment Bank (AIIB) was founded. China also took the lead in approving the Paris Agreement on climate change. All of these show China as an active participant in international affairs. Of course, the concept of "an international role" and some of the agendas involved are quite new to China. We are still in the process of exploring and learning.

Nevertheless, as a developing country, our participation and the role we play will both comply with the common beliefs of developing countries."

(3 minutes 12 seconds, about 560 Chinese characters)

I started with the "two sessions" to emphasise that China's political system is designed for the benefit of the Chinese people. It is the fundamental purpose of the CPC and the Chinese government to serve the people, so our working priorities are closely related to the people's interests. Then I clarified that our focus is on domestic development, which is to run our own affairs well. I then switched to the international angle and highlighted President Xi Jinping's remarks in Davos, Switzerland, on 17 January 2017. At the opening session of the World Economic Forum Annual Meeting, President Xi delivered a keynote speech entitled *Jointly Shoulder the Responsibility of Our Times, Promote Global Growth*. He said that:

"in the face of both opportunities and challenges of economic globalisation, the right thing to do is to seize every opportunity, jointly meet challenges and chart the right course for economic globalisation. We should develop a dynamic, innovation-driven growth model. We should pursue a well coordinated and interconnected approach to develop a model of open and win-win cooperation. We should develop a model of fair and equitable governance in keeping with the trend of the times. As long as we keep to the goal of building a community of a shared future for mankind and work hand in hand to fulfil our responsibilities and overcome difficulties, we will be able to create a better world and deliver better lives for our peoples."

When I referred to President Xi's Davos speech, I noticed that Rita and many other foreign journalists nodded. I think that was a gesture of understanding and acknowledgement.

CHINA AND INDIA ARE NOT ENEMIES

The questions from foreign journalists usually reflect the focus of attention of the people of the countries they represent on China and on the bilateral relationship. Journalists from other countries tend to raise critical questions. For instance, the *Press Trust of India's* Beijing-based journalist KJM Varma once asked me about China-India relations and his expression was rather critical. Varma and I also knew each other. We had had conversations on several occasions, and he would always refer to bilateral disputes. Personally, I had interacted a lot with the Indian side during my diplomatic career and visited India several times. I noticed that modern India was also developing fast, the people were proud, full of self-respect and boasted a magnificent history and culture. Many Indians had mixed feelings, even prejudice towards China, but more importantly, little knowledge of China. Although the two countries are neighbours, bilateral exchanges and understanding remain inadequate. For China to grow into a world power, it must learn to deal with all countries, to earn their understanding and trust. Yet, there is still a long way to go.

Varma often complained about not having the chance to interview or raise questions to Chinese officials. He also admitted that the Indian people did not have much knowledge of China and called for more bilateral exchanges. Every year when I prepared for the press conference, I needed to learn about China's relations with other countries and the outstanding issues, in case I got asked by a journalist. As to the relations with India, I had also done plenty of homework and paid special attention to the ins and outs of the related issues.

When Varma got an opportunity to ask a question during my press conference in 2017, as expected, he mentioned some of the differences between China and India:

> "India and China just had a high-level strategic dialogue a few weeks ago. Last year, the relationship encountered some difficulties. Especially over certain issues like India's admission into the Nuclear Suppliers Group (NSG) and the listing of terrorist

groups by the UN Security Council, our two countries still have divergent views. During the high-level strategic dialogue, India's foreign secretary expressed apprehension over the possible negative impact on India of the development of the China-Pakistan Economic Corridor and he therefore was not sure whether he would take part in the Belt and Road Summit organised by China. The year 2017 has just begun. How do you see the relationship shaping up this year?"

At a press conference, whenever a foreign journalist throws out a question with some critical opinions, tension starts to build up. A spokesperson needs to consider not only the feelings of the journalist and the country and people they represent but also the expectations of the people on home ground. In such a situation, a spokesperson should first control their emotions, think about the clear stance and ideas they wish to express, and try to quickly find the right angle to answer the question that can balance both domestic and overseas concerns. In terms of technique, when facing critical questions, a spokesperson should avoid being dragged along by the question, otherwise, the answer will just sound like some self-justification. Furthermore, a spokesperson should try to take the initiative and claim the moral high ground. On occasions such as live TV broadcasting, one should try to ease the atmosphere from time to time and avoid having one's rhythm disrupted by nervousness.

While Varma was asking his question, I raised my head to look at him in the eye and nodded now and then to indicate that I had heard him. Giving respect is how you start to earn respect. When I was about to start responding, I noticed that he seemed to be having trouble adjusting his earphones. They were a pair of red earphones, not the kind of black earphones most people were using for the simultaneous interpretation. I was not sure if he could hear the English interpretation, so I paused to ask if his earphones were working well. He replied a minute later: "OK." As short as it might have been, the pause changed the mood.

As to his specific question, the two foreign ministries had already engaged in talks, we could not discuss or solve those issues at the press conference. To respond to his question, I considered it necessary to start on a positive note — after all, India and China are both major developing countries and our disputes and differences are not hostile in nature. So I chose to talk first about the outcomes of the China-India high-level strategic dialogue and expressed some comments in a personalised tone and with some historical depth.

"I have read some coverage on the China-India high-level strategic dialogue, which I thought was pretty positive. The dialogue touched upon a wide range of areas. When we consider China-India relations, we must look at it like looking at a forest, observing both the individual trees, as well as the forest as a whole. I think the relationship between China and India has been advancing rather fast. In the 1990s, when I first started diplomatic work in Asia, the trade volume between China and India was only US$2 billion. I remember there was a young man at my office who mistakenly added one more "0" to the figure in his report. I remarked to him that the figure was too large, that I would never see the number reaching 20 billion in my lifetime. However, last year saw the bilateral trade figure surge beyond US$70 billion.

In the early years, there were only a few flights between the two countries, it took lots of trouble for us to visit India. Today, there are 40 flights bound for India from China every week. Not only do our state leaders meet regularly, but also the Chinese and Indian military exchange visits every year. A cooperation mechanism for combating transnational crimes and terrorism has been established. And China and India share a wide consensus on international and regional affairs. But indeed, there are disagreements and problems, many of which have existed for a long time. You have expressed your opinion, and I have also heard concerns from the Chinese side. I am sure that the two sides clarified their differences to each other thoroughly through diplomatic channels, and arrangements are being made for this year's exchanges.

As I see it, as major developing countries, China and India both face many challenges and difficulties in development. We need to try to understand each other and that can help us address the concerns. There are some problems we cannot solve for now, but we should not stop moving forward and refrain from cooperation just because of the existence of differences. In past years, China and India have continued to negotiate on outstanding issues while moving forward with bilateral cooperation and have been able to arrive at the current level in the relationship. A good example is the BRI with the construction of its interconnectivity projects, which are designed to bolster economic growth, and will ultimately benefit India. It is therefore very important that, although there are differences between us, we need to look at the bigger picture."

(3 minutes 7 seconds, about 590 Chinese characters)

The metaphor of forests and trees and the historical perspective on China-India relations were suggested by my colleague at the Chinese Embassy in India. I also learned from some scholars about the underlying reasons for India's pessimistic attitude towards the BRI. Most people I consulted spoke highly of the value of the relationship and yet were disappointed at the gap in understanding between the two countries. They believed that only by achieving respect and trust at the macro level could the two countries take steps forward towards addressing the specific issues. I expressed these thoughts in my response to Varma, hoping that India could view positively the cooperation with China as part of a larger picture and take initiatives to address problems and advance cooperation. Likewise, the Chinese side should do the same.

BEFRIENDING FOREIGN JOURNALISTS

Having been stationed abroad for years myself, I understand some of the difficulties foreign journalists may encounter, as they have to work and live in totally unfamiliar foreign countries. The language, culture and social atmosphere can all be different from their home country and every day they endure the pressure of work, selecting topics, interviewing and reporting. We are not enemies. To encourage foreign journalists to report on China in an objective manner, we need to provide them with the opportunities to learn about China, interview Chinese people and raise questions at press conferences, thereby drawing them close to China. Fundamentally speaking, news reports are about relaying the observations and understanding of people as well as the interaction of people. The root basis is how people look at and communicate with each other. If we have good understanding and establish sound partnership with foreign journalists, we can not only help them to learn about

China, and convey our policies and news, but also learn what the world thinks of us.

The first foreign journalist friend I made was Jaime FlorCruz from the Philippines. Having lived in China for over 40 years, he became a real "China expert." In 1971 Jaime, with a group of 14 young Filipinos, visited a student organisation at the invitation of the Chinese People's Association for Friendship with Foreign Countries (CPAFFC). Later that year, President Ferdinand Marcos ordered a curfew and arrested hundreds of people following a bomb blast in the Philippines capital Manila. Jaime, along with other college students who were attracted to "communist" ideals, were put on a "blacklist," which made it impossible for them to return to their homeland. He applied to stay in China and his application was approved. When the Chinese youth were encouraged to live and work in the countryside or mountain areas, he also went to work in a people's commune. In 1977, China's universities reopened and Jaime had the chance to take part in China's national college entrance examination which had a special arrangement for international students. He was enrolled into Peking University, studying history. Upon graduation, he started a career in journalism, first as a journalist with the Beijing office of *TIME* magazine, and then as the chief correspondent with the Beijing bureau of CNN.

We met in the late 1980s. He invited the young interpreters at the Department of Translation and Interpretation of the Ministry of Foreign Affairs (MFA) to his house for tea and helped us tackle some of our language difficulties. Jaime knew China well, and our exchanges were free of cultural barriers. I learned a lot from him about the views of Western society and how the Western media operated.

In 1988, I was a member of a delegation to visit New York. At Jaime's recommendation, I visited the headquarters of *TIME* magazine and for the first time observed at close quarters the operation of an international mega-media company. One occasion impressed me the most. It was a heated discussion among the editors about topic selection for the next issue. The office was small and there were very few chairs, some people were standing, others just sat on the table or on the floor, but everybody took part in the lively, attentive and sometimes intense debate. Although I could not fully absorb what was being discussed, the experience, atmosphere and environment stayed with me.

The offices at the headquarters of *TIME* were separated by partitions, and a small room at the corner of the corridor was a cartoonist's office. The walls were plastered with attractive illustrations and cartoons. I asked him a question which had been on my mind: why do magazine cartoons show people in a deformed way and often with twisted faces? He said: "That's to interest people. The primary purpose of any image is to attract readers."

Having stepped out of that room, I strolled around the building for a while before ending my visit. I should say that my initial views of the foreign media were influenced by the visit to *TIME*. Years later, I still like visiting the headquarters of mega-media organisations to observe their operations, always feeling intrigued. I joined a delegation that visited Russia in 2017 and went to the headquarters of *Russia Today* (RT). Over steaming-hot Russian afternoon tea and sweet bread, we watched some hyper-modern news presentations and learnt about some cutting-edge perspectives of young Russian journalists.

Another friend of mine from the media was Lionel Barber, Editor-in-Chief at the *Financial Times*. We met when I was the Chinese Ambassador to the UK. Knowing that I had taken interviews with the British media, he praised my courage to communicate with British society. During a weekend in the summer of 2008, he invited me to a party at his house. I noticed in his collections there was a small statue sculpted during China's "Cultural Revolution," so I asked him about his experience and views on China. Our discussion flowed naturally towards China's way of communicating with the world. As a senior media expert, he advised me against complaining about the Western bias against China, but instead to think more about how to express the Chinese view so that China could be heard by the world. He said the reporting of Western media was based on the information they received, and as the information directly provided by China was scarce, they had to learn about China through what was available and what they were given.

He admitted that the Western world might still be carrying the historical burden of the Cold War, but that did not matter. What did matter was whether the Chinese people could touch the hearts of people elsewhere in the world and convince them with their own ideas and propositions. He encouraged me to take more interviews with the media so that the thinking of the Chinese people could be heard by more British people. Otherwise, the public could only get news about China from indirect sources or from those with an anti-China tendency. The world wanted to hear the Chinese voice, but where was it? The conversation with Barber inspired me. Maybe we did not see the problem because we were too entrenched in it to notice it. We had probably not realised, or were not able to imagine, how eager the world was to learn about the rapid changes in China and how thirsty people were for direct information from China.

ANSWERING CHALLENGING QUESTIONS

In 2013, I left the Foreign Ministry and started my post with the NPC. I wanted to have a conversation with some foreign journalists in Beijing, to get their views on China's current affairs and the NPC, as they were a window through which the world observed China. Then I thought of Jaime. Though it had been a while since we last met, I knew he had been in Beijing. He was familiar with the foreign journalists and I hoped he could help me invite some of them for the meeting.

Jaime readily agreed and with his recommendations, I organised my first forum with the foreign media in Beijing. It was also my first chance to listen to them as a deputy of the NPC and hear their views and experience in China. I observed that their sentiment and attitude were rather negative, as if China did nothing right. This made me a bit frustrated: they had worked and lived here – why couldn't they see China's growth and progress? At the forum, I responded to their questions frankly. Many of them hoped to have the opportunity to raise questions at ministerial press conferences and media sessions. While I agreed that foreign journalists should be given more opportunities to ask questions, I had to stress that communication at these sessions was two-way. When the journalists asked questions, they were not only talking to the speaker but also to the Chinese people. From their words and the tone of their questions, the Chinese public could see how the foreign press perceived and viewed China.

At my first NPC press conference in 2013, I gave Jaime the opportunity to ask the last question:

"I've seen dramatic changes in Chinese society and the economy in the past 30 years. But reform of the political system seems to be lagging behind. Both the Chinese public and China's leaders agree that there is the need for reform of the political system. I'd like to ask, what does this reform entail? The NPC is a very important political institution. What can China undertake to do regarding the institutionalisation of transparency, accountability, and governing this very complex and fast-changing China?"

Such questions are not uncommon from Western journalists. Jaime's question reflected the attitude and concern of many foreign journalists about China, including those in Beijing.

Over 30 years ago, Western countries welcomed China's decision to reform and open up, and developed comprehensive economic cooperation with China, expecting that the country would move towards political reform and follow a Western path after gaining economic prosperity. Now, China had achieved prosperity without changing its political system and development path. Despite the huge economic benefits Western countries had gained from China's development, they still opposed China for not following Western political ideas and systems.

Western journalists rarely raised questions to invite self-praise. Foreign journalists in Beijing were not a friendship association, their job was to question. This was certainly not a "friendly" question from Jaime, although he was more polite than in our private discussions, and used as courteous words as possible. When confronting questions of a critical nature, I would try to turn the question around to convey the ideas and information I wanted to convey, and tough questions gave me the room to respond with tough language without sounding offensive.

I answered:

This has been one of the hot topics in the world of late. Jaime, you must have noticed that there is a broad political consensus in China on how to further deepen the reform and opening up. I have visited and observed many countries in the world and have rarely seen a country like China which has been engaged in such relentless reform over three decades. The reform and opening up has been China's weapon, without which we could not have made today's achievements.

You may remember the days when you first came to and stayed in China. In the 1970s and 1980s, China's economy had shortages and even used food coupons. Indeed, food shortages plagued our country for many generations. But now, we have grown out of that stage. During the "two sessions", you can see what questions are raised by Chinese netizens and the concerns expressed by the delegates. Searching on the internet, you may notice that the questions raised are mostly about people's needs and aspirations toward a higher level. For instance, people want to have equal access to education and employment, better care for the sick and elderly, a greener environment, a richer cultural life, and a more efficient and open government.

The changes in people's focus of attention reflect China's progress, which has been brought about by the reform and opening up. China's reform has been comprehensive and systematic, and it is hard to separate one from another. Time has proved that the reform has been successful, and that our path is the right one for us. At the same time, we are facing many more challenges and difficulties, and there is a strong sense of pressure and responsibility when we talk about the hard work ahead. The common understanding here is that the way to solve problems is through extending reform and opening up. The Second Plenary Session of the 18th CPC Central Committee once again noted that reform should be expanded and many tangible ideas have been proposed.

With regard to political system reform, let me quote from the report of the 18th CPC National Congress, in which there is a special chapter on this topic: "Keeping to the Socialist Path of Achieving Political Progress with Chinese Characteristics and Promoting Reform of the Political Structure." In it, there is the important idea of supporting and ensuring the exercise of state power by the people through the NPC, promoting law-based governance of the country, and strengthening supervision of the enforcement of the Constitution and laws.

This is an important aspect of the reform of China's political system and is also the key element when it comes to the accountability issue that you raised.

I already talked about the work of the NPC Standing Committee earlier, so I will not go into more detail due to time constraints. I would just like to say that, for a long time, questions have been raised abroad regarding China's political system reform. I have got the feeling through international discussions on this issue that some people still tend to view things ideologically. Although the Cold War ended long ago, there are still people who are more or less influenced by it.

It should be made clear that China's political system reform is the self-improvement and development of the socialist system with Chinese characteristics. We cannot accept the view that political system reform means blindly copying from others or otherwise China is not making any political system reform. Denying our efforts is neither fair nor accurate. I have observed in some developed countries serious difficulties that may be more complicated and difficult to solve than in China. However, I did not hear them saying that they needed to change the political system or copy other models. In contrast, when developing countries like China encounter some difficulties, there are voices telling them to adopt others' political models.

This is a misperception and is perhaps also why there is a lack of knowledge and understanding of the Chinese political system. In general, China has now found itself on the right path, and we are making a success of it. We have no reason to give it up. China has a population of 1.3 billion people, whose courage is enough for us to overcome difficulties, forge ahead along the right path, and realise the great rejuvenation_of the nation. Thank you.

(7 minutes 13 seconds, about 1,290 Chinese characters)

I started my response by explaining the changes that China's reform and opening up have brought to people's lives and the objectives of the ongoing "two sessions," while drawing on Jaime's own experience in China over the past decades. On political system reform, I made explanations with some relevant content from the report to the 18th CPC National Congress that I quickly found by searching on my computer. Then, I talked about the NPC's legislative and supervisory functions and, using simple language, I commented on concerns over China's political system and reform.

My response to this question was a bit too long, but I did have a lot to talk about. It was not easy to control the length of a reply on conceptual issues, especially when there were no prepared key points written down as a reminder. I learned from this experience and became more careful in choosing my words and refrained from elaborating when confronting a challenging question. Instead, I would try to quickly identify the core message in the question and connect the essential information I wanted to convey with the question and avoid vague and rambling answers.

Later, when I asked Jaime for a comment, he said that my answer was clear and reasonable. Admittedly, more communication like this was needed with journalists and audiences in the US and other countries to help them understand China's political system and policies as well as the Chinese people's thinking, but this was not going to happen overnight.

INTRODUCING THE NPC SYSTEM

After Jaime retired, a journalist of Chinese origin – Jiang Xin, took his place and reported on the "two sessions" in Beijing for CNN. I did not know him, only noting there was an American journalist who looked Oriental who often came to our briefings for foreign journalists. It was not until he sent me an application and outline for an interview in the days running up to the "two sessions" in 2016 that I got to know him better. I often received interview requests from domestic and international journalists for the "two sessions", which I mostly declined due to heavy workload during the session days. The CNN journalist's interview request aroused my curiosity. It was a major international media outlet with a profound bias against China. A voluntary request for a special interview with the NPC spokesperson was, therefore, refreshing. I went through his interview outline.

His questions included the nature of the NPC, how to effectively exercise power and avoid "rubber stamping," what new bills would be discussed or passed this year, and how delegates carry out their work. He also asked how I coped with the shift in my personal role. Following a discussion with my team, I decided to accept Jiang Xin's interview request. As CNN enjoys high global popularity and has a wide audience, I figured that taking his interview could help to spread NPC-related information internationally and familiarise more people with China's NPC system. Admittedly, a special interview at this time put great pressure on me. Considering the preparation time, I agreed to do the interview late on the afternoon of 4 March 2016, after the NPC press conference.

I did some research and preparation for Jiang Xin's interview and prepared key points for my answers. Since the Western audience knew little about China's political system but were highly prejudiced about it, I needed to make my answers persuasive, using language that was easy to understand. The interview was to be conducted in English, so I needed to find the English terms for some of the legal concepts and terms involved.

The outline he provided was quite detailed, which helped me prepare my answers in a targeted manner. For journalists, a successful interview could not depend entirely on raising surprise questions. Professional journalists would want the interviewee fully prepared so that every question was sufficiently addressed. Only in this way could the interview turn out to be informative and attractive to viewers.

My team was split on how to prepare for the interview. Some suggested a guarded approach, requesting Jiang Xin to strictly keep to the questions listed and the time allotted, in order to mitigate the chance of a "surprise attack". Others saw in Jiang Xin's request a signal of American public interest. They advised me to trust him and be friendly, suggesting that I would get a better result by being relaxed. I prepared for both situations, but based on the pre-interview communications with him, I opted for a friendly approach and the interview went well.

At 5:00pm on 4 March 2016, in a Chinese-style reception room on the second floor of the Media Centre，I took the interview with Jiang Xin. He and the photographers had already set up their cameras and sound equipment. We started by making small talk and then the interview began.

Jiang Xin asked his first question:

"Thanks for taking the time to speak with us. I understand you are very busy at the moment, so my questions will be very simple, and you may explain to our audience in plain words. Many overseas people may not know much about the NPC, except that it is China's legislative body. Could you tell us something about the NPC, and compare it with the US Congress and the UK Parliament?"

I answered:

Thank you for taking an interest in China's NPC. This week, China enters the season of "two sessions," which refers to the annual sessions of the NPC and the CPPCC, attended by all the delegates and members of the two institutions totalling over 5,000. More than 3,200 journalists have registered to cover the events, of which over 1,000 are from overseas. This is indeed a grand occasion. During the "two sessions," the Party and State leaders, as well as heads of provinces, ministries and commissions, will all join with the participants of the sessions to discuss state affairs.

The NPC of China, briefly speaking, is the highest institution of state power in China, which exercises the power entrusted by the people under the leadership of the CPC.

I would not simply compare the NPC to the UK Parliament or the US Congress. Every country has its unique system and its own way of doing things. For instance, China's State Council, namely the Chinese government, is subject to the supervision of the NPC. The role and purpose of the NPC is not to criticise the government for the sake of opposing it but to ensure that the government exercises its power within the framework of the Constitution and laws, and that the laws are strictly enforced.

Jiang Xin then asked:

"I suppose you have also heard about the comments or criticisms of some Western media that the NPC is a ceremonial or symbolic body to a large extent; and some even describe it with the term 'rubber stamp.' How do you respond to such criticism?"

I answered:

If we're talking about ceremonies and symbols, no one can compete with British institutions. While ritual is always necessary, the substance is more important. In China, the NPC is responsible for making laws that safeguard social stability and individual rights. For instance, when the Anti-Domestic Violence Law came into effect on 1 March, a 61-year-old woman who had suffered 30 years of domestic violence from her husband, was given a personal protection order. You could see that laws are critical to social progress as well as fairness and justice in China.

He followed this by asking about the highlights in the legislation work during the 2016 session and then turned to how delegates worked during the sessions:

"You mentioned that the economy and the budget would become hot topics, which is very interesting. It is often impossible for us to see how delegates work, as the conference is held behind closed doors most of the time. Do they argue and discuss with each other at the conference? Are there different opinions, or does everyone agree with the government? What is the conference like?"

I answered:

Firstly, the NPC has nearly 3,000 delegates from all walks of life and we even have an astronaut delegate. Each ethnic minority, even the smallest, is represented by its own delegates. So, we can say that the delegates to the NPC are highly representative. With such broad representation in a country of 1.3 billion people, there is inevitably very active participation in the conference. This session will last for eleven and a half days with one day off in between. There are several plenary sessions at which we will hear the report on the work of the government, given by the Premier, the report on the work of the NPC Standing Committee, given by the Chairman of the Standing Committee, and some other important reports. Voting will take place on the closing day of the conference.

The bulk of the time is for group deliberations, usually divided by region. For example, I belong to the Inner Mongolia Autonomous Region delegation and participate in the discussions of the Inner Mongolia delegation. The group discussions focus more on regional issues, but the delegates also need to understand the overall policies of the country. The new five-year plan, also known as the 13th Five-Year Plan, is very important, as it will be the final one before the first centenary goal is achieved by 2020. Therefore, I believe that each delegation will try to fully understand the central government's thinking on policy, and then consider how their local development can be integrated with the central planning. If there are things they do not fully agree with in the proposed plan, they can offer alternative suggestions. Although there are ten and a half days, the conference is very intense, as there is so much to work on. There are nine items on the agenda to be discussed, and the printed draft budget is especially thick. The discussions at the conference are often heated and lively.

I think you may have also noticed that, in practice, NPC resolutions are rarely vetoed, so some may think we are not that important. Actually, before putting any resolution to a vote, we would have thorough discussions and good suggestions are adopted. When people finally enter the Great Hall of the People to vote, most likely their concerns and opinions have already been taken into account, and they are normally already satisfied with the text. Naturally, there are votes of opposition or veto, which is normal.

My responses were long, as Jiang Xin's questions involved fundamental knowledge that required some explanation. To avoid being interrupted, I tried to show a clear, consistent line of continuity between each point.

He then raised a question about the agenda of the NPC:

"You just mentioned that there are some issues that delegates are concerned about. Are they usually domestic issues? From the perspective of the the international media community, there are many global issues of concern, for example, the South China Sea issue, the North Korea nuclear issue, and human rights issues. Will these also be discussed at the NPC?"

I answered:

Certainly, but foreign policy is seldom the focus of discussion. The Premier would include it in the government work report, and the delegates would suggest some ideas. For example, the Nansha Islands issue is likely to be of great concern to Hainan Province, as it is under their jurisdiction. Depending on the local circumstances, different provinces may have a different focus. Some might offer proposals about the BRI, which is of interest to many provinces, and some might want to know more about foreign aid issues. In short, anything that the people care about will be touched upon in the NPC without exception. This is why we get so many proposals every year. Last year the NPC got over 8,000 policy proposals, which is a heavy workload. One thing that is clear is that the delegates know and understand China's problems and challenges well, much better than the Western media.

He followed up with another question about the NPC:

"As China is changing and rising rapidly, the NPC is also evolving. What comments do you have on the changes of the NPC's role? Can we expect more heated discussions? Will more delegates voice dissent or vote 'No'? What is your view?"

My answer was:

An effective law must reflect the will and consensus of the people, and the making of it must be open and transparent. From my experience with the NPC over the past three years, one step in the law-making process is to widely solicit public opinion, including from interest groups, government bodies, social organisations as well as from experts and universities. Before a law is officially put to a vote, its argument and reasoning undergoes full discussion and debate. Usually, there are three rounds of deliberation on a single law, and the full draft is put online to solicit public opinion. This is a constantly evolving process. So far, there are 247 laws which cover all aspects of society and constitute the foundation and framework of the rule of law in China.

You have travelled to many places in China, so you must have seen what great progress we have made. And you are living in one of the safest countries in the world, which owes a great deal to a well-developed legal system. I believe that the success of the Chinese people mirrors the success of China's political system.

But there is no room for complacency. As President Xi Jinping often says, we are always on the road of reform.

As the interview drew to a close, Jiang Xin raised a personal question:

"On a personal note, do you find it challenging or difficult to work in a legislative institution as the former vice foreign minister? What have you learned from your three years in the legislature? Is there something that you didn't know before?"

I answered:

This has been a tough learning process for me. It is just as challenging as going through college again. For instance, I only had general knowledge of the Constitution when I worked in the foreign ministry, but now I have to understand each and every article. There is a lot to learn indeed. Take North Korea as an example. I have visited North Korea many times, so I know the country well. I have also attended the six-party talks. But at the time, I looked at the country through the lens of international affairs. When I worked with the Foreign Affairs Committee of the NPC, we would travel to various places to investigate law enforcement or to do research on some specific projects. One time, I spent a week with a few committee members inspecting the China-North Korea border by river boat or by car. Part of the border is the Yalu river and when we were on the boat, we could see people's activities on the other side, children swimming, women washing clothes in the water, and guards patrolling. It was so close that we were practically face to face. That was how I came to better understand China-North Korea relations, as well as the unique geology and geopolitical reality. That was quite different from my understanding before.

The place looked peaceful. We could observe people across the river. They were relaxed, working and getting on with their lives. I asked a question to many people on the Chinese side: what is your biggest hope and biggest fear? Officials, civilians, and even my chauffeur gave similar answers: the biggest fear was nuclear fallout and chaos across the border, and the biggest hope was to have an open border so that they could do business with the other side and live a better life. This was a pretty unique experience. It allowed me to see the deeper aspect of the issue and better appreciate our country and its policies.

The interview went quite smoothly. Although sometimes Jiang Xin went beyond the outline he provided, it was still a pertinent interview about the NPC. The CNN broadcast used excerpts of it and posted it on its website. I think this was the first time they used images and sounds that were actually from China to report on the "two sessions." Since then, I have established a good working relationship with Jiang Xin. Each time I had a briefing for foreign journalists, he would be there and was willing to share his thoughts with me. Every year during the "two sessions," he would request interviews with the delegates, providing detailed outlines, and he often asked me to make recommendations for him.

Before the "two sessions" of 2017, I continued to receive interview requests from foreign media outlets. From them, I chose to take an interview with Janis Mackey Frayer, a correspondent for NBC. It took place at 4:00pm on 4 March, in the same place as the previous year: the reception room on the second floor of the Media Centre. It was a brief interview which lasted for about eight minutes. She more or less followed the interview outline provided to me beforehand and mainly asked about China's NPC system and China-US relations. I talked about the progress achieved by the 12th NPC and its Standing Committee over the past four years in deepening reform and advancing legal progress, as well as China's view on the international order and vision for peace. I also said that the US should recognise China's rise in an objective manner and engage in active cooperation.

"REBUFF" WAS NOT MY INTENTION

In my contact with foreign journalists in China, one impression was that Japan had more media and journalists based in China than most other countries, and they usually participated actively in NPC activities. In each special briefing I organised, they would have a strong presence. They were particularly interested in economic issues. Many of them spoke Chinese, though not very fluently, and they worked hard to learn, never hesitating to use it. At symposiums, Japanese journalists would do their best to ask questions in Chinese. But they seldom put their hands up at my press conferences. Some say this was because they did not want to be "rebuffed" which would result in a loss of face for them. This might have something to do with a Japanese journalist's experience with me earlier.

On 4 March 2013, at my first press conference, a journalist with Kyodo News Agency asked me a question in Chinese:

"I have a question about maritime issues. What's China's blueprint for growing into a maritime power? How will it ease the tension with neighbouring countries, including Japan? Will China's diplomacy become even more aggressive?"

His question gave me a good opportunity to talk about China's maritime policy, so I said:

Building China into a strong maritime country is an indispensable component of our modernisation drive, which is clearly stated in the report of the 18th CPC National Congress. China is a large land-based country, it is also a big maritime country. Therefore, to further open up and integrate into the world, we must also build up our marine capabilities. Our path to achieve the objective remains peaceful, and we want to achieve this through mutually beneficial cooperation, especially in our cooperation with neighbouring countries. I was personally involved in working with ASEAN countries on maritime cooperation which has been quite fruitful.

In his question, there was a tone of concern over China's perceived aggressive stance, a feeling which was shared among neighbouring countries at the time, so I thought I needed to respond to that point too:

You asked if China's diplomacy would become even more aggressive. I have lately heard similar comments. Some American and European counterparts also asked: why do the Chinese talk like this? What do you mean by doing that? Don't you think it is a bit too aggressive? So, Japan is not the only concerned party, some other countries share this feeling and such comments can also be found in some media reporting.

China, which was poor and weak for a long time, has now grown strong and is entering the centre stage of the world arena. We are already placed at the centre of some world affairs. But there are many traditional powers on the world stage who have been there for a long time, and it is natural that they take an interest and observe China as a newcomer. They want to watch and comment on our words and actions. They want to know about us. What role is this newcomer going to play? What is it going to do? Will it get along with the others and integrate into the region and the world or will it not be able to fit in?

China is different from the traditional powers in many ways. We have our own political system. We have a large population. We are growing fast and will continue to grow. Not many people fully understand us. Some may anticipate our future based on the 500-year-old logic that power seeks hegemony, and even try to justify this logic with anecdotal evidence. This does happen sometimes, and I do not find it surprising.

The Japanese journalist raised that question, reflecting the perspective of the Japanese public. But as a Chinese citizen, considering the painful memory of the history of war between our two peoples, his comment was hard for the Chinese public to swallow. So, I also wanted to tell him and, through him to let the Japanese people know, how we felt. Actually, his question had already stirred the audience, so I used that atmosphere to my benefit and turned the conversation to the views and feelings of China's general public:

You may have noticed that many Chinese journalists in the hall laughed when you raised the question. Actually, in China, the story is completely the opposite. Many Chinese people, including those from the media, want China to be tough, especially in the face of provocations. This reality and the difference in the way we perceive things needs to be noted.

In terms of the policy, as I just mentioned, China is committed to an independent foreign policy for peace. On the one hand, we firmly safeguard our sovereign rights, and on the other, we are dedicated to maintaining regional and world peace. This is a fundamental principle that has not wavered for over 30 years. But when problems occur, for example, on territorial disputes, when we are confronted with provocations, how should we respond? We decisively face up to them, which I believe is our way of sending a clear message to the region that we want to maintain regional peace and a peaceful order. For countries in the Asia-Pacific region to defend peace in the world, we should trust each other, keep promises and abide by agreements. Otherwise, there would only be disorder.

You asked me about how we resolve disputes with neighbouring countries. I will not dwell on the specific differences between China and Japan, as it has been talked about a lot and both sides know the issue well. China wants to resolve the differences and disputes through dialogue and consultation. But it takes the willingness of both sides, as the saying goes, "one hand alone cannot clap." If the other side decides to take tough measures and walk away from the previously agreed consensus, we have another saying: "it is impolite not to reciprocate." I hope the journalist from Kyodo News will bring this message back to the Japanese government and knowledgeable people. We would like to know whether the people and leaders of Japan are aware of how the Chinese people think. Do they really know the historical facts behind the Diaoyu Islands, and can they face them objectively?

The basic facts about the Diaoyu Islands are clear. First, Japan stole the islands from the Qing government of China in 1895 after the First Sino-Japanese War. This clear fact is recorded in Japanese government documents, archives and academic books. I really hope this fact can be truthfully told to the Japanese people.

Second, after the victory in World War Two, according to the Cairo Declaration and the Potsdam Proclamation, any Chinese territories occupied by Japan had to be returned to China. This is also a clear historical fact. This is why when talking about the Diaoyu Islands, we often say that what was achieved in the victory of World War Two should be respected.

Third, last year the announcement of the Japanese government to purchase the Diaoyu Islands was a breach of the consensus reached with China when we established diplomatic relations. If the consensus is no longer valid, there is no reason for China to hold back either. It is only logical for China to send marine surveillance ships to cruise in the Diaoyu Island waters.

I hope through your report the message can be truthfully sent to Japanese society and that the voice of the Chinese people can be heard by people in Japanese society. With this knowledge they may be able to see objectively what happened in the past and what is happening now, so that the two countries can find a basis for dialogue.

Thank you!

My answer was unusually long and took over 10 minutes, the

longest in all my press conferences. I normally avoid speaking at length at press conferences as it would bore the audience. But this answer, although long, was a truthful reflection of the Chinese people's thoughts, and the audience stayed focused from the beginning to the end. But still, lengthy answers should be avoided. When I tried to cover all the points, it was easy to lose control of time. I told myself to learn from it and remember to be concise and professional.

The initial response of the Japanese journalist appeared to be positive. When he was asked to make a comment by a Chinese journalist after the press conference, he said he was satisfied with not only getting the chance to ask a question but also the answer he received. Indeed, in such an event, it is quite impossible for the person who asked and the person who answered to be in full agreement. Journalists want to ask questions and hope for honest answers, but should not expect the answers to support their own point of view.

After the conference, the Chinese media reported: "Fu Ying responds to a question about 'China's aggressive foreign policy' raised by Japanese journalist." Some commentaries indirectly criticised the journalist's question and his view on Chinese diplomacy, claiming that I was mocking the Japanese journalist by saying: "You may have noticed that many Chinese journalists in the hall laughed when you raised the question." Such opinions seem to have put pressure on Japanese journalists and caused criticism back in Japan. Word even spread among Japanese journalists based in Beijing that they should avoid asking Madame Fu Ying questions, in case they also got mocked.

In 2017, some domestic media reported on my answer to the CNN journalists during the NPC press conference as well as on my attendance at the Munich Security Conference. They highlighted my response to pointed questions on those occasions, using headlines like: "Fu Ying rebuffs US journalist," "Backseat drivers criticise China's military spending, only to be roasted by Fu Ying" and "Fu Ying gives a masterclass in how to rebut difficult questions". However, to "rebut" or "rebuff" was not my purpose. If one shows anger every time one is confronted with an uncomfortable question or criticism, the message one wishes to send might get lost. And anger makes one look insecure.

At international forums or in one-on-one news interviews, the interviewer and the interviewee can win over the audience only with honesty and wisdom. They may disagree and criticise each other's views, and sharp and heated debate is what's expected in such cases.

The knowledge and understanding of China in the international community is far from sufficient and there are both historical and present-day reasons for this. In developed Western countries, prejudice about China runs deep and unfair criticism is not uncommon. In spite of the difficulties, there is every reason for us to use possible opportunities to communicate and let more people know about our ideas and policies. We need to make our case by presenting the facts and first-hand information, revealing prejudice and narrowing gaps. China has endured poverty and weakness for a considerable part of its history, and has come to this stage through enduring hardship and making tenacious efforts. It will probably take another long process and conscious efforts to nurture the kind of confidence and mental strength that befits a great nation.

The interactions between countries is similar to those between individuals. There is the need for mutual respect, understanding and accommodation, rather than bickering and arguing for the sake of it. We should establish an international image of wisdom using persuasive skills. Sometimes using strong words is unavoidable, but to say it in a lighter tone works better. From my experience, when responding to a journalist's questions or in international debates, besides trying to win the argument, my focus is more often on winning over the wider audience behind the camera. Presenting the facts and reasoning things out allows more people to know our views and opinions and, in turn, we may gain more understanding, trust and support. This also better reflects the confidence of the Party, the nation and our people.

SECTION II
STORIES BEHIND THE PRESS
CONFERENCES

4

WORKING FOR "THE TWO SESSIONS"

From March 2013 to March 2017, I attended the five sessions of the 12th NPC. They all had, without exception, diverse agendas and tight schedules. For instance, at the first session in 2013, there were important personnel appointments, including the Presidential election and the appointment of the Premier of the State Council; we heard and deliberated on the reports from the NPC Standing Committee as well as those from the State Council, the Supreme People's Court and the Supreme People's Procuratorate; we examined and approved the government budgets and the reports on their implementation. Additionally, the "two sessions" involved the enactment of, and amendment to, basic laws on criminal offences, civil affairs, the State organs and other matters.

Article 2 of the *Constitution of the PRC* (hereinafter referred to as the *Constitution*) states: "All power in the PRC belongs to the people. The NPC and the local people's congresses at various levels are the organs through which the people exercise state power."

The *Constitution* defines the NPC as the highest organ of state power. The annual session of the NPC held on 5 March marks the "highlight" of the NPC and delegates' fulfilment of their duties. According to the *Election Law of the PRC for the NPC and Local People's*

Congresses at All Levels, the number of NPC delegates is limited to 3,000. They come from all walks of life, including representatives at the grassroots level and ethnic minorities. Additionally, the law states that there should be a certain number of female delegates. For example, 23.7% of the delegates to the 12th NPC were women.

Traditionally, the annual session of the National Committee of the CPPCC convenes two days before the NPC and the two are commonly known as the "two sessions". In 2017 there were 2,924 NPC delegates and 2,237 members of the CPPCC National Committee in attendance, which meant there were more than 5,000 participants gathered in Beijing to discuss national policies and principles. The Party and State leaders and heads of all ministries and commissions join "the two sessions" and listen to the views and opinions of NPC delegates and members of the CPPCC National Committee. At the same time, the progress of the "two sessions" is made available to the general public on television, internet and radio. Given their important and representative nature, the "two sessions" period is also regarded as China's annual "political season" and a moment when the entire country and the world's eyes are on Beijing.

Journalists are an active group during the "two sessions". As correspondents and chroniclers of this important occasion, they witness the evolution of how democracy and the rule of law perform in China and assume the responsibility of communicating the ideas and visions of the "two sessions" to the Chinese people and the international community. In 2017, of the more than 3,400 domestic and foreign journalists registered for the "two sessions", over 1,500 were from overseas. The "two sessions" attract media attention not only because of their importance but also their high level of openness. Take the NPC as an example; all the plenary sessions are open to domestic and international journalists. At every plenary session, the media sections on the second and third floor of the Great Auditorium of the Great Hall of the People are invariably packed with journalists from all over the world. NPC delegates proceed with their agendas under the intense gaze of the media who witness the process and see the voting results on the big screens in the hall at the same moment as the delegates. The journalists are invited to the delegates' special media reception days to observe the group discussion, sometimes taking on-site interviews.

The annual "two sessions" provide a huge, multiple dimensional platform to enable real-time interaction between the State and its people. NPC delegates and members of the CPPCC National Committee come to Beijing with questions and messages they have gathered over the past year from their local communities, as well as well-thought-out suggestions and opinions. This is also a time when journalists extensively report on public concerns and important social issues. All of the information is collected and assessed at the "two sessions" and then conveyed to relevant government authorities. This process ensures that the people's voice is heard clearly and accurately at every level of governance.

The "two sessions" also offer channels for the government to respond to public concerns. A series of press conferences and media sessions are held as a way to give prompt feedback and responses. The press conference held the day before the opening session of the NPC rings the "opening bell". From that day on and throughout the "two sessions", press conferences are held every day with heads of ministries and commissions responding to the concerns and questions in society. Journalists are also allowed to wait at the so-called "ministers' corridor", a passageway in the Great Hall of the People where high-ranking officials pass through when attending plenary meetings of the NPC and the CPPCC National Committee. Here they take questions directly from journalists. mostly about the latest hot topics.

Following is a summary of media interactions during the "two sessions" in 2017. The NPC Press Centre held 17 press conferences for government ministers. Along the "ministers' corridor", 45 ministers and one vice minister took 95 questions from the media. The 34 NPC delegations hosted 37 open-day events. For the media, the grand finale comes after the closing session, when the Premier of the State Council attends the last press conference and takes questions from domestic and international journalists. This is the most direct channel for them to listen to the leaders of the Chinese government. All these events make the "two sessions" an ideal opportunity for news agencies both at home and abroad to learn about and communicate China's politics and policies. It therefore has become known as "a feast for the media."

It goes without saying that the NPC's responsibility to respond to people's concerns and to supervise the government continues throughout the year. The "two sessions" alone cannot find solutions to every issue, and many complicated and deep-seated challenges call for comprehensive and long-term measures. Nevertheless, we want to take full advantage of the important platform of the "two sessions" to promote policies and push for progress.

During my five-year term at the Foreign Affairs Committee of the NPC, I learnt a lot about the People's Congress system and the "two sessions" and often thought about what was the essence of the system and its process. With close observation and direct engagement in the work of the "two sessions", I realised that the essence was "the people". The report of the 19th CPC National Congress pointed out: "The people are the creators of history; they are the fundamental force that determines our Party and country's future... We must regard as our goal the people's aspirations to live a better life, and rely on the people to move history forward."

On 5 September 2014, General Secretary Xi Jinping commented in his speech at the conference to celebrate the 60th anniversary of establishing the NPC that: "The key to the people's congress system's strong vitality and marked strengths is that it is deeply rooted in the people. The name of our country and the names of our state organs at all levels start with "the people", which indicates the basic orientation of China's socialist government." The people's congress system is a fundamental political institutional arrangement that unites the three most important elements in the Chinese system, namely: upholding the Party leadership, the running of the country by the people and law-based governance.

I have gained a deeper understanding of the system and first-hand experience of how it works – the NPC represents the interests of the people and serves the people. One of the important channels for the NPC to achieve its purpose is to listen to the voice of the people and respond to their concerns on the platform of its annual sessions. When preparing for the annual NPC sessions, I need to hold a series of symposiums with the support of the staff from the Foreign Affairs Committee to hear the opinions from experts and media, and identify the main concerns in society, and then communicate with the relevant government agencies for their response on these issues of concern. We then put them together and compile them into a handbook on questions and concerns on the latest issues, which is provided to the "two sessions" delegates as background information and reference materials.

The following chapter records some of what I have witnessed in the "two sessions" en route to its success.

ANNUAL PREPARATION PERIOD

The NPC's Standing Committee normally meets once every two months, during the last week of every even month, to deliberate on draft laws, and to listen to and deliberate on reports prepared by the State Council. Following its last meeting in December, the NPC Standing Committee and its institutions move to preparations for the annual session of the NPC in March the following year.

Traditionally, a number of working groups with well-defined duties and responsibilities are set up to work on the pre-session preparations and take up the coordinating role during the session. For example, the proposal group works on initial examination and prioritisation of the proposals and suggestions submitted by the delegates. It then puts forward draft plans for the distribution and handling of these proposals and suggestions, and classifies them before giving a comprehensive analysis. The secretarial group oversees the implementation of meeting agendas and schedules, and communicates with delegations and different divisions under the Secretariat. It also prepares and distributes ID cards and arranges meeting venues. As for the news group, it develops plans for news reporting, organises important news coverage during the session interview events such as news conferences and media sessions. It also is responsible for managing media and offers services to journalists covering the events.

After the conclusion of the NPC session, the Premier meets the press in the Golden Hall on the third floor of the Great Hall of the People. The NPC and CPPCC hold their own press conferences a day before the opening of their respective sessions in the Press Hall of the Great Hall of the People. All the other important press conferences, including those convened by the State Council ministries, take place at the spacious Media Centre.

Procedurally speaking, the spokesperson for the NPC, who is also a Deputy Secretary-General, is decided on at the presidium meeting the day before the opening session. As the Chairperson of the Foreign Affairs Committee, I would have already been involved in the news-related activities during the preparation period. An important aspect of my role was to provide news analysis and recommended talking points on important questions for the NPC and its delegates, as well as a media information and public opinion digest to government agencies. These materials are provided to delegates to help them prepare for meetings with the media. Government agencies are also urged to pay attention to the materials and provide answers to questions raised by the delegates, the press and the general public.

The news-related work comprised two parts: (1) collecting questions; and (2) filing recommended answers.

Our work began by finding out public concerns and hot topics by consulting with the media and relevant government agencies; we then sorted and categorised the numerous questions collected. The questions were sent to relevant government agencies who were requested to provide clear and detailed feedback on the issues that included: "What are the facts? How is it handled? What are the challenges? What are the solutions?"

To do this, we would first host a series of symposiums to exchange ideas with members of NPC special committees, government ministries and commissions, and the domestic and international media.

But how to identify social concerns? We would hold symposiums with the heads of news agencies and frontline journalists to get a clear picture of public opinion, hot topics and key concerns. Holding symposiums with government agencies was also an important channel for us to identify questions, as the information provided by the agencies on their priorities and key tasks over the passing year could be equally informative. I noticed that hot topics concerning the media and the public often coincided with the policy priorities and key tasks mapped out by government agencies. This also reflected the efficiency of the Chinese government in performing its duty of serving the people and improving their livelihoods. Importantly, such efficiency is guaranteed by the functional structure of the Chinese system with its institutions and mechanisms, including the people's congress system.

Based on the questions accumulated, we would then proceed to analyse and prioritise the key issues and concerns in the fields of politics, the economy, people's livelihoods and diplomacy over the past year and compiled them into what we called a "handbook on questions" for the two sessions. For instance, I still keep the 2017 book, entitled: *A Summary of Issues Most Discussed by the Media for the "Two Sessions"*. The 120-page book contained about 700 questions, of which 72 were on political and legal matters, 274 were about economic issues, 96 were about people's livelihood; four related to ethnic and religious issues, 77 on judicial and anti-corruption issues, 48 on Taiwan, Hong Kong and Macao, and 128 involved diplomatic and defence issues. We gave the categorised question lists to the relevant government agencies. Environmental issues, for instance, were handed over to the Ministry of Ecology and Environment (MEE) and the Environmental Protection and Resources Conservation Committee of the NPC. Trade and business concerns went to the Ministry of Commerce (MOFCOM) and diplomatic issues were passed on to the Ministry of Foreign Affairs (MFA). These materials could help them prepare for press conferences and news-related work during the NPC session.

Collecting questions was just the beginning of the work. What was more important was to come up with authoritative, professional and convincing answers to the questions. Our next step was to select "top priorities" from the "handbook on questions" concerning national development, people's livelihood and public interests. These were the questions we would discuss with relevant agencies and to which we would ask them to provide explanations and recommend answers. The government agencies often gave prominence to responding to our requests. They would conduct research on specific issues and send comprehensive feedback, comprising extensive background information including the causes of the issue, handling progress, and any existing challenges. Recommendations for an answer were offered based on the information provided.

Our next step was to set up a special working group to handle the huge amount of materials contained in the feedback, condensing the pages, polishing the language and re-examining the answers. Finally, *a Handbook on Questions and Concerns* was compiled with every question given 50 to 500-word answers attached with background information when necessary. That was an important part of the preparation work and would be made available to NPC delegates and government agencies. The 2017 handbook, for example, included 134 questions.

As I was in charge of this process, it also prepared me for my own press conference as I could acquaint myself with social news and learn useful facts along the way. It was a warm-up for the press conference I was going to chair. In particular, those highly informative symposiums helped me identify key concerns, be aware of current issues and prepare the key points for my own answers.

News-related activities at sessions of the NPC and CPPCC frequently overlapped, so I often coordinated with my counterpart, the spokesperson for the CPPCC, Lü Xinhua, and his successor Wang Guoqing. They both attended the meetings I hosted, and we would sometimes take turns chairing the symposiums.

STARTING FROM THE INTERNAL INFORMATION: OFFICE SYMPOSIUMS

Among all the symposiums, those held for NPC special committees and institutions came first. This was to ensure that we first learnt about "our own job". The NPC delegates and the general public would first want to know what the NPC and its Standing Committee had done regarding legislation and oversight over the past year. I normally invited representatives from departments of the Standing Committee to attend the symposium, including the special committees and commissions as well as the 16 units under the General Office of the NPC. The participants would have wide-ranging knowledge on issues regarding politics and social issues, economics and the law as well as foreign affairs, culture and the environment.

Topics discussed at an internal symposium are often considered as a lead to the follow-up symposiums for government ministries and commissions. For instance, during the symposium in 2017, the Financial and Economic Affairs Committee raised several hot topics, including the Rmb exchange rate, China's foreign exchange reserves, supply-side structural reform, real estate regulation, challenges in the real economy and the drafting of the *E-Commerce Law*. The Legislative Affairs Commission (LAC) mentioned the formulation of the *General Provisions of the Civil Law*, amendments to the *Cybersecurity Law* and the *Securities Law*, and the renewal of the expiring land-use rights, the enforcement of the *Labour Contract Law* and the pilot reform of the national supervisory system. The Budgetary Affairs Commission talked about local government debt, the real estate tax and progress in the promotion of the principle of statutory taxation. The Hong Kong Special Administrative Region (SAR) Basic Law Committee and Macao SAR Basic Law Committee drew attention to issues such as restraining "Hong Kong independence" activities, the interpretation of Article 104 of the Hong Kong SAR's *Basic Law*, the election of the Chief Executive, the issue concerning "two inspections at one place" for the high-speed railway, and whether Hong Kong would re-initiate its political reform. The Environmental Protection and Resources Conservation Committee spoke on the inspection of the enforcement of the *Environmental Protection Law* and special enquiries in 2016, the State Department's 2015 report on the environment delivered to the Standing Committee and the issue of smog control, which was a matter of great concern to the public. The Education, Science, Culture and Public Health Committee talked about their inspection on the enforcement of the *Food Safety Law*, progress in the implementation of the two-child policy, and amendment of the *Law on the Red Cross Society.* The Ethnic Affairs Committee, the Agriculture and Rural Affairs Committee, the Internal and Judicial Affairs Committee, the Bureau of Secretaries, and the Liaison Bureau also briefed us on the concerns and hot topics in their respective areas.

These extensive and thorough discussions provided a comprehensive review and summary of the past year. At the same time, as it turned out, the majority of these issues overlapped with those brought up at our subsequent symposiums with the government ministries and commissions.

What was highlighted at the internal symposiums was the "the NPC perspective": the roles and responsibilities of the NPC and its Standing Committee with a priority on the oversight over legislation and law enforcement. The NPC institutions often saw things from a different angle to the government agencies. For instance, the Environmental Protection and Resources Conservation Committee looks at the issue of smog control differently from the Ministry of Ecology and Environment. As for key economic and legislative issues, the Financial and Economic Affairs Committee and the Commission of Legislative Affairs hold different views from those of the National Development and Reform Commission (NDRC), the People's Bank of China, the Ministry of Finance (MOF), and public security bureaus, procuratorates and courts. As the participants in the internal symposiums were from the NPC institutions, they were well aware of the role and responsibility of the NPC, and they attached importance to fulfilling the NPC's functions and duties through legislation and oversight. When discussing specific questions, they offered views and suggestions based on their professional experience and knowledge. They would offer advice and inform me about the latest legislative progress and law enforcement inspection they had conducted as well as the result of their special enquiries and other progress in their work.

One experience by members of the Internal and Judicial Affairs Committee in 2017 left a deep impression on me. When they went to provinces on an oversight trip or on law enforcement inspections, what they saw was not necessarily what was truly going on. In order to find out the real problems and the true situation, they had to take measures to make "undercover investigations". They would not carry cameras or camcorders so as not to "reveal their identity," or they would wait until the last minute before disclosing their schedule to the local authorities, to make sure people could not be prepared and "put on a show" to look good.

Those who came to these internal symposiums were "veteran NPC members" with years of work experience and exchanges with them were very helpful. They would share information and engage in extensive discussions with me: What had been done by the NPC and its Standing Committee? How should we respond to social concerns? Which ministry or commission had the information we needed? We sometimes came across very difficult questions and their participation in the brainstorming was valuable.

The internal symposiums laid a solid foundation for preparing the news work of the two sessions. It was like a movie trailer, a prelude to the intensive symposiums with the media, and government ministries and commissions later on.

THE MEDIA SPEAKS FOR THE PEOPLE: SYMPOSIUMS WITH THE MEDIA

Following the internal symposiums were three more rounds of symposiums with media outlets and news agencies, the purpose of which was to identify the main social concerns and hot topics over the past year.

Typically, our first media symposium invited the state-run news agencies, including *People's Daily*, Xinhua News Agency, *Guangming Daily*, *Economic Daily*, *China Daily*, China National Radio (CNR), China Central Television (CCTV), China Radio International (CRI), China News Service, and *Legal Daily*. The second symposium was for the news agencies that focus on reporting on social affairs, such as *Beijing News*, *Beijing Youth Daily*, *Beijing Evening News*, *Legal Evening News*, *Caixin Weekly*, *Southern Metropolis Daily*, and *Southern Weekly*. The last round of the symposium was reserved for the online media, including people.com, xinhuanet.com, china.com, sina.com, sohu.com, qq.com, ifeng.com, thepaper.cn, and guancha.cn. Most of the participants in our symposiums were seasoned "two sessions" journalists or heads of news agencies. They came with a lot of questions and did not attempt to sugar-coat or evade bad news, so the discussions were often lively and passionate.

If internal symposiums and those with government agencies look at important social issues from the perspective of governance, then the media largely represents the views of the general public and reflects their opinions on social issues. The media is focused on how the state is performing in terms of its governance and the results. The issues of concern represented by the media are often what the people are concerned about.

In my experience, the media symposiums worked best in identifying questions for the "two sessions". To begin with, they were good at pointing out the topics and issues. Some topics had been there for years, such as smog control and anti-corruption, while others were new - social emergencies or the South China Sea disputes in 2016, and the 13th Five-Year Plan and the *General Provisions of the Civil Law* in 2017. People in the media could help us to come up with a "map of hot topics" based on how much the public was concerned about certain issues and the frequency of some keywords. Journalists from different news outlets frequently asked similar questions, and that was exactly where the value of the symposiums lay. The more frequently a topic popped up in the media, the greater concern it was to the people; hence the more necessary it was for us to follow it up and respond.

Secondly, once the topics were clear, the media people could help us to identify the exact "questions". The "map of hot topics" informed us what people's concerns were, but that was not enough. We needed to know the spin-off questions from these topics. Let's say you already knew that anti-corruption was a key issue being followed by the media this year. That was not enough. You still needed to find out what specifically the media was focusing on. Was it the progress of some "major cases" or hunting down corruption fugitives and recovering ill-gotten gains from overseas? Was it the drafting of the anti-corruption law or the reform of the national supervisory system? Extending the discussion from a topic to a specific question was a process through which we better understood people's concerns and wishes.

As we tried repeatedly to identify the common concerns, we also needed to pay attention to individual concerns. Listening to the questions from each of the news agencies on the same topic, it was not difficult to spot the differences in their focus. From the state-owned media and independent news agencies to the online media, they all had their own perspectives. Given the diversity of news agencies, having three separate rounds of symposiums allowed us to get a wider perspective of the issues and enabled us to better understand them.

The state-owned media typically sent senior journalists, who often had many years of experience in reporting current political events and were able to raise highly insightful questions with a broader perspective. You could tell these questions were based on both their profound knowledge and sound preparation. It was often these people who raised the "tough" questions that provided me with inspiration. For example, they asked, regarding the pilot reform of the national supervisory system, shouldn't the reform require amending the Constitution? Who should oversee the supervision committee? These were important questions which needed to be looked into and I took a lot of ideas from discussions with those professionals in the mainstream media, especially from their tough questions.

In contrast, journalists from the metropolitan media often paid more attention to "grassroots'" issues. When it came to national policies, they were able to approach the bigger picture from a more rudimentary perspective and raised questions or asked for explanation about things closely related to people's daily life. Their questions were varied, ranging from smog control, the legitimacy of traffic control policy, regulating online ride-hailing, the prevention of bullying in schools, the price of housing, and telecommunications fraud, to personal information security and hospital disputes.

The online media was more interested in current affairs. Symposiums held with these news agencies were refreshing and interesting. They would come up with a lot of new perspectives, new issues as well as new buzzwords. At the 2016 symposium, a journalist mentioned the online debate on large hadron colliders. To be honest, this was not a subject that I was familiar with, and many of my colleagues and other journalists were intrigued as well, so we asked him to tell us more. As it turned out, the focus of concern was not the specific issue, but the wider topic of the state's examination, approval and oversight of large projects.

For me, even a "little-known" "niche" issue like this should not be neglected. No individual or institution could have knowledge of everything. The purpose of inviting a variety of news agencies to attend my symposiums was to make sure that we got to see and hear views that we otherwise might miss or neglect. In an era with a highly developed internet, you never know when an issue could morph into breaking news. The "long-tail" theory on the internet describes how a "little-known" issue could turn out to become very valuable or powerful. Symposiums with the media enabled me and my colleagues to hear voices in various corners of society.

Apart from identifying concerns and questions, media symposiums also offered a perfect occasion to listen to suggestions on how we could improve our work. How to raise efficiency in providing services to the media during the "two sessions?" How could we manage press conferences and media sessions better? How could we speed up the application process and issuance of press cards? How could we encourage the delegations to be more open? How could we better apply new media and emerging technologies at the "two sessions"? There were always new suggestions which we readily heeded. Technical issues were easily fixed, and deep-seated issues were not neglected either. Many participants naturally "touted" and "advertised" their news agencies, but even this deepened our understanding of them.

These symposiums were not one-way, not just for us to "receive information" and take suggestions from. We also used the opportunities to inform them about our endeavours and clarify any misunderstandings. As far as I could tell, it was always good to spend time and effort to share information with the media. The more they were informed, the easier it was for them to report objectively. Since the media represent the people, journalists' knowledge and understanding of issues inevitably influences their coverage and the perspective they communicate to the public.

Holding media symposiums over the years gave me a lot to think about regarding the role of the media in the "two sessions". It came down to the "meta-question", namely, what was the essential purpose of the "two sessions"? As I wrote earlier, the "two sessions" were a platform for the government and the NPC/CPPCC to engage in a dialogue with the people. On the one hand, we used this platform to convey the major policies and principles of the Party and the State, on the other hand, journalists helped us to understand people's concerns by asking questions, acting as monitors and urging government agencies to perform even better.

When speaking to journalists during symposiums, I often emphasised the importance of communication. Admittedly, the "two sessions" could not resolve every issue or answer every question; however, it could be where the issues or questions were raised. In the same way as putting a question mark or comma instead of a period at the end of a sentence, the discussions would continue. For instance, those questions unable to be answered during my press conference could be asked again and be answered at the press conferences held by heads of relevant ministries and commissions. Some questions which had no answer at the time would be likely to trigger discussions, which would make them known to more people who would push for solutions. There would definitely be tricky problems that could not be solved in a short period of time, but by using the "two sessions" as a platform to cast light on them, the relevant ministries and commissions could be better informed of people's concerns, enabling them to develop clearer responses and solutions in future.

The public was constantly raising the bar for good journalism, which meant journalists were held accountable to people's expectations and they needed to do their homework and raise the kind of questions that reflected the public's concerns and produce meaningful reporting. People expected journalists and news agencies to be professional and, in the main, they were. Only with accuracy and thorough understanding of the issue and relevant facts could there be objective and balanced reporting.

Essentially, the NPC and the media should both take the side of the people. The NPC plays its role by performing its duties as prescribed by the Constitution and the law, whereas the media does so by communicating public opinions and government policies. Despite their different roles, the NPC and the media share the same goal: to serve the people following the direction, guidelines and policies of the Party.

MESSAGES FROM THE FRONTLINE: TALKING WITH THE MINISTRIES AND COMMISSIONS

The symposiums held with government agencies, including the ministries and commissions, were a major part of the preparations for the "two sessions".

In 2017, eight separate symposiums were held, inviting a total of 61 ministries or commissions. As China's economy was a hot issue that year, we devoted two symposiums to economic and financial affairs. The first one was attended by the NDRC, the Ministry of Commerce, the National Audit Office, the State-owned Assets Supervision and Administration Commission (SASAC) of the State Council, the General Administration of Customs of China, and the National Bureau of Statistics. The second one involved the MOF, the People's Bank of China, the State Taxation Administration, the former China Banking Regulatory Commission, the China Securities Regulatory Commission, the former China Insurance Regulatory Commission and the State Administration of Foreign Exchange (SAFE). All these government agencies sent a responsible representative to attend.

Wang Guoqing, the CPPCC spokesperson, and I stayed in the meeting room at the NPC office building in the days after New Year's Day for continuous and intensive meetings, talking with representatives from different ministries and commissions. During these symposiums, we discussed topics covering a broad spectrum of government work and shared an extensive amount of information. Every day, when we finally walked out of the meeting room, although feeling exhausted, our minds were active and excited.

The symposiums focused on the major work across the fields and the hot issues attracting public interest. The participants came with lists of their prioritised items and learnt from us what was discussed in the previous symposiums. We then engaged in heated discussions over the key topics and exchanged views and suggestions.

Based on the discussions, the ministries and commissions would mobilise their resources in the following weeks to produce background analysis as well as authoritative and professional responses covering the many social concerns. These materials would be sent back to us within a set timeframe to ensure that the NPC team had enough time to compile the information.

If the media helped us map out the current top issues, the ministries and commissions helped us piece together the jigsaw pieces of the country's development and policy implementation. As each agency brought us its piece of the jigsaw, we could gradually piece them together and complete the picture of China's general development over the past year.

During the symposiums, the questions that often lingered on my mind were: "What is the core issue in the hot social topics? How should we respond to public concerns? Who is the best person to answer these questions? Is the answer convincing?" I found the suggestions and views given by the government agencies highly instructive.

Another important matter to be discussed was about inviting the leading officials to host press conferences, take interviews or speak to the press in the "ministers' corridor" during the "two sessions". As the ministries and commissions were primarily responsible for many of the areas identified, they had first-hand information regarding the specific issues that concerned people; should they face the press directly, they could provide the most authoritative and professional answers. Therefore, we would try to confirm with the participants their press arrangements. In the end, of course, we would leave the matter for them to decide, as they knew better which issues needed a response and what was the best way to respond to public concerns.

We would also listen to the opinions and requests of the ministries and commissions to improve our press services during the "two sessions". Establishing the "ministers' corridor" was one of the creative improvements introduced during the 12th NPC. Previously, prior to every plenary session, high-ranking officials would enter the Great Hall of the People from either the East or the North Gates leading up to the Hall together with all other delegates. Before every plenary session, the wide staircase in front of those entrances would be packed with people walking through. They also became the ideal place for an "ambush interview" and reporters would certainly not miss this rare chance to raise questions to important figures. It was understandable, as the public crave first-hand information, and the reporters were there to get it. But the scene was difficult to control and often looked like a "battlefield". Many reporters waiting on the staircase would swarm around the ministers or celebrities forcing questions upon them.

The "two sessions" were solemn occasions, and this situation was not appropriate as they showed neither sufficient decency nor dignity for reporters or interviewees. To address this problem, we tried to put some order into the process by making special arrangements. At the "two sessions" in March 2013, a 200-metre passageway was created, leading from the North Gate to the main Auditorium in the North Hall for ministers and high-ranking officials to walk through. This passageway was open to the press, and the reporters could set up their cameras and wait alongside the passageway and question people passing by. The arrangement worked quite well and there were continuous improvements in subsequent years. It was now affectionately known by reporters as the "ministers' corridor". Increasingly, high-ranking officials were more willing to take questions in this corridor. The arrangement turned out to be an effective communication channel between the government and the people and was therefore welcomed by the general public.

For the government, whenever a social concern arises, the earliest response to the public is the best way to build people's trust and broaden their awareness of the Party policies, and win their understanding and support for the work of the government. Chinese government officials possess rich practical experience. They are mostly highly qualified with political and professional expertise and can be quite eloquent. However, speaking to journalists requires preparation and this is also something we often discuss and share experiences about during the symposiums.

Young people say they are "winging it" when taking an exam

without preparation. For government officials, when taking interviews or hosting press conferences, it is like taking exams. The difference is that we are speaking to the people responsible for communicating the Party's policies and governance messages. We are not conveying personal opinions, so we must not "wing it". All the government agencies attach great importance to their media interactions during the "two sessions" and have dedicated teams to work on the preparation. We would provide them with the lists of hot issues of concern to the media and the general public which serve as important references in their preparation.

As the Chinese saying goes: "One minute on the stage takes years of practice." This is the motto of Chinese opera training and is also what I believe in, borne out of my own experience. I would share with them my lessons and tips for handling press conferences.

I would suggest that the recommended answers prepared for the speaker should be as concise as possible, because meticulous and complicated formal statements were not necessarily appropriate for spoken communication. Statements on our accomplishments, clichés and slogans should also be kept to a minimum. Instead, we should try to respond directly to questions: "What are the existing problems? What policies and measures are in place? What are we going to do next?" We should provide more information that the people needed to know. One further suggestion was that the answers should be presented in clear, plain language whenever possible.

I would also pass on the requests and opinions of the media to the ministries and commissions. For instance, a journalist once reminded me that when a speaker was reading a script or statement without looking up and making eye contact with the audience, they sounded very dull and could not capture people's attention. A press conference was not a place to make a policy report; the journalists and the general public behind the cameras were looking for responses and answers to their concerns. Those of us sitting on the stage had the responsibility and an obligation to speak clearly and unambiguously when responding to people's concerns. This was how we gain people's trust and support.

Attitude and body language also played a role. As government officials, we needed to realise that although we were speaking to journalists, it was the people that we were communicating with. Therefore, our attitude needed to be humble, unpretentious and courteous. The relationship between the government and the media should not be confrontational nor competitive. On the contrary, we worked together to satisfy the people's need for information, informed them and conveyed to them the policies and the thinking of government. To fulfil our unshirkable obligation to respond to people's concerns, we should keep our "heads bowed like a willing ox" instead of "coldly defying a thousand pointing fingers with an angry glare", as Chinese poems describe.

Admittedly, officials are only human and, like any normal person, have their own character, we cannot expect them to behave perfectly all the time. I believe, however, that being brusque to your superior may only be a matter of personality, but being brusque to ordinary people is a matter of attitude. Therefore, when facing the public, we need to have an appropriate attitude to reassure the public and put them at ease.

The general public's expectations are that government officials should be both rational and sensitive, that they should be authoritative, professional, objective and as accurate as possible when answering the public's questions and, at the same time, confident, honest and approachable. When people say "I can count on this official" or "I can trust them with these things" after watching a press conference or an interview, then the goal of effectively communicating between the government and people is achieved. In this way, the Party's guidelines and policies can be better understood by the people whose support serves as the foundation of Chinese governance.

TELL THE CHINESE STORY: HOST BRIEFINGS FOR FOREIGN MEDIA

Foreign media and journalists are a special group of people who pay close attention to the "two sessions" and play an important role in covering the occasion. China's success and growth achieved through reform and opening up has attracted increasing international attention and a growing number of foreign journalists to come to

Beijing. According to statistics provided by the Information Department of the Ministry of Foreign Affairs, the number of resident foreign journalists based in Beijing was more than 170 in 1990 and was approaching one thousand in 2017. Furthermore, at major events in China there would be a remarkable number of additional "parachute reporters" temporarily dispatched to China.

The foreign media is an important bridge and window through which the rest of the world can learn about China and hear the Chinese story. The growing foreign media presence represents the increasing interest and attention China is receiving from the international community. They can inform the world about China's policies and development, and when there are major or interesting events, they can give the world eyewitness accounts. Over the past few years, China has been making an effort to speak directly to the international public, which has been effective, particularly in developing countries, such as those in Africa. In the Western developed world, however, China's voice is still insufficiently heard. This is partly due to political barriers left over from the past and also to an improvement in China's ability to communicate.

Exchanges with the foreign media were an important component of my media work before the two sessions and my office held special symposiums and briefings for the foreign media. The purpose was to touch base with them and exchange views on current affairs. Foreign journalists actively participated in them and in 2016 they were attended by over one hundred journalists including dozens of news agency heads. They were from the BBC, CNN, *The Economist*, Japanese news agency Kyodo News, German newspaper *Die Welt*, AFP and *Lianhe Zaobao* from Singapore. They were given briefings on the work of the NPC and its Standing Committee over the past year by leading members of relevant committees, which was followed by a Q&A and warm discussions. Through them, we were also able to find out international concerns and questions about China.

I noticed that the foreign media was mainly focused on three issues: China's economic development; the South China Sea issue; and the ongoing deliberation on the *Draft Law on the Administration of Activities of Overseas NGOs in China*. All these issues were too complicated to be explained thoroughly in a few words, and if they were left until the "two sessions", there would be limited opportunities for them to be raised and clarified. It was therefore necessary to hold briefings on specific topics such as these for foreign media.

On 3 February 2016, Gu Shengzu and Shao Ning, Vice Chairpersons of the Financial and Economic Affairs Committee of the NPC, at my invitation, gave a three-hour briefing on China's economy in Conference Hall One in the Great Hall of the People and over one hundred foreign journalists attended. The two of them gave fairly comprehensive accounts, one on China's current economic development, while the other reviewed and detailed the historical path to reform of China's SOEs. They then took questions from the journalists. The briefing provided a stage for lively discussions. Many news agencies, including the Japanese television network TV Asahi Corporation, and the Dutch newspaper *Het Financieele Dagblad*, asked questions that concerned them and received professional answers. It was a more effective mode of communication compared with the short Q&A occasions available during press conferences or media sessions during the "two sessions". The briefings provided more time for fuller discussions and there was also time to talk extensively about related background information and relevant knowledge. There were more chances for journalists to raise questions. Holding briefings before the "two sessions" could help spread information, build understanding and trust. These briefings added positively to our media relations.

Another hot topic for the foreign media was the South China Sea issue. A BBC journalist attending the briefing mentioned that China's activities on Meiji Reef (also known as Mischief Reef) affected normal civil aviation activities and limited the freedom of overflight, and that an aircraft had already been affected during its flight. I was familiar with the situation of the South China Sea and Meiji Reef, but I did not know to which incident he was referring. As I could not give a direct answer to his question, I stated China's policies and position instead and promised him I would look into it. Afterwards, I found a video released by the BBC on the internet. In early December 2015, a BBC reporter and his crew rented a light civil aircraft in the Philippines and flew over Meiji Reef, which was 140 nautical miles from the Philippines. Their stated intention was to "investigate" China's construction work on the reefs, but the act was obviously provocative. It could be seen from the video that the Chinese personnel stationed at Meiji Reef had spotted the aircraft and requested them to leave. The crew on the aircraft, however, claimed that they were going to Palawan Island and were only passing by. The video was less than five minutes long and the narration was about how fast China's construction work was proceeding on the reef and how threatening China was.

I was somewhat annoyed by this video. According to international law and common practice, a sovereign state is allowed to take defensive measures when its sovereignty is intentionally challenged. The behaviour of the BBC reporter on the small aircraft was obviously trying to stir up trouble. This was what the Chinese call "*pengci* (i.e., deliberate behaviour intended for blackmail)." Considering the special circumstances in the South China Sea, the Chinese side was already exercising restraint. The misleading video had been widely distributed. I therefore needed to at least clarify the case with the Beijing-based foreign media and inform them of our position regarding the South China Sea and the construction work on the reefs. In this way I could also help lay some groundwork for the "two sessions".

On 21 January 2016, I invited Wu Shicun, President of the National Institute for South China Sea Studies (NISCSS), to brief foreign journalists on the South China Sea issue in Conference Hall One in the Great Hall of the People. He spent more than two hours explaining in depth the South China Sea disputes from the perspective of history, laws and policies, before answering questions. The participants listened to him attentively, reminiscent of students attending a seminar in college.

A briefing couldn't clear all the doubts and concerns of the foreign media about the current situation and the history of the South China Sea. But they at least learnt more about the current situation and history of the South China Sea disputes and felt our sincere intention to communicate with the rest of the world. It was regrettable that the BBC journalist did not attend this briefing, as he too could have learned a great deal.

Before the "two sessions" in 2016, the foreign journalists were also paying close attention to the drafting of *the Law on the Administration of Activities of Overseas NGOs in China* (hereinafter referred to as "the *Law*"). Since the very start of its drafting process, the *Law* had drawn considerable attention from overseas, especially governments and NGOs in Western countries. In December 2014 and April 2015, the draft of the *Law* was deliberated by the Standing Committee of the 12th NPC before being made public in full to solicit public comments. Many international organisations, institutions and foundations as well as some foreign embassies and consulates in China, and foreign government leaders expressed their opinions and concerns. During my overseas visits and when I attended events in China, I also received verbal or written suggestions, which I passed on to the Legislative Affairs Commission of the NPC Standing Committee for consideration.

It was understandable that the *Law* came into focus. As the word "Overseas" in its title suggests, the main subjects to be regulated by the *Law* include people, organisations and funds from foreign countries. People who were concerned wanted to know how to perform registration and filings when the new law came into force. "What would be the prerequisites for setting up an organisation's representative offices? What are the regulations on funds? What are the conditions for taking the post of chief representatives or representatives?" Some of their concerns about the uncertainties could be resolved through communication and explanation.

There has been a large number of overseas NGOs actively operating in China for a very long time, and many of them have played a positive role. For example, in my homeland, the Inner Mongolia Autonomous Region, there is a place called Engebei which suffered severe desertification. In the 1980s, Japanese Professor Toyama Seiei and the Japan Association for Greening Deserts came to Engebei to plant trees. They encouraged and supported the local people and worked with them. Professor Toyama Seiei spent eight to nine months in Engebei every year, working ten hours a day helping the local people plant trees. After he passed away his children followed in his footsteps, and many more Japanese joined in to carry on his mission to green China's deserts. The vast desert which once was barren has now been transformed into an oasis. I visited Engebei and met Mr Toyama. I was amazed when looking at the before-and-after photos and how it had changed. My family and I also planted saplings to taste a bit of the hardship.

There are many other overseas NGOs that are playing an active role in fields such as environmental protection, education and scientific research. They are more than welcome in our country. China did not want to make the *Law* to "drive them out", rather, the intention was to standardise and regulate NGO activities and provide them with legal protection, which had previously been absent. Indeed, there are people and organisations under the guise of "NGOs" who conduct activities that undermine China's security and interests, and this is something we cannot allow to continue.

On 28 January 2016, I invited Guo Linmao, Director of the Social Law Department of the Legislative Affairs Commission of the NPC Standing Committee, to host a briefing on law-related issues in Conference Hall One. During the briefing, Mr Guo spoke for about two hours, first about the purpose of the *Law* and the progress made. He then patiently and professionally responded to various questions raised by foreign journalists. Guo made it clear that China fully recognised the meaning and value of overseas NGOs and that the *Law* was created to expect a more regulated manner of the activities of these organisations in China.

At my NPC press conference on 4 March 2016, I was asked by a journalist from the German newspaper *Die Welt* about the NGO Law. My answer conveyed three points: first, I explained how the *Law* was being deliberated, emphasising that we had been soliciting and considering opinions from various interested parties; second, there was no doubt that many overseas NGOs brought experience and funds that benefited China, and they also acted as important conduits of communication between China and other countries. The *Law* was intended to provide a more regulated environment for NGO activities rather than prohibiting or restricting their legal and beneficial activities; third, I provided a more detailed explanation of what was meant by "registration with public security bureaus" as required by the *Law*.

With my experience over the past few years, I became more familiar with communicating with foreign media. When preparing for the "two sessions" in 2017, I found out that the Beijing-based foreign media's primary interest was China's economic progress, so I invited Wu Xiaoling and Gu Shengzu, both Vice Chairpersons of the Financial and Economic Affairs Committee of the NPC, to brief the foreign media on 18 January 2017, about China's economic development. The briefing lasted for over two hours, during which the two vice chairpersons made professional and comprehensive presentations on China's current economic and financial issues and answered dozens of questions from journalists. They helped clarify many misconceptions and concerns among the foreign media. Their briefing certainly helped to increase understanding before the "two sessions".

As the annual session of the NPC in 2017 was going to deliberate the draft of the *General Provisions of the Civil Law*, I also asked Zhang Rongshun, Vice Chairman of the NPC Standing Committee's Legal Affairs Committee, and Jia Dongming, Director of Civil Code of the NPC Standing Committee's Legal Affairs Committee, to offer a briefing for the foreign media on the *General Provisions of the Civil Law* on 9 February. He explained the compilation and the progress of this Law.

In five years, from starting the preparations for media work of the "two sessions" in late December until the opening of the "two sessions" the following March, all the NPC institutions would be on very busy work schedules, exciting and at the same time, orderly. All of us were working for the same purpose, that was to serve the "two sessions," no matter what their role; chairpersons and vice chairpersons, special committee members, colleagues at NPC institutions, or conference hall staff and cafeteria chefs.

The "two sessions" are not just an occasion for those who work for the sessions. They are for our country and our people. Moreover, as a grand platform to hear people's voices and answer people's concerns, the "two sessions" also serve as a critical link in the modernisation of China's national governance system and governance capability. Therefore, apart from those who work directly at the sessions, the delegates to the sessions, committee members, people in government agencies and friends from the media, are all engaged in the "two sessions" in their own ways. We have only one goal, which is to work together for the betterment of China.

5

"FORGED" INTO A NEWS SPOKESPERSON

MY FIRST EXPERIENCE WITH A PRESS CONFERENCE

My first experience with an NPC press conference was in 1988. That was the first session of the 7th NPC held from 25 March to 14 April. The session elected new government leaders and heads of ministries and commissions, and Qian Qichen became Foreign Minister. He gave his first press conference in this new capacity on 13 April at the Great Hall of the People. I was his interpreter for the occasion. It had been two years since I had returned from studying at the University of Kent, in the UK, and I was working at the English Division of the Translation and Interpretation Office (now Department of Translation and Interpretation) at the Ministry of Foreign Affairs.

Interpreting plays a key role in communication. If an interpreter does not clearly express what the speaker is saying, however eloquent it might be and however profound the meaning, the listener won't be able to get it. Consecutive interpretation at televised press conferences is more challenging than usual as there is little room for correction, placing the interpreter under greater stress.

In order to get into the right frame of mind, I arrived 40

minutes early and waited in the Shaanxi Hall of the Great Hall of the People for the press conference to begin. It was the first time I had interpreted for such an important press conference which was broadcasted on live TV. I had never been more nervous in my life. The Shaanxi Hall, which was located next to the hall where the press conference was about to take place, felt empty and seemed very chilly. As I was sitting there in expectation of the "big event", my anxiety grew, my heart raced and my hands were cold.

A moment later, Foreign Minister Qian arrived. As always, he walked in briskly, looking composed and confident, and his eyes were brightly piercing as usual.

"Are you nervous?" he looked at me and asked in a caring tone.

"Yes, I'm very nervous," I replied honestly.

"Today is a test for you as well as for me," Foreign Minister Qian said.

It rang a bell in my heart. No, how could I be so absorbed with my own feelings? He was going to do the talking and I was just going to be interpreting. The new Minister must be under greater stress given the burden on his shoulders. On realising this, I felt remorse and endeavoured to get rid of my anxiety quickly. An idea flashed into my mind: I remember reading in a book that keeping one's muscles tense and active could ease the brain and mental tension. I ran to the washroom and jumped on the spot 50 times. Soon the strenuous exercise made me pant, my heart rate quickened and my body warmed up. It seemed to work and relieved my anxiety and stress, and I no longer felt cold.

When I returned to the Shaanxi Hall, Minister Qian was still sitting there quietly. He watched me running out and back in with a gracious smile. His composure affected me and I gradually found my peace. As I calmed down, I began to empty all those troubling thoughts out of my mind and got ready for the intensive interpretation work of the upcoming press conference.

The time was up and I followed Minister Qian onto the stage to begin the press conference. He spoke fast and kept his answers concise. The grammatical differences between the Chinese and English languages made it difficult to process short sentences when interpreting from English into Chinese. I found it was not easy for me to organise his briefly constructed sentences into complete English sentence structures. I also found it quite challenging to grasp the gist of his response and convey his intended meaning and attitude promptly to the audience. I tried my best to keep up with his train of thought, decode his intentions, grasp the key points and implications of his answers, and then use the most appropriate expressions I could think of to articulate them in English. Everything went well. When you are concentrating intensely on something, time passes quickly. The press conference was over before I knew it.

This first experience at the NPC press conference left a deep impression on me and helped me better manage my emotions. From then on, I tried to pull myself together, remove the chaotic thoughts that sometimes cluttered my mind, and remain calm to focus on what needed to be done. This experience has proved to be very helpful whenever I have an interview or speak at a press conference.

In my career as a diplomat, Premier Zhou Enlai was my "first idol" and I learnt mainly about his ideas and diplomatic skills from historical archives which have always been my guide. Qian Qichen was my second idol. To me he was a strict but amicable leader and teacher. During my two years working for him as an interpreter, I was deeply influenced by his modesty, dedication, perseverance and broad-mindedness. When I transitioned from an interpreter to a diplomat in late 1990 and started working on Asian affairs, I still had many opportunities to work for him when he attended multilateral meetings and diplomatic negotiations. I was able to continue to learn from his great diplomatic skills. For example, when confronted with diplomatic dilemmas, how to prioritise interests and achieve better and more results, and how to realise a win-win outcome by compromising on nonessential matters. Another example is how to be confident without being overbearing, show respect for others without diminishing oneself, and eventually winning respect and trust in diplomatic engagements. As an old saying goes, "those who do not plan for the future will find trouble at their doorstep." Minister Qian would approach an issue from a long-term and strategic perspective first, then decide on the tactics and the steps to deploy. In this way, he could uphold the general direction while dealing with the details flexibly to achieve optimum results. Minister Qian was always even-tempered with his staff and got along well with everybody. He did not talk much, and yet he had the ability to inspire and rally those around him. Each and every one of us who worked with him felt trusted and important, and were imbued with a sense of responsibility. At the same time, he furnished us with ample space to do our own work creatively and develop a sense of achievement.

Minister Qian became the first spokesperson of the MFA in 1982, when he was the Director-General at the Information Department of the MFA and it established the MFA's spokesperson system. It all began in March 1982 when China and the former Soviet Union finally saw a window of opportunity to turn around the relationship after more than two decades of antagonism and tensions. Leonid Brezhnev, then First Secretary of the Communist Party of the Soviet Union (CPSU), delivered a speech in Tashkent. Despite the habitual "attacks" against China, he released a rare signal indicating that his regime was willing to improve relations with China. Deng Xiaoping seized this opportunity immediately and instructed the MFA to make a gesture of response. On 26 March, Qian assumed the role of spokesperson, and gave a response in three sentences: "We have noticed the remarks of Chairman Brezhnev of the Soviet Union on China-Soviet relations in Tashkent on 24 March 1982. We categorically refute his attacks against China in the speech. In China-Soviet relations and in international affairs, we attach importance to how the Soviet Union acts."

This press conference was held at the entrance hall of the main building of the MFA without any seats for attendees. Still, it marked the outset of establishing a press conference system. On 23 April 1983, the All-China Journalists Association introduced to the Chinese and foreign journalists for the first time the spokespersons of the ministries and commissions under the State Council and people's organisations.

The spokesperson system for the "two sessions" was established later. When the first session of the 6th NPC and the 6th National Committee of the CPPCC were convened in Beijing in June 1983, Zeng Tao, then Deputy Chairperson of the Foreign Affairs

Committee of the NPC, served as the first spokesperson of the NPC sessions. On 4 June, he and the CPPCC spokesperson released the news regarding the holding of the "two sessions" to Chinese and foreign journalists. Since then, the "two sessions" have maintained the tradition of holding a press conference prior to the opening day.

There had been six spokespersons of the NPC sessions, namely Zeng Tao, Yao Guang, Zhou Jue, Zeng Jianhui, Jiang Enzhu and Li Zhaoxing. They were either veteran diplomats or outstanding journalists who had made great contributions to the NPC press conference system. Some were respected former leaders of the Foreign Ministry whom I knew well. Their adroit and responsive demeanour at press conferences was admirable. It had never occurred to me that I could take their place years later. What is so wonderful about life is that it always takes you by surprise, and nothing you have learnt is wasted. That is to say, everything that you learn turns out to be an invaluable asset at some point in your life.

IT'S NOT JUST ME — IT'S A TEAM

It looks like a spokesperson at a press conference is able to skilfully deal with any situation and take assorted questions from journalists in a composed manner. "How do you manage to pull it off so easily?" is a question I get asked a lot.

If you think the success of a press conference depends on the spokesperson alone, then you are mistaken. Today's society is always thirsty for all sorts of information and the division of labour in a society has become more and more refined. Consequently, it is next to impossible for an individual to become proficient in every field or profession. A spokesperson of the NPC sessions is assigned complicated and challenging responsibilities, which cannot be fulfilled by the efforts of a single person.

Social governance in an industrialised society depends on specialisation and people are becoming more and more influenced by the advancement of globalisation and have begun to gain international vision.

To fulfil my role as a spokesperson, I had a supporting team of professionals. What is so great about teamwork is that it pools the wisdom of many people enabling one to penetrate the surface and find the truth beneath.

I held my first press conference in March 2013, there was not much time to prepare and I was overwhelmed by the many social and economic issues, as well as the specialised legal subject matter. I struggled through the whole process and quickly realised that working alone could not produce a satisfactory result.

Given that the country was fast-tracking the comprehensive rule of law, and the NPC was proceeding with its endeavours following the 18th CPC National Congress, I needed to stay in sync as the spokesperson. I kept asking myself a question: How can I chart out a more rational and effective way to prepare for press conferences?

In 2014 when the new preparatory work began, I started to build a team. The members were veteran experts specialising in law from NPC institutions. They had good knowledge about the NPC's work and were able to provide me with legal expertise. The following year, I increased the number of members by inviting a couple of scholars from universities and think tanks to come on board, drawing on their expertise in the areas of law, economics, international affairs and communications. At that point, I had built a versatile, talented team from within the NPC and beyond, who were mostly young and worked part-time for the team. Still, they participated in the work with great passion, a hardworking spirit and devotion.

This group of diverse talents could generate an intriguing "chemical reaction" during brainstorming sessions, as they complemented, informed and inspired each other. They had many different opinions and perspectives to offer, which reflected the look of today's Chinese society — the co-existence of diverse views and demands. This process deepened my understanding of the issues, helped me grasp the full spectrum of public opinion, and guided me to consider different interests and perspectives without bias.

My work with the team followed a three-phase process:

In the first phase, we screened and sorted out questions based on the information we accumulated from the symposiums held earlier with the media, various ministries and commissions, and discussions with experts and think-tank scholars, through which we could identify and determine the key concerns and hot issues of the people and the media. Those symposiums were held for the NPC's general press work and I often met with my team on the sidelines to analyse and select questions to ensure my own preparation for the press conference was also correctly targeted and efficient.

In the second phase, we would start conducting surveys and outlining key points for recommended answers to key questions. To achieve this, I would assign priority research topics to team members in accordance with their expertise and interests. They could then figure out the intricacies of the questions and consider possible responses to them in combination with the priorities of the NPC and its Standing Committee. Then we would sit down and discuss, before splitting up to write the proposed key points for the recommended answers. Finally, I needed to rephrase these key points in my own words.

The last phase was rehearsal. In a simulated press conference, my team members would ask questions from different angles, then comment on and analyse my answers by pointing out gaps before making modifications and adjustments. I encouraged them to be "strict and critical", and they certainly were tough on me and especially harsh when it came to pointing out my recurring mistakes. Thanks to their rigorous training, I was able to deliver my press conferences with greater confidence and ease.

Driven by similar beliefs, members of our "squad", as we called it, got together before every "two sessions" and worked harmoniously and efficiently, and with a strong sense of team spirit. We were like a family, learning from each other, meeting challenges, and growing together. Many times, when I felt tired or discouraged by challenges or setbacks, they gave me confidence, encouragement and strength.

Many other people helped me along the way, aside from my team. I used to ask colleagues in NPC institutions to critically proofread and revise my key points in recommended answers. They would come up with important corrections and suggestions. Xin Chunying, Deputy Secretary-General of the NPC Standing Committee, was one of my stern teachers. I regarded her opinion as the "authoritative quality control". Deputy Secretary-General Li

Lianning, who was once in charge of the press activities of the NPC Standing Committee, was also a legal expert. He guided me when I was first preparing for press meetings and continued to share many insights with me. There were so many colleagues who helped me along the way, and the list was too long to name everyone here. I benefited greatly from all of their suggestions and advice.

I would also seek suggestions and advice from think tanks, as well as experts and scholars, when faced with specialised and difficult issues. I could never have acquired so much information and knowledge without their help. It was wonderful to have their support, and I am deeply grateful for all that they did!

FINDING OUT PEOPLE'S QUESTIONS

In the early days as a spokesperson, there was the sense of being overwhelmed by a sea of questions and concerns that needed to be looked into and addressed. The main challenge concerning preparation back then was to find the right direction as soon as possible.

China, as a large, densely populated country, has secured remarkable achievements in economic, social and cultural domains through nearly 40 years of reform and opening up. We have successfully addressed the issue of poverty, which has troubled the country for centuries. Nevertheless, new challenges keep emerging. As General Secretary Xi Jinping stated in his report delivered to the 19th CPC National Congress: "As socialism with Chinese characteristics has entered a new era, the principal contradiction facing Chinese society has evolved. What we now face is the contradiction between unbalanced and inadequate development and the people's ever-growing needs for a better life." This shift has been demonstrated over the past five years, and has been reflected in public opinion during the NPC sessions.

On occasions like the NPC press conferences, the media expects us to respond to all kinds of questions which may cover a wide range of subjects, including the rule of law, justice, security and the environment. However, a press conference is constrained by time and space. In a routine press conference of one hour, one may be able to answer approximately twelve questions, with sufficiently short answers. What are the primary concerns of the people? What questions are most likely to be raised by journalists?

In our preparations, the key issue for my team and myself was: how to effectively engage and respond to the most pressing concerns of the media and the public, the most important and most frequently raised question, while also conveying important messages from the Congress - all in the space of an hour?

Where to start? We would select important questions from a host of media concerns. The "handbook on questions and concerns" compiled from earlier symposiums for the Delegates served as the basic reference material for my team. Next, we would develop a "matrix diagram" of the questions from the media. On the vertical axis were the names of different media outlets, and on the horizontal side were their questions. The overlapping questions were marked in black. We could then make a list of the hot-button social concerns based on this diagram. It was not as easy as it sounds, so Liao, a young team member who majored in media studies, helped to do the analysis, sorting and ranking of the collected questions.

Guided by the diagram, the team worked together to select about 70 key questions from among the list, taking into consideration the relevance of these questions to the work of the NPC and its Standing Committee.

Why did we choose exactly 70 questions, no more, no less?

Let's just say the number was based on previous experience.

I could not deal with more questions. A person has a limited amount of time and energy. Instead of going through countless questions, I needed to delve into the most important ones and study them thoroughly. Also, there was no need to have more. The 70 "questions" represented 70 "topics", such as smog, anti-corruption, the 13th Five-Year Plan, the North Korea nuclear issue, the South China Sea issue, etc. Condensed from a broad range of questions, they could essentially cover all media and public concerns. However, journalists might come up with completely different questions on the same topic. All I needed to do was to make sure that I was fully prepared for each topic and then adeptly respond to questions.

We could not narrow the scope further because we might have

missed some public concerns. Therefore, as far as I was concerned, the meticulous selection of 70 pertinent questions was the necessary foundation for our subsequent work.

The criteria for selecting questions was whether they were the people's most important concerns. We also needed to consider whether it was appropriate for the NPC spokesperson to answer.

While talking to journalists at media symposiums, I often reminded them to consider whom their questions were targeted at when they designed questions for the "two sessions". For example, if they wanted to ask a question at the NPC opening press conference, they should ensure it was relevant to the session or the functions of the NPC and its Standing Committee, preferably questions about legislation and oversight. If they had a question about government administration, it would be more appropriate to bring it up at the press conference held by the head of a relevant ministry/commission, or the Premier.

For me, I preferred to keep close ties with journalists, as a press conference was not a one-person show for the spokesperson. Instead, the spokesperson and journalists were in a symbiotic relationship. Only through the interaction of answering could messages to the public be effectively conveyed. An informative press conference depended not only on a good performance from a spokesperson but also from journalists. A successful press conference often produced astute questions asked by journalists which were met with enlightening answers from the spokesperson.

I could not "customise" journalists' questions, but I would encourage them to mull over their questions and focus on concrete issues so that they could come up with excellent questions which addressed people's concerns. When you hear a question that gets to the point and is presented from a unique angle and in a witty style, you are dealing with a journalist who has thoroughly researched the subject. I have found through years of experience that journalists who have done their homework well are often able to raise good questions.

My team and I would divide the 70 questions into three broad categories, according to their level of public attention, their importance and urgency. We named the process "question prediction".

"Category I" comprised about 20 "must ask" questions based on our initial assessment, including hot-button issues and the current top priorities of the Party, the State and the NPC and its Standing Committee. For instance, in 2017 questions in this category included the *General Provisions of the Civil Law*, anti-corruption efforts, the reform of the supervisory system, smog, the defence budget and military reform, protection of personal information, school bullying, the individual income tax threshold and other issues which were attracting wide attention nationally.

"Category II" also comprised around 20 questions. They were less pressing than "Category I" but had already triggered some social discussion, so we assumed they could pop up during the process. For example, this category in 2017 included questions on the *E-Commerce Law*, the *Cybersecurity Law*, the *Securities Law*, China-US relations and North Korea's nuclear program.

"Category III" consisted of longstanding questions followed by domestic and foreign media over the years. Even though I was quite familiar with these frequently asked questions, I still needed to update my information with new data and the latest developments.

Actually, our preparations consisted of a lot more than this. There was a large database of possible questions, you never know what you might be faced with and it was always better to be prepared.

Normally, we could finish working on "Category I" in the first half of February and continue monitoring current affairs in case any new issues cropped up.

At this point, it could be said that we had located the most important questions on the mind of the media and the general public.

DETERMINING OUR POSITION AND PERSPECTIVE

Once we were clear on the questions, the next step was to find answers to them. Most importantly, we needed to first determine our position on these questions which could lead us to the correct angle to handle the questions with a pertinent and effective response. So what should be my position when facing the media and the public?

General Secretary Xi Jinping delivered an important speech on China's political system at the Great Hall of the People after he was elected President of China at the First Session of the 12th NPC. He stated: "We must uphold the leadership of the Party, the position of the people as masters of the country, and the rule of law, uphold the principal status of the people, expand people's democracy, advance the rule of law, uphold and improve the fundamental political system of the people's congress and other basic political systems, including the system of multiparty cooperation and political consultation under the leadership of the CPC, the system of regional ethnic autonomy, and the system of community-level self-governance, build a service-oriented, accountable, law-based and clean government, and fully mobilise the initiative of the people."

In light of the instruction of General Secretary Xi Jinping, the position that we should adhere to is upholding "the leadership of the Party, the position of the people as masters of the country and the rule of law." China's system of the people's congress is the fundamental political arrangement which ensures the unification of these three most important political components. The role of the people's congress is the soul of this fundamental system and also the source of its vitality.

Being a Party member, I have gained a deeper understanding of our system as an NPC deputy and a member of the NPC Standing Committee. Party leadership is the fundamental guarantee in ensuring that the people exercise state power and govern the country through the people's congresses. The rule of law is the way to achieve this goal. Under the strong leadership of the Party, the NPC and its standing committee handled the electoral fraud case in Hengyang and the voter fraud case in Liaoning Province in strict accordance with the law. Every move has demonstrated the resolute will of the CPC Central Committee to ensure that all power in China belongs to the people and the fundamental objective of upholding the principal status of the people. The CPC Central Committee will not let any challenge threaten the essential system of the people's congress and remains dedicated to advancing law-based governance.

Since the 18th CPC National Congress, General Secretary Xi Jinping has proposed the "Four-pronged Comprehensive Strategy," which involves comprehensively building a moderately prosperous society in all respects, comprehensively deepening reform, comprehensively promoting law-based governance and comprehensively enforcing strict Party self-governance. More precisely, the rule of law is the basic strategy for the Party to lead the people to govern the country, as well as a basic approach to governance. The State promises and works in accordance with the laws and regulations formulated by the NPC and its Standing Committee to proceed with all aspects of work in a law-based manner. In addition, it will protect people's rights to equal participation and development, maintain social equity and justice, and respect and safeguard human rights.

With the position clearly outlined, the question is how to put the concept into practice? My experience over the past five years came down to three key points:

We should uphold the leadership of the Party — The guiding ideology, theories, principles, policies, decisions and the practical arrangements of the Party should be our basic position.

We should uphold the position of the people as masters of the country — The people's opinion should be our position, so we should always stand by the people and work to satisfy their desire for a better life.

We should uphold the rule of law — Law-based governance should be our position. The NPC and its Standing Committee, as China's top legislative body, should formulate and amend the law under the leadership of the Party, in line with the opinion of the people. A spokesperson should view every question from a law-based perspective.

For instance, at the press conference of the second session of the 12th NPC on 4 March 2014, a journalist with US-based outlet CNN asked:

"We hear every day of sad stories of ordinary Chinese citizens, known here as petitioners. And these desperate people write letters, complaints, petitions or demonstrate in the streets or in front of buildings, complaining of injustices, abuse of power or violations of their human, social and civil rights. What has forced these people to resort to petitioning? Why can't they get to address their grievances through the courts and the existing legal system? What is China doing to address this problem and, perhaps, to abolish the petitioning system?"

He raised a long and somewhat sharp question. But it was true that some people trusted petitions, namely public complaints and proposals in the form of letters and visits, more than they trusted the law. Regarding this problem, the NPC and its Standing Committee held the same position as the policy of the Party while the State Council, the Supreme People's Court and the Supreme People's Procuratorate also took the same position. That was to make sure people were able to protect their legitimate rights and interests through legal channels.

Then why was it so difficult for people to lodge a complaint against a government agency or official? When a citizen, legal person, a person or organisation intended to take a government agency and its officials to court, it was often difficult for them to file a case, progress the trial and enforce the court ruling. This was because administrative departments did not want to be sued, and the courts were reluctant to accept these kinds of cases. Even if they did, the plaintiffs would find it difficult to win, let alone enforce the court ruling. Consequently, instead of lawsuits which should be the normal channel, many cases went into the channel of petitions in the form of letters and visits to the authorities. People often chose to start a petition to draw the authorities' attention to their predicament when their rights and interests were compromised, as they did not have access to or were unable to resort to legal channels.

Law-based governance was the keyword in responding to this question. The CPC adopted the *Decision on Some Major Issues Concerning Comprehensively Deepening Reform*, at its Third Plenary

Session of the 18th Central Committee. One of the requirements of the decision was to bring the law and litigation-related petitions into the legal channel.

Since the early days of the 12th NPC and its Standing Committee, the amendments to the *Administrative Procedure Law* and the *Administrative Reconsideration Law* were included as agenda items in the five-year legislation plan with the aim of curbing administrative power, promoting law-based administration and building a law-based government. In December 2013, the NPC Standing Committee completed its first deliberation on the *Draft Amendment to the Administrative Procedure Law*, which marked the first major amendment to this law since it was enacted 23 years ago. Priority was placed on how to ensure that people's rights were better protected when taking legal action and how to resolve difficulties in administrative litigation. To address these issues, the amendments required heads of administrative departments to appear in court to answer questions; infringements relating to land requisition to be incorporated into administrative procedures; and people were allowed to file oral complaints against government agencies/officials. In addition, relevant departments under the Standing Committee were doing research on the *Administrative Reconsideration Law* in preparation for its future amendments.

That was the position of the NPC and its Standing Committee, and it also reflected what the people wanted. For me, to answer the question from the US journalist, I first needed to establish my position which should also be the position of the people and the position of committing to facilitating the settlement of problems. Once this was clear, the other points would be easy to articulate. Although it was a bit jarring to hear an American bring up China's domestic problems, it did not affect my using this opportunity to introduce China's policies and practices to Western journalists by telling them what the problem was and how we were addressing it. What was more, I was speaking in front of not only the US journalist but also the Chinese public.

My answer was as follows:

"The petition system is a rather unique institutional arrangement in China. Over the years, it has played an important role in communication between the authorities and the people. Certainly, as time has changed and Chinese society has evolved, social conflicts have become increasingly complicated. Therefore, we have come to face new pressures or challenges in petition practices, which now call for improvements. To address the issue, new policies and reform steps have been proposed.

One of the steps which is particularly related to the NPC is to take reform measures to guide the handling of law and litigation related petitions into the channel of the rule of law. Such issues are usually known in China as "litigation initiated by the people against the government", which can be realised in two ways from a legal perspective. The first is to resort to the Administrative Procedure Law, a law established more than two decades ago. It provides legal guarantees for people to safeguard their rights and interests. However, the experience over the past 20-odd years has shown that the law needs improvements. According to the research and investigation of the implementation of the Law, the rate of plaintiffs winning administrative litigations has declined dramatically in recent years. Furthermore, there are instances where an administrative department is unwilling to be sued, or a court is reluctant to accept an administrative litigation case. Some people complain that they do not dare sue the government, nor are they able to win such a case. As a result, a huge number of law and litigation related cases have been brought forward in petitions in the form of letters and visits. The NPC Standing Committee will work on an overhaul of the law, with the purpose of removing as many barriers as possible that are impeding people from suing the government. When amending the law, we will also listen to the opinions and suggestions of people from all walks of life.

The second way is through the Administrative Reconsideration Law, which was formulated 15 years ago. Theoretically speaking, it offers a more convenient channel for relief, but the results of law enforcement reviews suggest that its function has not achieved its full purpose. For example, people at the community level in some regions have not even heard of the existence of such a law. So, the NPC Standing Committee has also included the amending of this law in its five-year legislation plan.

By amending the two laws, we aim to exercise better oversight on administrative powers, which is an important aspect of the initiative to "confine power within a cage of regulation". With such improvements in place,

Two weeks later, on 19 March 2014, the General Office of the CPC Central Committee and the General Office of the State Council jointly published the *Opinions on Law-Based Handling of Issues Concerning Law and Litigation Related Petitions*. The *Opinions* required that all regions and government agencies took firm steps to intensify coordination and support, in order to improve the working mechanism of handling law and litigation related petitions, and strive to forge synergies for law-based settlement of issues concerning petitions. The amendment to the *Administrative Procedure Law* was passed on 1 November 2014, and took effect as of 1 May 2015. I learned from news coverage that in May 2015, the people's courts had accepted and heard 26,000 "litigations initiated by the people against the government", a year-on-year increase of 221%.

The point is that, whatever the question, construction of an answer can stand the test of time, as long as you are clear about your position and seek truth from facts.

I also came across some rather tough questions. When we were preparing for the press conference of the 2016 NPC session, a hot topic, namely "human rights lawyers", emerged. It was repeatedly brought up at the media symposiums and continued to be a heatedly discussed topic in the run-up to that year's NPC press conference.

The issue started with the public security agencies' action against the Beijing-based Fengrui Law Firm in July 2015, for its suspected involvement in a major criminal gang. Nine lawyers and several other staff members were placed under criminal coercive measures. They were accused of plotting to challenge more than 40 sensitive legal cases and incidents since July 2012 and disrupting social order. When this became breaking news, some in the foreign media played up the case, criticised China's legal system and human rights conditions, and blamed China for clamping down on "human rights lawyers".

Since the case was in the middle of judicial proceedings, the authorities were not able to reveal the details, thus leaving an information vacuum that was filled with conflicting voices and confused public opinion. It became a hot topic I had to face when preparing for the press conference.

Under our *Constitution* and according to the related laws, the people's courts and the people's procuratorates independently and impartially exercise judicial and procuratorial power in accordance with law. No Party or government agency or individual may intervene in judicial activities. Therefore, before the final judgment of a case, the NPC spokesperson cannot comment on the case. However, as the issue had drawn significant attention from the media and the public, I needed to respond if asked about it by journalists.

I decided to listen first to the voices of the interested parties, namely lawyers. I invited lawyers from among the NPC deputies and listened to their explanation of the circumstances. The profession of lawyers in China started from scratch during the reform and opening up, and has now grown into a strong group of professionals. The Chinese legal community has for years provided quality and efficient legal services that have improved the livelihoods of the people. Their work contributed to economic and social development, the development of law-based governance and guaranteed orderly social services. Most lawyers are conscientious and adhere to the law when assuming their responsibilities to safeguard the rights and interests of their clients. Some even moved from big cities to settle down in western regions or impoverished rural areas to provide legal aid for local people. These outstanding legal practitioners are the real "human rights lawyers" who live up to the policy requirements of the Party.

Indeed, in the name of being "human rights lawyers", there were a few lawyers, and some non-practitioners, who sought to capture public attention for personal gain. Some even developed ties with anti-China overseas organisations or individuals and violated laws. Nevertheless, we should not let the reputation of lawyers as a whole be tarnished by the actions of a few individuals. The lawyers we talked with expressed that they hoped to be understood, recognised and respected in their practice of law and called for better protection of lawyers' rights to practice law.

My team and I began studying the matter and considered

positions and perspectives from which to respond to the related questions. First, we needed to understand the relevant policies and uphold the position of the Party. The Party has always attached importance to the work of lawyers. China currently has 24,000 law firms nationwide, compared to 70 or more when the reform and opening up was first introduced. At the same time, the number of lawyers has grown from over 200 to more than 300,000, a clear indication of the substantial progress in developing the rule of law. Since the 18th CPC National Congress, the CPC Central Committee has further confirmed the status and role of lawyers, and set out new and higher requirements for the law profession and lawyers. General Secretary Xi Jinping pointed out that lawyers constitute an important force in advancing the rule of law, and intensive efforts should be devoted to enhancing the law profession and lawyers. The Third Plenary Session of the 18th CPC Central Committee regarded the work to reform and improve the lawyer system as an important step in comprehensively deepening reform. It has required the adoption of measures to improve the mechanisms for protecting lawyers' rights in practice, as well as the system for punishing illegal practices and strengthening professional ethics. Lawyers are expected to play an increasingly important role in safeguarding the legitimate rights and interests of citizens under the law. According to the "Four-pronged Comprehensive Strategy", law-based governance plays a fundamental and supporting role. Against this backdrop, the law profession is embracing unprecedented opportunities, and I considered this to be the necessary position when responding to this question.

Secondly, I now needed to consider the questions on the perspective of the people. With the all-round economic and social development of China, people's awareness of the law was rising. When people encountered social or economic problems, they would want to check the relevant laws and regulations, and therefore had grown accustomed to using the expertise of lawyers when there was a need. Lawyers began to have an essential role to play in terms of respecting and protecting human rights, and became an indispensable driving force in China's social progress.

Finally, I needed to consider the questions from the point of view of the NPC and its Standing Committee. In 1996, the NPC Standing Committee adopted the *Lawyers Law of the PRC*, stipulating that efforts were to be made to enable lawyers to play their role in the development of the socialist legal system. Lawyers were required to abide by the Constitution and laws while strictly observing professional ethics and regulations governing their legal practice. It also specified that the legal practice of lawyers should be protected by law.

At the press conference for the NPC session in 2016, a journalist with the China News Service mentioned "human rights lawyers" in a question. My reply was the following:

> *"Lawyers have become very important professionals in China. Be it in social affairs or economic activities, when people come across disputes or difficulties, they are likely to turn to lawyers first for help. Therefore, lawyers constitute an important force in the development of China's socialist rule of law. Our legal community is thriving. When the practice of lawyers restarted in 1979, there were just over 200 lawyers nationwide. Now there are approximately 300,000 lawyers in the country. This represents huge progress, not to mention the fact that the legal community continues to grow rapidly every year.*
>
> *With respect to specific individual cases that have attracted wide discussion, the judiciary will handle them in accordance with the law. But what I would like to say is that, "human rights lawyers" is not a term many people here agree to use, because it sounds like a political classification of lawyers. Lawyers above all should be models in observing the law. According to the provisions in the Lawyers Law, lawyers must abide by the Constitution and laws in their practice. They should also be held accountable should they knowingly commit any violation.*
>
> *As China is comprehensively promoting the rule of law, the healthy growth of the legal community is both necessary and critical for the execution of laws and safeguards for social equality and justice. Moreover, the rights of lawyers to practice in accordance with the law should also be guaranteed.*

Most of the content of this response derived from my discussions and research with my team. But I missed out an important paragraph in my talking point: "according to the *Lawyers Law*, all lawyers should be 'human rights lawyers' as lawyers' responsibility is to protect the legitimate rights and interests of their clients." This point was something my team and I saw as important and needed highlighting, and I regretted having forgotten to mention it. Indeed, I find that doing press conferences without regrets is unavoidable and can never be fully satisfactory. There is no perfect spokesperson and there is always the possibility to do better.

On 13 June 2016, the Xinhua News Agency reported that the General Office of the CPC Central Committee and the General Office of the State Council had published the *Opinions on Deepening Reform of the Lawyer System*. The document set out that the lawyer system is an important component of the socialist judicial system with Chinese characteristics and an important symbol of the advances in the rule of law. Lawyers are an important force in the implementation of the fundamental principle of the rule of law and the establishment of the socialist rule of law in China, and are a vital constituent of the contingent of professionals devoted to the socialist rule of law.

A PRESS CONFERENCE IS THE ART OF "LISTENING"

To communicate well, you need to first and foremost know your audience. The audience for a televised press conference comprises diverse groups with a variety of backgrounds. From civil servants keeping an eye open for new interpretations of important information or homemakers watching TV while doing housework, to retired officials and workers who are interested in political and social developments, and taxi drivers who listen to the radio while driving. They expect a spokesperson to give a clear explanation on issues of public concern and interest in plain and vivid language. The scholars, experts, entrepreneurs and students who are also watching and listening hope to get some important signals or learn about policy information which will influence the development of the country and society.

Communication is aimed at reaching people's hearts and minds. To attain this purpose, one needs to stimulate people's interest to listen by talking in a way that they can understand and, moving one step further, to convince them. For the public, a press conference is the art of "listening" while for a spokesperson it is the art of "speaking".

When speaking at a press conference, I wanted my voice to be heard by the journalists in attendance. But, more importantly, I hoped that ordinary people watching TV or listening to the radio could also understand and accept the messages I was trying to convey, and even could remember some of the key information. In other words, I wanted the audience to understand, enjoy and remember what they heard, regardless of their status in life, profession or age. All of our efforts would be worth it if we could make this happen.

The goal of making the audience "understand, enjoy and remember" was more easily said than done. It would take endless effort to achieve and this was exactly the objective that my team and I tirelessly worked towards.

The first threshold was ensuring that the audience could "understand what I say".

This seemingly simple requirement was, in fact, the toughest one. Each year, to address hot-button issues and the key questions, I would receive a great deal of relevant information from the NPC Standing Committee and the government agencies concerned. However, they were mostly official documents, with complex contents written in standard yet bureaucratic language, some of which was obscure. When responding to people's concerns, I could not use the kind of language that was specialised, theoretical and in the style of official documents. I needed to convert the official and literary-styled language into easily understandable answers for the press conference.

But how to achieve it? A question and an answer forms a dialogue. I should try to speak in my own language while conveying clearly the key messages.

First, I needed to be brief. It was better to wind up each answer in three minutes, making a point a minute. If the answer was too long and there were too many points, it would be hard to keep the audience's attention. Therefore, when working with my team on key points, we tried to keep every answer to within 300 words, breaking them into three paragraphs. We would then refine the language within this limit.

From my experience, if I had a prepared note to hand, I could improvise an answer based on the key points and generally gave a four minute, 600-word answer. However, if the prepared key points could not fully answer the question, I might need to say more to fully address the issue. In the case of a totally unexpected question, the answer was more likely to be unstructured and lengthy. So, in general, the answers based on prepared materials were compact and usually worked better than an unprepared or totally improvised response.

Preparing the key points for answers was a demanding job. Sometimes a piece of material was well structured, even brilliant, after being refined through expert discussion and teamwork. Yet to avoid being wordy, a great deal of information had to be cut out. My team members often exchanged their drafts for cutting as they could not bear the pain of removing things from their own work. The need for brevity was such a tough objective, my team and I often struggled over a single word or sentence, changing it again and again. The magic of language is that as you meticulously drill down, even by altering a single word or phrase, the impact can be different.

When responding to questions at a press conference, a spokesperson should try to use plain language as in everyday life. Back in 2013, when I was preparing for the NPC press conference, I needed to consider responding to questions about a reform step for "all government budgets and final accounts". After reading through lots of materials, I managed to understand its meaning and worked out a professional-sounding explanation. I tested it by reading it out to my family to see if they could understand. They let me finish and then looked at me, dazed, and asked: "What exactly are you trying to say?" I changed the language again and again, and read it to them a second and a third time. It was not until the fourth attempt that my husband, who was cooking, turned towards me and said: "Well, this time I got it." He could even repeat it back to me.

This process really inspired me. Our policies and major reforms are all designed to serve the people. We can only earn stronger support from the people if they know and understand the policies.

Therefore, when speaking to the public, I needed to, first and foremost, explain why an issue or reform was relevant to them. On this tax reform issue, my final version attracted the public's attention as it highlighted the points: "Simply put, to implement 'all government budgets and final accounts' is to include all government revenues and expenditures in the budgets and final accounts. That is to say; every penny the government spends is placed under supervision. This is a very important move in implementing the state's policy for law-based governance."

This showed that "how to say it" was as important as "what to say."

The second threshold was making the audience "willing to listen."

If making people "understand what they hear" is a technical issue, then making people "willing to listen" is more of an art. To cross this threshold, I needed to communicate with the journalists and the public at a more personal level and, where appropriate, exchange friendly chitchat — in this way, people naturally became interested in what I said.

So, what makes people willing to listen? From my experience, people are willing to listen to sincere words. Sincerity is not just a formality, but what people truly feel and are moved by, something that is intangible yet can touch the heart. As long as you are in awe of people and feel a sense of responsibility for them, your sincerity seeps into your words; words of substance, words of feeling.

Journalists raise questions to reflect public concern. They are usually about people's "personal interests", such as real estate taxes and the *Securities Law*, or their "major concerns", for example, food safety and smog. Others may be related to some painful issues, as in ending domestic violence and protecting women's rights and interests. There are also issues even described as "thorns in the heart", like corruption, wrongful convictions and protection of personal information. Responding to these concerns, a spokesperson needs to have empathy and to be able to relate to people so that they can accept and acknowledge the response.

Humour can help to make people "willing to listen".

Humour is a lubricant in human relations. When I was young,

my family experienced some misfortunes and life was difficult, yet my mother never lost her sense of humour and was always ready to make us laugh. For this reason, I did not become lost in my life and have kept a positive outlook. During my career as a diplomat, I have come to realise that humour can not only help me make friends but also help gracefully extricate me from dilemmas.

It is natural for a spokesperson to feel fear when surrounded by "the unknown" at a press conference. Journalists have the upper hand since they can initiate questions, while a spokesperson can only react and try to construct a good result. Such interactions create a kind of tension at press conferences, which can be unnerving. So sometimes humour is a good way to change the atmosphere.

For instance, at the NPC press conference in 2016, when responding to a journalist's question about the smog problem which had been the public's constant concern, I said that the Chairperson of the Environment Protection and Resources Conservation Committee of the NPC was already "under a mountain of pressure" (*yali shanda*). Using this internet catchphrase vividly described how the lawmaker felt about the problem and helped me to gain the public's understanding. These kinds of internet catchphrases are humorous, even witty, and can foster a more relaxed atmosphere at press conferences.

However, catchphrases need to be chosen sensibly and appropriately. I rarely used whatever first came to my mind and would use such terms only after I had thoroughly studied and understood them. I owed this to the young members of my team, as well as some friends in think tanks. When listening to them, I found that some modern words and phrases they used to elaborate on ideas were often refreshing and appealing which made it easy for people to comprehend and embrace. Learning from them greatly benefited me.

In 2016, the North Korea nuclear issue became a hot international topic. When considering how to respond to questions on this issue, I wanted to include a warning on the danger of the situation if things continued as they were. A team member suggested that we could use the "Dark Forest" theory in the science fiction novels *The Three-Body Problem*.

I enjoyed reading the trilogy and finished it almost at a single sitting. The theme running throughout the trilogy that astounded me the most was its depiction of, and consistent emphasis on, the greatness of humanity. What made humans was their humanity, of which kindness was set as a baseline. Humans had weaknesses and made mistakes and they were far from perfect compared to robots. Humans seemed to be more vulnerable than higher-level beings in the universe. And yet, the beauty of humanity displayed by earthlings was something that went beyond technology and power. The value that had carried the continuity of humans lay in its great essence of humanity, which enabled humans to find their way in spite of repeated trials and tribulations. The author Liu Cixin even placed the humanity of earthlings above all other beings in the universe: even when the planet earth was being destroyed, humans still held on to their humanity.

The trilogy portrayed the universe in a zero-morality competition. The "Dark Forest" theory, which derived from that kind of situation, was also an appropriate metaphor for the mutual distrust between the US and North Korea and the potential dangers ahead. The concept seemed an appropriate phrase to express my worries back in 2016.

At that year's press conference, a journalist with the Singapore-based newspaper *The Straits Times* asked about the North Korean nuclear issue. I responded by saying that China was firmly against North Korea's development of nuclear weapons because it would threaten not only regional peace and stability but also the security interests of China and its neighbours. I also expressed my wish that both the symptoms and root causes be addressed so that the fundamental problems could be solved. Then I used the term "dark forest" in the novel *The Three-Body Problem* as an analogy and commented: "That kind of environment characterised by utter insecurity and a lack of trust in others should not be today's reality." I said: "The ultimate solution to this problem is to break the vicious security cycle in Northeast Asia and to provide security in exchange for security."

I learnt that former US President Obama also liked the trilogy. But it is a pity that he failed to take bold steps to lift the US and

North Korea out of the morass of mutual distrust and allowed the situation to slide in a dangerous direction.

The third threshold was making the audience "remember what they hear".

To make people remember, I had to be concise and have a focal point. There needed to be a core message in the answer which was like its soul, expressed by a few key sentences that could make a deep impression. When I discussed with my team, we would first consider "what the question was about" and tried to make sense of it before moving on to "what to say" and figuring out the core message to convey.

Take my responses to the anti-corruption questions which came up in every press conference for five years. The media and the public concerns covered an extensive array of issues that included: future plans to combat corruption, moves to improve Party conduct and build a clean government, sentencing of corrupt officials, how to promote institutional development and the CPC Central Committee's eight-point decision on improving Party and government conduct in the long term, solutions to some government officials' inaction, and issues concerning corrupt fugitive officials and recovery of ill-gotten assets as well as international cooperation. We needed to attend to every aspect when making preparations. However, I needed to be concise and to the point, and avoid trying to explain everything at length in such a limited time.

From the perspective of the NPC and its Standing Committee, the most important message to convey was the commitment to "building a systemic anti-corruption regime" which could basically cover all media and public concerns on the subject. In response to the anti-corruption issue, I always had to emphasise this core message.

PRACTICE, PRACTICE, AND MORE PRACTICE

There can be both predictable and unpredictable developments at a press conference. What is intriguing about a good press conference is precisely the intertwining relationship between predictability and unpredictability. For a spokesperson, predictability is attributed to sufficient, effective and targeted preparations. Whether or not one can cope with the unpredictable depends on the knowledge base and management skill on the spot. In a nutshell, preparing beforehand to address as many aspects as possible can boost proficiency in handling the predictable, and diligent learning and accumulated knowledge can lay the foundation for tackling the unpredictable.

Hence, for me, constructing key points for answers to priority questions was only half of my preparation work. In order to be able to increase predictability, manage unpredictability, and improve my improvisation skills, I needed to do two more things. The first was to memorise the key points and the second was to improve my ability to respond to questions that could come from various angles.

This ushered in the second phase of the preparation: training, which was the toughest.

The first step in my training was to learn by heart the key points, especially the core parts. The goal was to be able to deliver replies in a smooth, clear and colloquial manner.

The process of memorising the key points was agonising and painstaking, as it required great effort and intense repetition. For example, when talking about legal issues, it was particularly important to articulate points in a logical and reasoned manner, using accurate definitions. For example, distinction must be drawn between "rights" and "powers", between "supervisory" and "procuratorial", and between "time limit" and "duration". For instance, when the *General Provisions of the Civil Law*, the *Public Cultural Service Guarantee Law* and the relevant issues were drawing a lot of public attention, I needed to familiarise myself with them and be able to explain them accurately. This was not easy as I needed to memorise, within a short space of time, the technical terms and legal glossaries and then be able to correctly articulate them in my own words.

There was no other way than practice, practice, and more practice. Due to the tight schedule and my other workload, all I could do was to memorise a bit more every day. I divided the day into three time periods: morning, afternoon and evening. At the beginning of each time period, I would first review the key points that I had memorised for the previous training session to remember them better, and then work on some new ones. I had some of the key points recorded on my phone and listened repeatedly while taking walks after lunch. To cope with easily mistaken terms and definitions, I would go to a quiet park after work and stand in front of a tree, repeating the legal glossaries and terms over and over again in order to build mouth muscle memory. This used to be my way to memorise vocabularies when I was an English student. Now my team jokingly reminded me that I should choose a different tree each time, in case the tree withered with boredom.

My team saw me struggling and suggested that I should not waste time memorising the legal terms that were particularly hard to pronounce. And when asked, I could just read the key points written on paper. But I was still determined to memorise as much as I could because I believed that only by having the terms firmly in my mind could I effortlessly express myself. Should I have developed the habit of reading straight from a script, I would be inclined to rely on written talking points. Then when unexpected questions were raised, I would be needing to look for scripts on the table or search for information in the computer, looking unprepared and unconfident which would inevitably undermine the effectiveness of my communication.

During this period, I continued to memorise, review and further polish the key points. My family was my first audience and my best teachers. They would listen to me and gave candid comments on whether I sounded verbose or ambiguous. Sometimes they would point out that there was no need to go into detail about something which was common knowledge.

The second step in my training practice was to do rehearsals.

At a press conference, despite the many unpredictable factors, a spokesperson needs to keep good control of the whole process and take full advantage of each question to convey the messages for the NPC conference. A spokesperson should be able to think fast under intense pressure, organise every sentence properly, and be aware of the possible effects and impact of what is said. These skills do not come naturally and need to be developed through training and rehearsals.

When asking questions, the journalists may have different focuses and perspectives. One should not respond mechanically with prepared key points regardless of the unique angle of the question. For me, I had to train myself to be able to connect my prepared materials to the question naturally while accurately delivering the core message.

Then how to practice? As the day of the press conference approached, I would invite two to three team members to do rehearsals with me and take turns to ask questions they had formulated. By this time, I needed to be fully focused. They would take notes of what I misspoke or missed out, and then go through them with me. With one rehearsal after another, I was able to get my messages out more and more confidently and fluently. My improvisation skills improved and, on occasion, I even had a flash of inspirational new ideas. But my assistants might not always agree as some of them were not appropriate or disrupted the logical structure. Gradually, my responses became clearer and smoother.

The third step was to have simulated rehearsals.

I know that one's ability can be affected by nerves when under stress and usually that inhibits the ability to think or express oneself. A speaker may perform at up to 70% of their potential under favourable circumstances but under extreme stress the performance can drop to around 50%. In order to become more comfortable and adjust to the tension of a press conference, I needed to get into the role earlier. Therefore, my team would organise a few rounds of simulations in the final few days before a press conference.

We would set up a video camera and make the environment look as real as possible. There would be one team member playing the role of the moderator and others acting as journalists asking questions. Somebody would be keeping the time and taking note of any mistakes. Everyone would perform in strict accordance with the timing and procedure of a formal press conference. I had the computer on the table loaded with information which I would use at the real event. The one-hour simulated press conference required great concentration and was as intense as the real thing.

Simulated rehearsals helped me adapt to the tense atmosphere and enabled me to keep on track and focus on the key points. It also helped me learn to behave naturally in front of cameras and release the stress brought about by the anticipation of the unknown. Initially, I even experienced brain fade and became entangled in an incoherent jumble of words. On occasion, I mumbled in such a funny way that my team members laughed and could no longer go on, while I was oblivious as to what had gone wrong. This was precisely what simulated rehearsals were all about: identifying shortcomings and making corrections.

My team and I would then watch the replays together to pinpoint mistakes. As the saying goes, "the devil is in the detail". The path towards improvement is through correcting one's mistakes. Successful expression is the combined result of a number of factors that include not only what is being said but also the manner, voice and tone of expression; even body language contributes to the result. For example, although some body language is necessary, a spokesperson should not use too many hand gestures, as television tends to amplify body movements. Eye contact matters a great deal in human relations as it is the window of a person's inner world and making eye contact with journalists is a good way to engage with them and express confidence. Of course, this requires good control of the interaction. When people talk smoothly and naturally, their eyes appear stable and bright. By contrast, if people speak as if by rote learning or try to search around in their mind for answers, their eyes look unfocused and dull, giving the impression of self-doubt.

At the end of these rigorous rehearsals, I felt happier and more confident in myself and the success of the press conference.

APPEARANCE IS ANOTHER FORM OF EXPRESSION

From my diplomatic career, I have learnt about the importance of appearances and have become accustomed to paying attention to etiquette. When deciding what to wear, it is important to not only follow established rules and customs but also to consider the environment. For example, I would choose Chinese-style clothing for formal protocol events, fashionable clothing for museum-based or other cultural events, and a suit for the workplace.

Press conferences of the NPC sessions are formal working

events. In 2013 for my first press conference, I first chose a light grey suit, which looked low-key and demure. However, when visiting the venue of the press conference, I discovered the colour of my outfit was almost the same shade as the marble backdrop. Unsurprisingly, a CCTV director recommended that I changed to a more colourful suit. My husband encouraged me to wear a sapphire-blue blazer which, although it was a casual jacket, had an eye-catching colour. I matched it with a black silk skirt to add a touch of formality. Just as I had hoped, the effect on the camera turned out well.

In 2014, I came across a stylist, Meiduo, who started to advise me. Her critical eye and emphasis on detail helped me dress more professionally. For instance, for the NPC press conference of 2015, I chose an iron-grey Chinese-style brocade blazer with a barely visible navy-blue pattern. Meiduo suggested that I pair it with a soft-grey light sleeveless sweater and a pair of navy-blue trousers. My shoes had to be blue as well to avoid having more than three colours for the outfit. Although these details were inconspicuous, the pieces fitted together well on camera.

Over the years, I have maintained one principle when choosing outfits for press conferences: they must deliver a subdued image both in terms of colour and style. According to Meiduo, a subdued image could help me cope with tensions arising from tricky questions and make people feel close, amicable and calm.

Appearance is a subtle feeling which is hard to describe in words and it takes many factors to deliver. Every time when the door opened, and everything was in place, the last important tip for me was: to wear a smile. From my career experience, a smile was often a simple yet useful key to opening up communications. It was an indispensable lubricant, especially when speaking with journalists and the public. I learnt about its importance and eventually made a habit of it. But in the early years, when interviewed by the media, I did not realise the importance of a smile and often looked serious, especially when responding to tough questions, and therefore tended to appear quite nervous on camera. People watching on television would feel detached and find it difficult to apprehend. Admittedly smiling does not work for every occasion and it all depends on the subject.

Smiling may seem an easy gesture, but it is not always easy to put on, especially under pressure. At a press conference which is being televised live, there can be many unpredictable factors, and a spokesperson needs to stay highly focused. I often forgot to smile, so my assistants constantly reminded me during rehearsals not to be stone-faced. They would also use a variety of ways to remind me when I was on stage doing a press conference, like having the first sentence displayed on my computer screen as: wear your smile, and having a smiley face at the corner of the screen as a constant reminder.

Smiling strengthens affinity, demonstrating a sense of confidence as well as calmness. Ultimately, smiling is an attitude. In my view, it should represent not only a spokesperson's attitude towards the public but also China's attitude towards the world.

SECTION III
STORIES OUTSIDE THE NEWS CONFERENCE

6

FRIENDLY AND FIERY MOMENTS
AT INTERNATIONAL FORUMS

I often attended international forums when I was a diplomat and continued to receive invitations after joining the Foreign Affairs Committee of the NPC. Every year I would choose to attend some of them that were relevant to China and deliver speeches or participate in debates. Speaking on China at international forums can be challenging, as it is a place where old and new concepts collide, and history and reality intertwine. It is not rare for Chinese and Western voices to confront each other back-and-forth. I often felt duty bound to stand up for my country on occasions like this. It is comforting to know that I could maintain and explain my country's policies and position, convince some people and gain support, or reduce some of their prejudices.

Opportunities like these tested and sharpened my ability to express myself and deliver persuasive presentations, so they also provided me with valuable personal experience. Frequent participation in international discussions pushed, and continue to push, me to enrich and improve myself. Nothing is more inspiring and rewarding than direct involvement in front-line debates. More importantly, while engaging in international discussions, it also informs me about current international thinking, the international community's understanding and expectations of China, how it misunderstands us and why it is sometimes dissatisfied with us.

CHINA NEEDS MORE REPRESENTATION AT INTERNATIONAL FORUMS

International forums are mostly symposiums with specific objectives, either held regularly over many years or irregularly. The form and content of these forums reflect the needs of the host country as well as the international community for exchanging information and views on political, security, economic, scientific and technological, and cultural topics across national boundaries. Often consensus grows on these important issues through debates and discussions. Every year, there are numerous international forums held in the world on various themes. Many new but important international propositions and agendas emerge from such discussions.

Most international forums encourage open discussions. Even though some are chaired by governments, more are sponsored and organised by semi-governmental or specialised non-governmental institutions. Forums frequently take place in Europe and the United States, and some developing countries are now catching up and offering their own international forums. Dignitaries, renowned experts and academics regard international forums as important channels to acquire the latest information and to influence others. International forums often come up with forward-thinking and cutting-edge ideas. More often than not, participants hold conflicting opinions driven by different positions and interests. Inevitably, some discussions are friendly, while others are intense or result in fierce debates. This is how, through brainstorming and confluence of diverse information and views, people find inspiration and solutions to daunting challenges. This is exactly what international forums are intended for. Participants can also use these international platforms to spread and promote their countries' policies and visions or undertake important diplomatic engagements. As participants return home after each forum, they spread newly acquired knowledge and information to all corners of the world, like a dandelion's seeds in the wind.

Prestigious international forums can influence where the world is going. The Geneva-based World Economic Forum, also known as the "Davos forum", for example, holds its annual meeting every winter in Davos, Switzerland and has become an influential international forum that takes the pulse of the world's economy and exerts an impact on its global direction. President Xi Jinping attended its annual meeting on 17 January 2017, and delivered a keynote speech entitled "Jointly Shoulder the Responsibility of Our Times, Promote Global Growth". He called for efforts to uphold economic globalisation and build a community with a shared future for mankind, against the backdrop of the emerging trend towards full-on de-globalisation, rising trade protectionism and declining confidence globally. His speech was warmly received and struck a chord across the world.

Another significant forum is the Germany-based Munich Security Conference (MSC), which is hailed as the "Davos for defence", indicating its influence on security and strategic domains. While in Asia, the Asia Security Summit or Shangri-La Dialogue was initiated by the UK's International Institute for Strategic Studies (IISS) and co-organised by the Ministry of Defence of Singapore. As a highly-charged security-themed summit covering the Asia-Pacific region that is attended by high-ranking defence officials from major countries in the region and beyond, fierce debates frequently occur. In addition to these forums, the government-backed ASEAN Regional Forum is also an important venue in which I used to be involved. China's presence at the forum has grown along with the expansion of its contacts in the neighbourhood and has helped nurture the mutually beneficial cooperation between China and ASEAN as well as with its member countries. Three international forums in Russia established with the support of President Vladimir Putin: the Valdai Discussion Club, the St Petersburg International Economic Forum (SPIEF), and the Eastern Economic Forum; have also proved to be heavyweight meetings. The Russian government has been consistent in its support of international forums in spite of the difficult external environment it has faced in recent years, as a way to maintain positive international communication and narrow the gap between the world and Russia.

I have noticed that in many international forums, there are often US senators and members of the House of Representatives actively participating in the discussions. The US Congress is in session for about a third of the year, with long recesses in summer and winter. Many senators and members use this time to attend international forums, either individually or in groups. The hosts of international forums value their participation and arrange schedules to suit their needs so as to ensure their routine attendance at these forums. At influential international forums, you can hear Americans expressing their position and views on major international issues, which tends to not only influence the forums but also the direction of subsequent opinions.

For example, I came across senior US Republican senator John McCain at a number of international forums. Born in 1936 and known for his deeply conservative views, McCain was a frequent visitor to various international forums, particularly some very important European ones. For 22 years, he never missed a single MSC. Our last conversation was at the Ambrosetti Forum in Italy in September 2017. He had been diagnosed with primary glioblastoma two months before the forum but he still managed to show up after his chemotherapy. I was impressed by both his optimism and perseverance. His speech was received with long applause from the audience, out of respect for his unbreakable will against the disease, as well as an appreciation for his enduring support for the forum. He told me afterwards that he had attended this European forum for 14 years in a row.

There was a time when Chinese faces were rare at such international events, let alone making China's voice heard. As our country advances its reform and opening up, and increases its understanding of international development, Chinese officials, scholars and young students have begun appearing at international forums to present China as a country growing in confidence and vitality, and making constructive contributions to the world. Certainly, it is important to ensure China has adequate representation at important forums. Only by having greater numbers of people involved, can we effectively raise awareness and present our views to the wider world. It is equally important to encourage every participant to develop the ability to engage with others through learning and gaining more knowledge and experience.

China is also initiating and sponsoring international forums. Among them the Bo'ao Forum for Asia (BFA), which dates back to 2001, is considered influential. When I was Chinese Ambassador to the Philippines, there were frequent fishing disputes involving Chinese fishermen. In 1999, when taking a home leave, I went to visit the fishing village of Tanmenzhen in Hainan Province. On my way, I was invited by some young people to stop over in Bo'ao where they proposed the idea of an Asian Forum. The ground was muddy from previous rainfall, and in a shed beside a half-finished building, I listened to, and discussed with them, the design and planning of the forum, picturing a vision for a China-based Asian forum. A seed will sprout and grow once planted in the right soil. This idea came right on time. In 2001, the BFA was officially launched, and former President Jiang Zemin gave a speech at the inauguration ceremony. From then on, it has become a tradition for Chinese leaders to attend the opening ceremony and deliver a keynote speech at the annual session. Notably, former President Hu Jintao attended three of its opening ceremonies. Much progress has been made since, and it is now an important platform that connects China with the rest of Asia and beyond. Bo'ao, once a small fishing village, has also developed. The BFA brings in dignitaries, entrepreneurs, and scholars from Asia and other parts of the world every year to listen to Chinese leaders talking about policies and proposals, and to discuss issues of common concern. President Xi Jinping has attended the opening ceremonies of the BFA three times since 2013 and delivered keynote speeches on each occasion. The theme of his speech at the opening of the BFA on 10 April 2018 was: "An Open and Innovative Asia for a World of Greater Prosperity." He made a commitment to carrying forward the reform and opening up, which was launched four decades ago. He also announced the introduction of several new measures, including expanding market access, improving the investment environment, strengthening intellectual property (IP) protection and increasing exports. The implementation of these measures would take China's opening up to a new level.

I was there when President Xi Jinping made this speech. Domestic and international guests spoke highly of China's commitment to the opening up and reform, and expressed high expectations.

As China's international status and influence grows, many renowned international forums have begun to favour China as their meeting venue in order to better understand and relate to China. For example, the World Economic Forum Annual Meeting of the New Champions, also known as the "Summer Davos", is an international gathering permanently held in China. The first session was held in Dalian, China, in September 2017. It now alternates between Tianjin and Dalian every September, and Chinese leaders attend the gathering and make keynote speeches.

The increasingly active interaction by international forums with China is also driven by the growing demand in the world to hear China's voice and to acquire information about China. At the same time, China, as an emerging power, also needs to be more active at these platforms and to share the Chinese story, with the aim of increasing its influence and participation in international affairs.

In the following chapter I will write about some of my personal experiences in a few selected international conferences including the Munich Security Conference and the Valdai Discussion Club.

MY FIRST ENCOUNTER WITH THE MSC

The Munich Security Conference, which is held annually in Munich, Germany, is an international defence meeting that focuses on transatlantic partnerships. It evolved from the "Internationale Wehrkunde-Begegnung" ("International Meeting for Defence Experts") established in 1963 by Ewald-Heinrich von Kleist-Schmenzin, a German politician and publisher. It provided a debating platform for the North Atlantic Treaty Organisation (NATO) led by the US to counter the Warsaw Treaty Organisation led by the former Soviet Union. When the Cold War came to an end, it was renamed "Münchner Sicherheitskonferenz" or "the Munich Security Conference"(the MSC). Since 2002, the MSC has shifted its focus from European security affairs to global defence and diverse security issues. In doing so, its participation has also been expanded to include non-NATO members and regions beyond Europe. It now touches on many new topics, including anti-terrorism, prevention of the proliferation of nuclear weapons and efforts to maintain regional stability. The MSC enjoys effective support by the German Government and the President and Chancellor take turns to attend and address the meeting each year.

The MSC is attended by senior defence and foreign affairs officials, and experts specialising in security affairs from countries across the globe. Almost all high-ranking officials in charge of strategy and security affairs in Europe and the US attend. The US Vice President, Secretary of State and Secretary of Defence attend the MSC and deliver policy speeches every year. Joining them is a big number of senators and members of the House of Representatives, demonstrating the importance the US attaches to its alliance system. The Russian Foreign Minister seldom misses the MSC session either. In recent years, as conflicts between Russia and the European countries as well as the US have grown, it is quite common to hear unrelenting criticism and accusations against Russia at the MSC. Even so, it has never discouraged Sergey Lavrov, the Russian Foreign Minister, from showing up, giving his speech, taking questions from the audience and defending his country. There has also been greater interest in the event in recent years from Middle Eastern and Asian countries, with the foreign ministers and defence ministers of Japan, South Korea and Singapore frequently attending. The forum also offers an important venue for heads of state and high-ranking defence and foreign affairs officials to talk to each other, and the reception rooms at the venue are always fully booked.

I met with MSC Chairman Wolfgang Ischinger many years ago. He was a senior German diplomat and held important positions, including Political Director-General of the Federal Foreign Office and German Ambassador to the US and the UK. Gentle and polite, he is an observant man with great insights into global changes and trends, which makes him the perfect chairman of an international forum like the MSC.

The *Munich Security Report* compiled by Ambassador Ischinger has been released on the eve of the opening session of every MSC since 2015, to set the theme and tone for each year's conference. The theme of the first report of 2015 was "Collapsing Order, Reluctant Guardians?" to encourage discussions on the US-Russia geostrategic conflicts in Ukraine. In 2016, the theme was "Boundless Crises, Reckless Spoilers, Helpless Guardians." The report focused on anti-terrorism and the refugee issues challenging Europe. In 2017, the report went under the title "Post-Truth, Post-West, Post-Order?" in response to the tremendous "uncertainties" that were troubling the Europeans, arising from the UK's referendum to leave the European Union (Brexit) and the election of US President Donald Trump. "Post-Truth" in the title referred to the substantial impact of fake news on the direction of international politics. These themes fostered head-on discussions on the challenges troubling international society. Another highlight of the *Munich Security Report* lay in its style of posing questions and presenting facts without offering pre-determined answers. This helped it to achieve the purpose of defining the general direction of discussions at the MSC while leaving enough space for brainstorming.

Given that the world is paying more attention to China's international role, Ischinger held that, without a Chinese presence, any discussion on international and regional security issues involving China would be incomplete. He had been trying to invite China's high-level delegations to the conference and paid visits to Beijing for this purpose. In response, both the Chinese State Councillor and Foreign Minister attended and addressed the MSC.

The 50th MSC, which was held from 31 January through 2 February 2014, coincided with China's Lunar New Year holidays. That was also the first time I attended the MSC. The focus of issues that year included the transatlantic security landscape, emerging countries and global governance, the European debt crisis and the future of the EU, the situations in Mali and Syria, and Iran's nuclear programme. But, above all, people attending devoted much of their attention to the domestic situation in Ukraine. I arrived in Munich by plane with a small team of assistants on 30 January 2014 which was the eve of the Chinese New Year.

I was invited to attend a conference hall panel under the title of

"Europe, America and Asia" which was intended for discussions on global power configuration and regional stability. The panel was moderated by James G. Stavridis, a US senator and retired admiral. Apart from me, it was also attended by Ivo Josipović, President of the Republic of Croatia, Lindsey Graham, a US senator, and Shivshankar Menon, National Security Advisor of the Republic of India. I knew two of the panelists personally, but not the senators. I had paid a visit to President Josipović during a visit to Croatia. He was fascinated by China, and we had a pleasant conversation. Menon from India was an old friend of mine. It was obvious that the panelists came from vastly different backgrounds, probably with differing priorities. I was wondering how this forum was going to find a common focal point for discussions.

However, our moderator, Senator Stavridis, identified what he took as a point of focus effortlessly. He began the discussion by saying, of the five panellists on the stage today, four were from democratic countries. This introduction immediately defined me as his opponent. Unfortunately, this was perhaps how China was perceived through the eyes of many Europeans as well as in other Western countries. For them, "China is a non-democratic country with an incorrect political system." Western countries, having fought a half-century Cold War with the former Soviet Union, had assumed that they had won over communism and it was "the end of history." They could never have imagined that China, a country led by the Communist Party, could survive and even thrive. How this happened was beyond them. The US senator seemed unhappy at having a Chinese delegate by his side, and I was not very happy with his unfounded provocation either. But I managed to remain composed, thinking about how to get out of his pre-set trap.

The topic of that session had nothing to do with China's political system. In their following remarks, no other guests responded to his comment or mentioned anything about political divergence. When it was my turn, I was hesitant about whether or not to simply ignore the senator's provocations and stick to the topic, conveying China's position and views. Dr Henry Kissinger was present that day and took a seat near the stage. I looked in his direction and saw him smiling at me. We'd previously crossed paths on multiple occasions and had many discussions, including on political divergence. Today, the panel was not the occasion to argue about political differences and yet I still felt the need to refute the senator's seemingly careless but very intentional political provocation. How should I go about it? Watching Dr Kissinger's expectant smile, an idea came to my mind.

I smiled and said: "Yesterday was the first day of the seven-day holidays of the Chinese Lunar New Year, which is the most important festival for the Chinese people. People, wherever they are, try to arrive home before the New Year's Eve to join the family reunion dinner with their parents. While the people were either at home or on their way home, my colleagues and I spent nine hours on a plane headed for Munich. We all missed the family reunion. But for what? We did so with the purpose of improving mutual understanding between us."

I heard a wave of chuckles and saw Dr Kissinger nodding at me smilingly out of appreciation for my subtle response to the provocation. Likewise, the audience was quick to understand that this was my way of countering Stavridis' bitter attitude. Having gained the upper hand, I continued: "Of course, this should be based on mutual respect, including respect for every country's political system derived from their different history, experience and development path. More than 30 years have passed since China launched the reform and opening up, and the remarkable economic and social achievements we have secured also speak to the success of our political system."

I chose not to start a head-on confrontation with the moderator, otherwise, it would mean that I had accepted his division. The best way to refute his provocation was to subtly find an appropriate angle to deconstruct his value judgment and wipe out the resultant atmosphere. In order to do this, I moved the conversation to another level and was able to state my views on the panel topic more freely without being constrained by the moderator's value framework. The discussion then proceeded smoothly and the panelists expressed their views and interacted with the audience.

While more than 800 people were invited to the MSC, its conference hall has only about 200 seats. The principle of "first come, first served" is adopted. Many participants who were not in the hall could watch live streaming on their computers at the coffee shop or in the corridors outside. The conference hall was full the day I was on the panel, with many people standing in the aisle. When the floor was open, I started to receive many questions and I could sense a keen interest in China from the audience.

After the session ended, Ischinger came on the stage. When he approached me, he congratulated me on the panel performance and then apologised for making my team and I miss the Chinese New Year holidays. He promised that they would try to avoid a clash with the Chinese New Year dates when planning future MSC schedules. He also expressed appreciation for my participation and invited me to attend the MSC more often. He said that China's image needs to be represented and established by Chinese participation, and the MSC discussions on international security issues needed a Chinese voice.

WHO IS "CONTROLLING" NORTH KOREA?

In 2016, I was invited to speak at an MSC panel discussion with the topic of "Doubling Down? China and International Order(s)" which was held in the conference hall. I gave a speech entitled "Putting the Order(s) Shift in Perspective," in which I talked about how the issue of a world order was looked at differently. The gist of my speech was that the US-led world order rested on three pillars: first, the American value system, which was also accepted as Western values; second, the US military alignment system, which was claimed to be the security foundation for US leadership; and third, the international economic system, which included but was not limited to the international institutions within the framework of the UN. This world order structure led by the US was rooted in history, but continued to play a role during modern times. The US had long been playing a leadership role in this order while reaping huge benefits from its role. This order was exclusive in the political and security areas but more open in the economic area. Therefore, globalisation had mainly occurred in the economic sphere. However, as globalisation became deeply embedded, and international politics was increasingly fragmented, this world order was being challenged and finding it harder and harder to provide effective solutions to contemporary difficulties.

I explained to the audience that what China supported was the international order, which referred to the international institutions and norms underpinned by the purposes and principles of the *UN Charter*. China felt a strong sense of belonging to this order, as one of its founders, as well as being a beneficiary, a contributor and a party to its reform efforts. Chinese President Xi Jinping, during his visit to Seattle in September 2015, stated that "a great number of countries in the world, especially developing countries, want to see a more just and equitable international system. But it doesn't mean that they want to unravel the entire system or start all over again. Rather, what they want is to reform and improve the system to keep up with the times."

I ended by asking the question: where do we go from here? I said, China was not going to be the last developing country to ascend to the world's centre stage. Many more countries would want fairer treatment in the international order and institutions alongside China. Changes were needed, as the world's power was set to become more decentralised and challenges become more complicated. As we could not remake each other in our own images, could we not work together to build a more inclusive framework or "common roof" that accommodates as much as possible the world's diverse interests, needs and ideas on governance? "Naturally, this would take time."

The moderator of the panel was Professor Sebastian Heilmann, President of the Mercator Institute for China Studies (MERICS) in Germany. According to the schedule, the guests would discuss issues concerning China, the international order, China-US relations and then take questions from the audience. The other guests on this panel discussion included Kevin Rudd, former Prime Minister of Australia, Ng Eng Hen, Minister of Defence of Singapore, and Robert Corker, Chairman of the US Senate Committee on Foreign Relations. Corker had previously visited China, and we had a long conversation about the North Korean nuclear issue. He attached importance to my opinions, but we saw things so differently that we found it hard to convince each other. Now we were sitting together on the stage and when I started speaking, he could not hear me clearly so he went back into the audience to listen until I had finished.

Every time I decided to attend an international forum, I would do some homework not only about the theme of the forum but also about the moderator and other guests. It was important to know their views and stance from their published articles and speeches, especially those of the moderator. If the moderator held strongly biased views about China, it would be important for me to prepare for a possible confrontational debate. Sebastian Heilmann, the moderator of this panel, was a China expert. His previous remarks indicated that he had a fair approach towards China and even called for establishing new connection points between Germany and China. For example, when he was asked in an interview with a German media outlet whether China's development threatened Germany, he said that Germans appreciated China as an economic entity and many people hoped to benefit from China's growth. But they were also afraid of competing with China. He believed that Germany and China would maintain positive and complementary development in the future. In terms of China's foreign policy, he believed that China, as a responsible major country, had realised where its geostrategic interests lay and was more interested in seeking development in Central Asia and East Asia. However, China's increasing military spending had caused some misunderstandings. Also, some Southeast Asian countries were concerned about the pressure brought by China's rise on the neighbourhood and that China's economic and military dominance worried them. As an observer, Professor Heilmann hoped that China would make an effort to increase trust and ease tensions.

Based on this information, I assumed that the moderator would be relatively balanced. To my surprise, Professor Heilmann appeared somewhat aggressive and repeatedly turned to the North Korean nuclear issue and targeted his questions towards me, questioning China's stance and actions. Apparently he was trying to lead the audience to the conclusion that the reason the North Korean nuclear issue was sliding into such a dangerous situation was due to China's "inaction". His remarks struck a chord during the panel discussion and I guessed that it enjoyed an echo on the floor with the European public under media influence. Facing his barbed questions, I did not push back immediately and waited until his provocations forced me into a corner. At that moment, he seemed to feel that he had the upper hand, so he stared at me, looking serious, and pushed further by asking:

"Has China lost control completely over its former ally the DPRK?"

I could feel the tension in the hall and saw it was time to fight back. Only by responding at the right moment could I use his momentum against him.

To answer his question with a"yes" or "no" would mean that I agreed with his premise that China controlled North Korea and that China was to blame for North Korea's development of nuclear weapons. The question per se was based on a flawed assumption of China-North Korea relations and China's foreign policy. Therefore, I had to prevent myself from falling into the trap of "yes" or "no". Instead, I needed to respond to Professor Heilmann by questioning and deconstructing the underlying rationality of his question. However, given that the overwhelming majority of the audience agreed with him, if I appeared aggressive and antagonistic, it would not only be difficult for me to win over the audience but also make me appear to lack confidence.

I noticed that in his question, he inadvertently violated the basic principle of sovereign equality set out in the *UN Charter*, which I could take as an opening point for my rebuttal. I started my reply with a smile:

"That sounds very Western... losing control over a country, a sovereign country?"

The audience broke into laughter.

The moderator immediately realised his fault and looked rather uneasy. I could feel the audience beginning to move to my side. Building on the momentum, I continued:

"That's not what China thinks. We don't control any country. We have never controlled any country, and we do not want to be controlled."

Then I explained China's stance on the North Korean nuclear issue, emphasising that

"we firmly oppose the nuclearisation of North Korea. We understand their security concerns and we hope that the US can come around to addressing the issue with them. But in the meantime, we hope that North Korea will stop this dangerous move."

"The Chinese Foreign Minister Wang Yi and the US Secretary of State John Kerry had a meeting in Munich about this issue. Afterwards, the Chinese Foreign Minister made a few points to the media: 'First, whatever happens, there should not be any nuclear development on the Korean Peninsula; second, we should not solve the problem with the use of force; and third, the solution should not undermine China's national security interests.' I hope that China and the US can work in the same direction and be able to communicate with the parties concerned."

Over the years, I have a strong impression that there is such a lack of information on China in the Western world that prejudice and misinformation can easily be sold. As a result, when Chinese appear in international forums, especially those held in Western countries, they often encounter an unfriendly atmosphere. If they react strongly when provoked, their ideas may not be well received and they have difficulties connecting with the audience and winning their understanding. In order to achieve better results, it is always important to look for the right moment and find a clever angle to fight back. Of course, this requires good preparation, including practicing and polishing arguments and expressions as well as a constant effort to learn and gain more knowledge.

For me, whether it is a press conference or a forum, my ability to influence hinges on whether I can successfully get my points across to most of the audience, or better still, be accepted by them. It is a game of wits. What I need to remember is that I am not competing with journalists, moderators or other panel guests, but trying to win the hearts and minds of the audience offstage and the public beyond the camera lens. Now that I have dared to step into the international arena, I must accept the challenges and try to win over people instead of being intimidated by failure. I have, therefore, never stopped learning, for example, how to speak clearly and reasonably on international occasions so that people can understand what I am saying and hopefully agree with, or at least acknowledge, my points. Attending international forums gives me the opportunity to put what I have learnt into practice.

DEBATE AND ARGUMENT

The 53rd MSC was held in 2017. Chinese Foreign Minister Wang Yi attended the plenary session and delivered a keynote speech entitled: "Adhere to Ideas of Cooperation and Make Correct Choices." He talked about the idea of building a community with a shared future for humankind as proposed by Chinese President Xi Jinping. He said that the international order and the system built after World War Two are still playing a key and irreplaceable role in maintaining world peace and development, and that it should be upheld and maintained. There is no one-size-fits-all development path and model, and there is no so-called "end of history." The path and model should be based on each country's national circumstances and be supported by the people. Countries should, in the spirit of mutual respect, learn from each other while making progress together. Peace and development remain the theme of today's world. As long as all countries observe the purposes and principles of the *UN Charter*, disputes can be addressed peacefully, confrontation can be avoided, and win-win cooperation can be achieved on the basis of peaceful co-existence.

I also attended the 2017 MSC and was invited to speak on a side panel entitled: "Pacific No More? Security in East Asia and the Korean Peninsula." It was moderated by Australian former Prime Minister Kevin Rudd, and also attended by Yun Byung-Se, Minister of Foreign Affairs of South Korea, Ng Eng Hen, Minister of Defence of Singapore, US Senator Dan Sullivan, and Lassina Zerbo, Executive Secretary of the Comprehensive Nuclear-Test-Ban Treaty Organisation (CTBTO). According to the set arrangement, the panelists were asked to each deliver a speech before having a discussion among themselves, and then take questions from the audience.

However, a new programme was added to the opening of the panel, which we were only informed of upon arrival. John Chipman, Director-General of the IISS was going to introduce to the panel his newly published *Military Balance 2017*, an assessment report on global military capabilities and defence economics. I got to know Mr Chipman when I was serving as Chinese Ambassador to the UK, where I delivered speeches and participated in seminars at the IISS. On this day he made a seven-minute introduction to the report, attaching importance to the military development of Asian countries and highlighting China's growing military build-up. He claimed:

"The IISS data shows that after overtaking Europe as the second largest defence spending region in 2012, Asia in 2016 spent 1.3 times more than Europe on defence when measured in constant 2010 US dollars. China spends the most in the region. Its official defence budget is 1.8 times higher than the combined budgets of South Korea and Japan, and 3.7 times higher than other states surrounding the South China Sea put together," he said. "In some capability areas, particularly in the air domain, China appears to be reaching near-parity with the West."

Chipman went on to raise more specific points:

"China's progress in military research and development, together with its improved military capabilities, means that it is now the single most important driver for US military technical developments. This year's *Military Balance* assesses that China's air force has just introduced into service a highly capable short-range missile that only a handful of leading aerospace nations are able to develop. The introduction of this weapon – called the PL-10 – reflects the sustained and continuing investment China is making in air-launched guided weapons. Work has started on building three Type-055 cruisers. At least 13 Type-052D multi-mission destroyers are in service or under construction, and a growing number of China's modern surface combatants are being fitted with phased-array radars. China has already started to make its military training more realistic..."

His introduction with technical details gave the audience the impression that a crisis was looming in Asia. After a short comment, the moderator Kevin Rudd asked the panelists to speak. The South Korean Foreign Minister delivered a prepared speech on foreign and security policy. When it was my turn, I thought that I would miss the opportunity to refute Chipman if I only used my prepared speech.

Since I had no previous knowledge of his intervention and therefore did not do any homework on his report, I avoided making specific comments on the contents of the report. Instead, I started with an angle that fitted into the general atmosphere of that year's MSC.

> *"Europe is not irrelevant to the Asia-Pacific. For us, coming from afar, it is interesting to see how the Europeans examine and reflect on themselves. However, Mr Chipman seemed to examine Asia from a different angle. For example, yesterday and today, the prime ministers and defence ministers of European countries talked about how important it is for NATO members to increase their defence budget share to 2% of GDP. It is one of the hottest issues debated here, but when talking about Asia, Mr Chipman sounds like Asians are doing too much."*

With that said, I then pointed out that China has been keeping its defence budget at about 1.5% of its GDP.

> *"Today's world is more and more globalised. I hope that the standards for viewing things will become more consistent and that we can somehow look at each other through the same lens. We are not enemies. I agree that there should*

be good analysis on defence development and a good explanation to each other as to why countries are doing so, to make each other feel more comfortable about it."

"I share the feelings of many in China that we are proud that the country can finally develop a strong military to defend ourselves. China has suffered so much in the past and needs to be able to stand on its own feet. China's peace and safety is also an important part of the peace and safety of the world."

The key point of my comment on Chipman's speech was to point out his double standards towards China. He indicated that China's military build-up "brings threats" and "challenges" to Asia. However, at the same conference, NATO members were talking about the need to increase defence budgets to 2% of GDP so as to contribute more to European security expenditures. This push actually came from the US, a dominant member of NATO. My comment neutralised Mr Chipman's attempts to play up China's "military threat." I had been asked about China's defence budget at every press conference when I was the spokesperson of the NPC. This debate could be regarded as another rehearsal of my presentation at the press conference which I would be presiding over in March. After returning to Beijing, I saw the latest data on China's defence budget which accounted for approximately 1.3% of China's GDP in 2017, even lower than the 1.5% that I mentioned in Munich. I therefore used the latest figure at the press conference of the NPC session in March 2017.

After my comment on Chipman's remarks, I went back to my prepared text and talked about Asia-Pacific security,

"At the heart of the debate about security in the Asia-Pacific is the choice between exclusive security or inclusive security,"

The former is based on alliances rooted in the belief of a zero-sum game, which may protect one or several countries, but undermine the security of others. Whereas the latter, without excluding any country, is aimed at common security in a region, achieved through joint efforts. President Xi Jinping has talked about this issue on many occasions, and the answer given by China is unquestionably "inclusive security." After every panelist had spoken, the panel moved into discussion and the focus was unsurprisingly on the North Korean nuclear issue. The panelists were eager to find out each other's views and the audience were also interested in the subject. A day earlier, I had met and talked with one of the panelists, CTBTO Executive Secretary Lassina Zerbo, who was a professional in nuclear disarmament. When I attend international forums, as long as conditions permit, I try to get in touch with other panelists in advance to get an indication of their opinions and intentions. After all, it is not a comfortable experience to sit on a stage with people you know nothing about and have no expectation of what they may say. When meeting with Zerbo, I briefed him on China's stance on the North Korean nuclear issue, particularly the "suspension for suspension" proposal (calling for North Korea to halt its nuclear weapons and missile programmes and urging the US and South Korea to refrain from conducting military drills and return to the negotiating table) and the "dual-track approach" (calling for denuclearisation and the establishment of a peace mechanism on the peninsula), put forward by Chinese Foreign Minister Wang Yi. Based on his expertise, Zerbo immediately realised that China's idea would be the most realistic one and expressed support for the idea. I also gave him a long article I had written about the history of negotiations on the North Korean nuclear issue that was due to be published by the Brookings Institution. When we met the next day, he had finished reading my article. "Zerbo was completely convinced," his assistant told me. Then we started to discuss how to support each other during the panel discussion.

So, when it was his turn to speak on the panel discussions, Mr Zerbo insisted on urging the US and South Korea to respond to China's "suspension for suspension" proposal. He asked the South Korean Foreign Minister and the US Senator:

> "Madam Fu Ying is putting on the table today a proposal whereby
> North Korea agrees to stop testing or to stop any movement
> towards further developing its nuclear capability. And in exchange,
> China can ask North Korea to return to the negotiating table, and

you (the other side) are in a position where you are asked to postpone or stop military exercises, which have been a threat to them (North Korea). Fu Ying talked about reducing the threat and giving them more security. That's the question I'm asking; if something were to come to the table, how would you react to it?"

US Senator Sullivan had probably not anticipated the question, or did not know much about the issue, for his response was somewhat perfunctory.

"My first reaction would be that this question is not only for the United States but for our allies, South Korea and Japan. My view is that we should not be making any decisions that do not provide consensus with our two key allies on this issue in the region. The goal is a nuclear-free peninsula. Unfortunately, the proposition you just mentioned doesn't sound like you are getting there with a regime that doesn't necessarily have a good track record of keeping its own word. So, I'm not sure I'm giving up military exercises, which are important. But again, that would be a unilateral decision. The United States would have to get consensus from our allies [through negotiation]."

He was beating around the bush and evading the main question of how the US and North Korea can talk instead of fight.

This response invited more questions from Zerbo. At the end of the panel discussion, he returned to the issue, but there was still no clear response. Debates like this are often inconclusive, but today's discussion enabled China's reasonable propositions to be more widely known and appreciated. After the conference in Munich, I kept in touch with Zerbo, and I also talked with US Senator Sullivan when we met again in Washington. He hoped to learn more about China and was willing to play a role in dialogue between the US and China.

MY EXPERIENCE WITH THE VALDAI DISCUSSION CLUB

In 2016, I was for the first time invited by the Valdai Discussion Club to its 13th Annual Meeting held in Sochi, Russia.

The Valdai Discussion Club is a successful international communication platform created by Russia. The first meeting was held in Veliky Novgorod in 2004, near Lake Valdai, after which it is named. Russian organisers defined the club as "a platform for international experts where foreign scholars have the opportunity to get the most authoritative and credible information about Russia's national and social development from Russian elite representatives." The Valdai Discussion Club focuses on issues related to Russia and it attracts experts and scholars in politics, security and economics from all over the world, including those from China. Since 2014, the club has begun to concentrate on finding solutions to overcome the crises of the international system by promoting dialogue among the global intellectual elite. The club is also paying attention to the global agenda.

It was in 2008 that I first took note of the Valdai Club. At that time, a military conflict had broken out between Russia and Georgia over South Ossetia, and Russia was heavily criticised by the West for sending troops there. I was the Chinese Ambassador to the UK and during a reception, I happened to hear Professor Richard Sakwa of the University of Kent giving a detailed and objective explanation of why Russia sent troops to South Ossetia, which really impressed me. Later, he told me that it was because he had attended the Valdai Discussion Club, where he had the opportunity to listen to Russian leaders' explanations and analyses on this issue. International scholars like Professor Sakwa, having acquired first-hand information in Russia, would be able to bring back and share it after returning home. It proved that the Valdai Discussion Club was effective in its international communications.

There are a number of reasons why the Valdai Discussion Club is attractive; first, it has distinctly Russian characteristics. Its establishment and progress are directly supported by the government and guided by the Russian leaders, and the participants can have access to authoritative information and opinions; second, it takes an open approach to different opinions on Russia from the international community and it welcomes debate among participants. The Russian scholars and officials are not afraid to confront different opinions and enjoy taking part in the debates. By virtue of its reputation, it has become an important communication platform for international scholars who study Russia not to be missed.

China and Russia enjoy friendly relations, so I do not have to worry about facing hostility in the Valdai meetings. Nevertheless, since it is a gathering of international participants, confrontational and conflicting views are unavoidable. In recent years, the increasingly warm relations between China and Russia have aroused concern globally. To clarify some questions, I wrote a long article entitled: "Are China and Russia Partnering to Create an Axis?" Excerpts from this article, entitled: "How China Sees Russia," were carried in the January/February 2016 issue of *Foreign Affairs*. The full text in Chinese was published in *Contemporary International Relations* in April 2016. Probably because of this article, the Valdai Discussion Club invited me to its annual meeting. I am not an expert on Russia, so to prepare for the meeting, I did some homework to try to understand more about contemporary Russian politics.

With "The Future in Progress: Shaping the World of Tomorrow" as its theme, the annual meeting in 2016 consisted of six sessions, two special sessions and one plenary session. They covered almost all major issues of concern in world politics, including world order, democracy, security in Central Eurasia and the Middle East, the impact of migration, the world economy, Europe's future, the power of technology, the collapse of the Soviet Union and Eurasian cooperation.

I participated in the first session, "World order, quo vadis?" As it was a hot international topic that year the discussion was broad. The moderator was Fyodor Lukyanov, Research Director of the Foundation for Development and Support of the Valdai Discussion Club. Other panelists were former Australian Prime Minister Kevin Rudd, John J. Mearsheimer, Professor from the University of Chicago, C. Raja Mohan, Director of Carnegie India and Sergey Karaganov, former Chairman of the Valdai Discussion Club. While

I knew some of them, I was unfamiliar with others. Having studied their background and some of their published articles, I could see that the panelists had quite diverse views on issues related to world order. Even the Chinese and Russian scholars saw things differently. Being present at the Valdai meetings helped me better understand Russia and China-Russia relations, and it was also a platform where I could express China's perceptions and viewpoints.

I was the first to speak on this panel. My speech, entitled "Major Countries Need to Build Trust," was based on my observations of the international landscape at the time. On the one hand, cooperation among major countries had become more and more important; on the other hand, there was growing suspicion and concern among them. Their lack of mutual trust was not in the interests of the world as cooperation among major countries was badly needed. Therefore, I said that "there is every reason for us to foster the habit of coordination and building trust." I also talked about the differences between China and the US over the issue of world order. This was not the first time I talked about it at an international forum: the "world order" the US claims to lead is a power structure, resting on American values, rejecting other ideologies, and supported by a military alignment which does not take into consideration the security interests of others; what China supports is an international order centred around the UN. China is among its founders and is a beneficiary, as well as its active supporter and reformer. This international order structure overlaps, to some extent, with the aforementioned US-led "world order", but they do not match entirely. Chinese President Xi Jinping has talked about the concept of building "a community with a shared future for mankind" and the need for "a new model of global partnership" and that together with other countries, China wants to "make the international order more just and equitable." This cannot be achieved without trust.

When responding to the different views and even concerns about China's role in the world order, I said:

"There are a number of elements that China holds high in its foreign policy thinking. First, is mutual respect, which we see as the foundation of country-to-

Karaganov, who spoke after me, was a senior Russian scholar with old-fashioned gentlemanly manners. He believed that people's understanding of the world had changed and that the balance of power had been shifting. Facing many emerging hot spots and conflicts, the US-led world order could not adapt to the changes, and international mechanisms were reacting slowly. Against this backdrop, countries should improve their relations, start negotiations in economics and nuclear safety, and establish a stable and normal international cooperation mechanism. Just like China's BRI, Russia's Greater Eurasian Partnership (GEP) could start with the core countries of Eurasia. The future world system should be based on freer economic rules, respect for the interests, sovereignty and territorial integrity of all countries, and be politically diversified so that countries' choices of development path can be respected.

Then it was the turn of Mearsheimer, an outspoken American scholar widely known for his "offensive realism" theory. I visited him when I went to give a speech at the University of Chicago in 2015. We had a conversation in his office which turned into a heated debate, and our scheduled 40-minute meeting lasted for nearly two hours. He was convinced that China wanted to compete with the US for world leadership. For him, the disputes over the South China Sea and Diaoyu Islands were all evidence of "China's power projection in the Asia-Pacific." He used a saying to describe the inevitability of conflict for power between China and the US: "What's good for the goose is good for the gander," by which he meant that just as the Americans pursued world leadership, the Chinese would do the same. As for the existing world order, he did not deny that the US-led world order was not inclusive enough but claimed that this could not be changed and that China, as a newcomer, could either submit or challenge. He looked me in the eye and said:"I do not believe the Chinese will submit. If China continues to rise, competition for power between the United States and China is inevitable."

When we met in Russia again, Mearsheimer had not changed his view of China. His speech highlighted the return of great power politics and the re-emergence of security competition among the great powers. He said that the world went from bipolarity during the Cold War to unipolarity after the end of the Cold War, and now it is transitioning to multipolarity and the transition is going deeper. Structural changes in the distribution of power were driving the competition between the great powers. He said that great power politics was a zero-sum game, and any gains that the Chinese made would come at America's expense. At that time, the pressing issue for the US was the tension between the US and Russia. Mearsheimer believed that American leaders failed to appreciate Russia's security concerns and failed to give Russia the respect it deserved, causing deterioration in the relationship. But the greatest rival for the United States, he said, was not Russia but China. It was not the US-Russia relationship but the US-China relationship that would become the defining issue of the 21st century. Mearsheimer also tried to remind the Russians that it would be China, not the United States, that would pose a threat to Russia in the future.

The last speaker was Mohan from India. India is also growing strong and its national consciousness is imprinted with the characteristics of a developing country. Indians have high self-esteem, are sensitive to their own interests, and have unique perspectives on international affairs, while being reluctant to be involved in any bloc. Mohan listed three factors complicating the world order: First, the deglobalisation represented by Brexit; second, the technological changes that influenced the capital and power distribution; third, the rise of populism that was challenging mainstream politics in the West. In Mohan's view, the geopolitical conflicts between NATO and Russia caused by NATO's expansion and the disputes between China and the United States in the South China Sea boiled down to a struggle for spheres of influence. Great powers should exercise restraint towards each other's spheres of influence to create some space for each other's existence.

Later in the discussion, the focus naturally turned to the relationship between China, the United States and Russia. Mearsheimer remained on the offensive, stating bluntly that although the United States still held a favourable position in the great power competition, its dominance was being challenged by China and Russia. He suggested that the United States should align with Russia to confront China, as China was the biggest threat to the United States.

In this forum, there were more similar views among panelists from China, Russia and India as these three countries were all emerging economies in the globalised world, hence their stances were closer in many respects. Mearsheimer's remarks could not shake the foundation of their common interests. However, some young Russian academics were quietly captivated by his appeal. I found it necessary to counter his argument, so I said:

"The concept of geopolitical rivalry is rooted in the history of the Western world, but now the world has changed. When analysing China, it is risky to assume that it will fall into the same pattern. This can lead to misjudgment. The international community needs to revise its thinking. The tragedy of wars and conflicts in the 20th century should not be repeated in the 21st century. The United States is worried that China will push it out of Asia and take over its world leadership. But for many in China, the United States-led world order is a mess. Who is willing to take over such a mess? For many other countries, isn't it enough to have one such country like the United States?"

Other scholars on the stage mostly did not want to concede the prospect depicted by Professor Mearsheimer. Karaganov saw Russia and China as the main challengers to the US-led world order. For Kevin Rudd, a zero-sum game was not inevitable, and cooperation was still the primary way forward in international relations. He mentioned the idea of a "G3" in which the United States remained a geopolitical and geo-economic superpower, Russia was a re-emerging geopolitical power, and China, already an economic superpower, was on its way to becoming a geopolitical power. Only when the three powers of a G3, the major countries represented by the G20, and global governance under the framework of the United Nations worked together, could humankind effectively cope with future global disasters. Mohan stressed that the United States, China, Russia, India and other major countries should respect each other's "sphere of influence" to avoid unnecessary conflicts. He also suggested that powers like the US, China and Russia should do some self-reflection and reform the current order to make it more reasonable and effective.

The audience also joined in these heated discussions by asking tough questions. One of them asked me, what was the difference between China's strategic partnership with other countries and the United States'security alliances? I said:

"A military alliance is based on dominance and submission, where equality does not exist. In contrast, the strategic partnership between China and other countries is based on equality, mutual benefit and mutual respect."

Another commented that China's non-alignment diplomacy was too conservative and should be reformed. He then asked me whether China would agree to send troops to Central Asia in support of Russia if turmoil occurred there. I said: "We in China also discuss amongst ourselves what China's international role should be. China suffered from invasions in its history. Now the public often watch on TV the disastrous effects and the pain on women and children brought about by wars and conflict. Generally speaking, the Chinese support peaceful settlement of disputes and oppose the use of military means to interfere in other countries' internal affairs. Since China's reform and opening up, people's standard of living has improved tremendously and the per capita GDP has increased from less than US\$230 to US\$8,000. This can be attributed to China's peaceful development path, and there is no reason for us to give up on this path. If there is a request for China to send troops to other countries, I think we need to listen carefully to the arguments of all parties concerned. China is already an active participant in international peacekeeping operations within the framework of the United Nations."

During the 2016 Valdai Discussion Club, four high-ranking Russian officials came from Moscow to participate in the meetings. They were Russian First Deputy Prime Minister Igor Shuvalov, State Duma Chairman Vyacheslav Volodin, the President's Economic Advisor Alexei Kudrin, and Foreign Minister Sergei Lavrov. They attended meetings with scholars on separate occasions to explain Russian policies and offered their views on various issues. Shuvalov talked about Russia's economic situation and related policies. Kudrin also analysed the economy but from a different angle, mainly commenting on the effectiveness of policies and existing problems. Volodin elaborated on Russia's political parties and their stance on parliamentary election. Lavrov candidly and comprehensively analysed Russia's international environment and explained Russia's foreign policy.

The audience raised many questions, touching on the fraud in the Duma election, the low voter turnout and expanding presidential power. They also asked whether President Putin would continue to be in office after 2018. Western scholars in the audience said that Russia was experiencing a decline in democracy and increased populism as well as centralisation. They raised questions on how to look at the widening revenue deficit, the increased share of defence spending, tightening internet control and Russia's international role. Some Western scholars commented that Russia's political and military actions in Syria and Ukraine had undermined the foundation of the international order, while scholars from the Middle East and Central Asia approved of Russia's role in ensuring regional stability. In terms of the "GEP", European and American scholars argued that it was only a concept that Russia wanted to use as a bargaining chip to aid its return to Europe, whereas Central Asian scholars expressed their concern about Russia's political intentions behind the initiative.

What impressed me was that Russian politicians and scholars did not shy away from these sharp questions but rather responded candidly.

The final event, and the highlight, of the Valdai Discussion Club was President Putin's speech, followed by a Q&A. In this session, Tarja Halonen, former President of Finland, Heinz

Fischer, former President of Austria, and Thabo Mbeki, former President of South Africa, were also invited to deliver speeches. During the Q&A session, President Putin held the spotlight more than the others on stage. Almost 90% of the questions were for him, some of which were even hostile. President Putin responded to all questions skilfully and kept everything fully under his control.

While he criticised the shortcomings of the existing world order, he stressed that the United Nations "is unparalleled in its representativeness and universality." He also reiterated his support for harmonising the Eurasian Economic Union and the China-led Silk Road Economic Belt project to "promote an extensive Eurasian partnership which promises to evolve into one of the formative centres of a vast Eurasian integration area." He was very positive about Russia's relations with China and expressed optimism for its future. The session was extended to four hours to allow President Putin enough time to answer all the questions.

I also asked a question:

"The relationship between Russia and the EU did not go as expected 25 years ago. From your point of view, Mr President, what were the hopes that failed to materialise and, from a philosophical point of view, what is the lesson to be learned for the next 25 years?"

President Putin gave an honest answer. He said that 25 years ago, the Soviet Union and then Russia expected that once they switched to a more open ideology and policies, their differences with the Western world would disappear. But it turned out that the differences concerning national interest and geopolitics were much more complicated than just ideological differences, which led to many twists and turns in the relationship up to this day. But President Putin expressed confidence in the future and emphasised that when a new international security system was built, Russia-European relations would be better.

Some experts raised questions about the purpose of Russia-China cooperation and the United States presidential election. Putin denied that Russia intended to align with China against the United

States and reiterated that they would work with whoever the American people chose as president.

VALDAI 2017

In 2017, I received an invitation to attend the 14th annual meeting of the Valdai Discussion Club. The theme was "Creative Destruction: Will a New World Order Emerge from the Current Conflicts?" The term "creative destruction"[1] was coined by the economist Schumpeter, which was meant to explain the relationship between economic recession and technological innovation. Creative destruction means that every recession breeds the possibility of technological renovation and economic creativity grows from the same roots as economic destruction. There is a similar Chinese saying, "*Bu Po Bu Li* - There is no making without breaking." Given what Russia had gone through over the previous year, it was not difficult to understand what the organisers were thinking about.

When the 13th annual meeting of the Valdai Discussion Club was held in October 2016, the United States presidential election was still a month away. Many people in Russia wanted to see relations with the United States improve if Donald Trump was elected. However, after President Trump took office in 2017, the expected closer Russia-US ties did not occur. Worse still, Russia was implicated with "Russiagate"and other American domestic fraud cases, further souring the prospects for the relationship. The annual meeting of 2017 demonstrated a pessimistic mood on international politics. With "conflicts" as its keyword, the meeting included five sessions focusing on five aspects of conflicts: those among differing geopolitical worldviews, between rich and poor, between humans and nature, between (Western democratic values) universalism and self-identity, and between progress and humanism.

I was invited to speak at the first session: "The Conflict Between Differing Geopolitical Worldviews," along with former Valdai Discussion Club president Sergey Karaganov, former Egyptian Foreign Minister Nabil Fahmy, *Die Zeit* Editor at Large Theo Sommer, and Dartmouth University Professor William Wohlforth. The moderator was Fyodor Lukyanov.

The topic of this session was stimulating, indicating the emerging geopolitical disputes and conflicts of interest among the major powers. Russian scholars believed that the geopolitical confrontation in the world was intensifying. Karaganov said that the world was confronting a new Cold War and was becoming rougher, and that the destruction of the world order was moving international relations to the military-political level. The German and American panelists talked about major power relations from geopolitical perspectives and claimed that there were geopolitical intentions behind China's BRI.

However, in my view, China should not follow the old debate on geopolitics. China's development and its growing international status cannot be ascribed to geopolitical gaming. The kind of zero-sum-game geopolitics derived from the era of imperialism and colonialism can no longer explain today's world. China's success in reform and opening up over the past decades has demonstrated how a major country can become strong through its own hard efforts and wide-ranging international cooperation in a globalised and relatively peaceful world, without getting caught up in geographical restrictions and competition. The idea of building a community with a shared future for mankind, put forward by President Xi Jinping, has transcended these outdated world politics.

Before going to Valdai, I invited some Chinese scholars to join me in a brainstorming session on this topic. Their views varied, but most agreed that going beyond geopolitics should be the most realistic choice in today's world. I decided to talk about this at Valdai and to call for international cooperation, instead of a relapse into a zero-sum game, hence the title of my speech: "Conflict or Cooperation? Beyond Geopolitics."

I made two points in my speech. First, the geopolitical paradigm was insufficient to analyse the new phenomena in today's world. Over the past three decades since the end of the Cold War, mankind had experienced unprecedented economic globalisation, which had promoted an increased free flow of goods, capital and labour. As a result, the world's geopolitical space had been re-configured and could no longer be divided according to politics and blocs, and the "centre-periphery" model was not relevant any more.

We were all in the same economic system and geopolitical thinking could not offer answers to today's concerns. Nevertheless, this way of thinking was not fading but rather still weighed heavily on the established major powers' way of thinking.

I said:

"For example, in the Asia-Pacific region, the United States is still driven by the urge to keep control over strategic maritime transportation hubs. It is even trying to intervene in maritime and territorial disputes in the South China Sea, causing concern that local disputes might be turned into geostrategic rivalry among powers. Another visible case is the Korean Peninsula. It is because of geostrategic thinking that the US repeatedly missed opportunities to solve the Korean nuclear issue, and we are now witnessing a serious nuclear proliferation crisis. Global security cooperation is also lagging. Confronted with the threats of extremism and terrorism, unified world action is hard to achieve if the big powers only proceed from their own geopolitical interests."

My second point was about China's choice.

"China, as both a continental and a maritime large country, is itself a variable. The rise of China brings new changes to the world. China's success proves that there are other paths that major countries can take on their rise. China can reach world markets through its maritime connections and its interior land mass with vast economic depth also offers routes to reach Central Asia and beyond to Europe. This makes it a central point not only between sea and land but also between low and high-end markets in the international trade structure. We need to appreciate that the world has changed so much that we must encourage and cultivate a sense of community."

President Xi Jinping said at the Belt and Road Forum for International Cooperation in May 2017 that "in pursuing the BRI, we will not resort to outdated geopolitical manoeuvring. What we hope to achieve is a new model of win-win cooperation. We have no intention of forming a small bloc detrimental to stability. What we hope to create is a big family of harmonious co-existence."

The conclusion I offered was that, for China, the choice was to go beyond geopolitics and that this was also the global trend. In the future, countries should join hands to build a community with a shared future for mankind, instead of retreating back to their box of geopolitical competition.

My proposition against a new geopolitical rivalry stimulated debate and during the Q&A more questions were raised to me. Some raised doubts on the strategic intentions of China's BRI and others challenged my view by citing China's building of a military base in Djibouti.

I could see that most of the critical questions about China were due to a lack of understanding and first-hand information, so I prioritised informing people about "things as they actually are." I told the audience what the BRI was, how it was put together and how it was proposed and proceeding. I explained why it was an economic cooperation initiative and the principles it pursued such as extensive consultation, joint contributions and shared benefits. Its objective was to build an open and inclusive regional cooperation platform. As for Djibouti, I explained that it was a support base China had built to provide supplies for the Chinese Navy to aid their peacekeeping efforts in the Gulf of Aden, which had been going on for years and played a role in ensuring the security of that area. My replies and clarifications reinforced my viewpoint about the need to transcend geopolitics.

RUSSIA'S "VALDAI EXPERIENCE"

My participation in the annual meetings of the Valdai Discussion Club in 2016 and 2017 offered me a valuable and rewarding opportunity to observe how Russia managed this influential international communication platform. I came to understand how Russia, when faced with adverse international opinion, has fought its way out through effective international communication.

On the periphery of meetings, I talked with some regular participants to learn from their observations and perspectives. Although some Western participants did not think that they could be persuaded by the opinions and information conveyed by Russian officials, they nevertheless appreciated the format, and the Russians' efforts to promote international communication and their expanding influence. Some scholars recalled the meetings during the infancy of the Valdai Discussion Club. When the first meeting was held in 2004, President Vladimir Putin invited the scholars who came to the meeting to his holiday villa for a frank conversation on Russia's domestic and foreign policies. This move improved many foreign scholars' impression of Russia and Putin. The initial effect of the Valdai meetings bolstered the organisers' confidence and the meetings continued to be held annually. The direct communication between President Putin and participants had also become an essential part of the meeting and continue to this day. It had to be admitted that the reason that the Valdai Discussion Club, an international forum, could last so long and do so well was due to President Putin's personal consistent attention and input.

After 14 years, the Valdai Discussion Club's operation has become very international, its agenda-setting and conference organisation have matured, and it has accumulated a long list of names and institutions as potential participants. Its connections extend to many countries in the world and experts in various fields. Every year it invites approximately 100 people to attend, according to the topics of the year. The Valdai Discussion Club was founded with the objective of breaking the Western stereotyped misconceptions of Russia. It mainly invites world-renowned and senior experts on Russian affairs from around the world, including from Western countries, with the objective of influencing and broadening their knowledge and understanding so as to improve Western public opinion and the views of academia. Valdai also invites experts from major Asian countries that have close ties with Russia, including China and India. Valdai's conference arrangement is hardly extravagant and it is excellently put together by a small team of young reception staff.

The theme of its annual meetings is decided by the Valdai Discussion Club think tank together with the President's Office, keeping in mind the current affairs and hot international and domestic topics. The Valdai debates can help identify the focus of the international community on Russia as scholars from all over the world bring in various opinions and critical views. The meetings are committed to open exchanges, with no boundaries set, and while the participants get the opportunity to speak freely, the Russians also get their views disseminated.

Observing Valdai, the Russians, no matter whether they were young staffers, politicians or senior scholars, all left me with the impression of being professional and international. It is safe to say that the Valdai Discussion Club has contributed to Russia at least in the following respects.

First, it enhances communication with the international community. The scholars it invites from across the world are active both at home and internationally and involved directly or indirectly in foreign policy-making discussions in their own countries. Having had direct access to thorough and authoritative explanations of Russia's policies and strategic intentions, they can bring this information back and share and review it with academic circles and decision-makers at home. In addition, through setting the agendas of Valdai discussions, Russia can play a role in leading the trend of researching the international elites and, at the same time, raising their own ability and participation in setting the agenda on the world stage.

Second, it contributes to Russia's sensible decision-making and reduces the risk of misjudgement. Through direct exchanges and debate on conflicting views with international scholars, the Russians can keep an objective understanding of the external world, grasp the focus of world opinion, and obtain valuable information as reference for their decision-making. In addition, the Russian organisers pay attention to the consistency of their participants and value their feedback through which they can assess the relevant countries' understanding and judgment of Russia. I reckon this must be useful as it can help the Russians to assess the potential cooperation and conflict points, and increase their own space for strategic assessment. Besides, by providing a venue for in-depth discussions, the Russians can clarify any misunderstanding that appears and therefore help reduce misjudgment of its strategies.

Third, it helps strengthen Russia's intellectual reserves and capacity. Valdai offers a platform for senior Russian officials and scholars to debate with high-quality international scholars, broaden their horizons, deepen their understanding of international issues and sharpen their judgment. It also provides an opportunity for senior Russian officials to participate in international debates and face tough questions thereby testing and improving their capability to confront difficult situations.

In today's diversified international environment, the major countries need to have multi-layered and multi-faceted connections with the outside world. They need to win understanding, recognition, and support through successful international communications. Although Russia faces great external pressure and rejection, it does not want to close the door to communication. Instead, it persists in extensive engagement with the wider world. I find it admirable. Despite the Western world's negative views on Russia, the Valdai experience has been successful in achieving its purpose as it can accurately and effectively convey Russia's national policies and positions to selected international experts and scholars for targeted international communication. In this way, as a platform of public diplomacy, Valdai plays its part well.

At the annual Valdai Discussion Club meeting in 2016, a scholar asked Putin: "Every year you come here and answer tough questions... Why and what do you gain from this?" Without a second thought, Putin replied, "I can understand you and get to know what you are thinking, and let you get to know me and what I am thinking."

7

RECALLING MY TIME SPENT IN THE UK

China's international image should be established and improved by the Chinese people themselves. It is not impossible for us to communicate and develop mutual understanding with the international community, including the Western public. My experience tells me that we need to improve our awareness and ability to communicate with the outside world. When dealing with Western media, there are some special skills which we may need to learn.

When talking to the media, one needs to consider how to better express oneself and have an effective interaction, especially when confronting tough questions or biased attitudes. In my three years serving as the Chinese Ambassador to the UK, I had many encounters with the media and interactions with journalists. I realised that I needed to improve my skills and sought professional training. Gradually, my efforts paid off as I understood better and successfully applied what I learnt. And now I would like to share some of these experiences with readers.

Reflecting on my three-year tenure in the UK, 2008 is most memorable. It was the year that the world witnessed China's splendid transition into a global player. Yet it was also a year filled with not only great joy but also deep sorrow for the Chinese people.

It felt like a roller-coaster ride for China's international image, as China endured extraordinary tests while entering the international arena.

In early 2008, when winter storms hit more than 20 provinces in China with heavy snow, ice and low temperatures, millions of migrant workers going home for the Chinese New Year got trapped at railway stations, 400,000 in Guangzhou alone. China was under the spotlight of the world media and the government's ability to handle the crises was questioned. However, China's effective response to the disaster impressed the world.

Then in March, when the chill of winter was still lingering, "Tibet independence forces" instigated violent riots in Lhasa. The Western media collectively misreported the incident in complete disregard of what really happened, tarnishing the reputation of the Chinese government and its people.

In early April, when the torch relay for the Beijing 2008 Summer Olympics went around the world, it experienced disruptions in some countries instigated by the "Tibet independence forces". This again contributed to headlines from the Western media denouncing Beijing.

Then came the major Wenchuan earthquake on May 12. The heroic spirit and solidarity demonstrated by the Chinese people together with the government and the military won praise from the international media, marking a reversal of China's image.

In August, the Beijing 2008 Summer Olympics was successfully held. The fabulous performances at the opening ceremony impressed the world. Throughout the games, the high-quality services and enterprising spirit of the Chinese people dispelled previous doubts.

When September came, the melamine-tainted infant formula scandal became a hot topic internationally, leading to widespread discussions on China's food safety. Soon after the successful launch of Shenzhou 7, the manned spaceship, made the headlines globally and was celebrated as a new chapter in China's space programme.

In 2008, as the Chinese Ambassador to the UK, I had intensive interactions with the media. I noticed that most British journalists did not have a fixed image of China and their attitudes varied depending on what they were covering and what information they had. For them, China was like a kaleidoscope changing too much and too fast to comprehend. Though they were prone to buy into any negative stories about the country, they would not hesitate to report positive stories about China should the information be available and convincing.

The indifference and then the enthusiasm the British and Western media manifested before and after the opening ceremony of the Beijing 2008 Summer Olympics made me realise that, in a sense, international opinion reflects the performance of a country and it can be influenced only through candid engagement and transparent information. Admittedly, prejudices cannot be dispelled by just one or two rounds of effective communication. Like tides, public opinion rises and falls, as do the media's attitudes following each new event. As old prejudices persist, consistently providing first-hand information is one of the key factors in gaining public understanding.

Entering the second decade of the 21st century, the world media began to notice China's progress and accomplishments. Hence, how to communicate with the outside world became a new topic for the Chinese. The world's public opinion environment is strongly influenced by the Western media which has evolved out of a complex history and modern development. Its perception of China is tinted by the legacy of negative Cold War stereotypes. For this reason, it took painstaking efforts for me to learn about how to effectively interact with the British and wider Western media which turned out to be my most important experience during my term in the UK.

ARRIVING IN THE UK

On 12 June 2007, I presented my credentials to Her Majesty Queen Elizabeth II as the Ambassador Extraordinary and Plenipotentiary of China to the United Kingdom of Great Britain and Northern Ireland. Afterwards, I held an arrival reception at the Embassy of China at 49 Portland Place, London, which was attended by ambassadors from other countries and friends from local communities. I received interviews from CCTV, Xinhua News Agency and other Chinese media. Interested in the process of presenting credentials, the journalists asked me to share the details. That day, Her Majesty was wearing a pale pink dress. All smiles, she was warm and expressed friendship with China. Buckingham Palace had dispatched a horse-drawn carriage for my husband Hao Shiyuan and I. This 167-year-old carriage, though an exquisite antique, functioned perfectly. Its black paint cover was decorated with gilded trims and the wheels were painted bright red. Its interior was soft and comfortable. As we slowly travelled across the city, the passers by and tourists were friendly and waved to us. I expressed to the media my appreciation and gratitude to the UK for organising such a grand event to introduce me, a foreign ambassador, to its people.

I was the 10th Chinese Ambassador to the UK since the founding of the PRC. I felt very honoured to be able to carry forward the accomplishments of many of my predecessors. With reverence and awe, I was deeply indebted to the Party and the country for entrusting me with such an important mission. I had studied at the University of Kent in the UK during the mid-1980s and the topic of my master's thesis was China-UK trade. To collect materials for my thesis, I visited the 48 Group Club, a UK-based business organisation dedicated to facilitating trade relations between China and the UK. I learnt from my research that the relationship between China and the UK boasted a long history and had developed through many twists and turns, and continued to hold great potential for the future.

Years of progress nurtured sound and stable China-UK relations. As the new ambassador, I wanted to work hard to bring bilateral relations to new heights. As I observed, there were plenty of opportunities to improve China-UK relations. As industrialisation accelerated, China faced numerous new challenges and opportunities, and the UK could be a partner in our endeavour. As the world was being pushed by economic globalisation, the two countries faced many similar international and regional issues calling for coordinated efforts. However, there was insufficient knowledge about China in British society and the media's deep-seated prejudice about China could affect people's opinions and get in the way of expanding bilateral cooperation. Therefore, it was important for me to try to understand how the British media conducted itself, and the interaction between the media and the government, especially the roots and logic that underpinned the relationship. In this way, I could find the proper way to communicate across British society and help more people to understand China.

I followed the media closely and started every day by reading newspapers and watching TV news. I also read books and documents about anything that was of importance to the UK and its people. Day after day, I accumulated growing knowledge about this country and started to understand better how the British government, the media, and its people interacted with and influenced each other. Their relationship and interaction have hundreds of years of history and the three have become both competitive yet interdependent. The government is subject to media supervision and serves as an important information source for the media. The media serves as a vehicle for the government to communicate with the public concerning social governance, policy implementation and public opinion, and the government works non-stop to enhance its professional competence in dealing with the ever-critical media.

For instance, Tony Blair had two competent veteran media consultants who worked closely with him when he won the election in 1997 and became Prime Minister of the UK. They were Peter Mandelson and Alastair Campbell. Their style was regarded as a new phenomenon in the evolution of British media politics, for which they were given the name—"Spin Doctors". The name used to have the implication of manipulating the media. The verb "spin" means whirling around quickly. When it emerged as a buzzword in the 1970s, it meant that a person knowingly provided a positively biased or skewed interpretation of an event to enhance their position and influence on the public. The term stemmed from the idiom, to "spin a yarn", hinting at telling far-fetched stories. Originally, it was a nautical term describing how people would listen to unlikely stories of sailors' adventures while spinning a long yarn used to make ropes. Later, people used its symbolic meaning to refer to a form of propaganda designed to influence public opinion by changing their perception of certain facts. The word "doctor" means a qualified practitioner of medicine or a venerable person who holds a doctorate. Here, however, "doctor" is used in a derogatory sense, referring to someone who is skilled at manipulating a story.

The term "spin doctor" is more or less political satire in the modern world. American writer Saul Bellow first used the term in a speech delivered in 1977. Then the phrase appeared in an article published in the *New York Times* in October 1984 and has since become widely used. According to the article, spin doctors were political consultants specialised in communicating and dealing with journalists. They would make every effort to lead journalists to see things from their perspective. By the 1990s, the term came to refer to media or political consultancy specialists who work for politicians on election campaigns. Their task was to design every detail of an election campaign and try constantly to present the politician in the most favourable light to the public through the media.

I once exchanged views with the then EU Trade Commissioner Peter Mandelson. To me, Mr Mandelson looked like a typical English gentleman with a somewhat melancholy temperament who spoke slowly. It was a summer day in 2007 when I paid a visit to his office. He talked optimistically about China's economy, expecting it would continue to expand rapidly and suggested that the UK and China should effectively expand bilateral trade. We also discussed outstanding trade problems and possible solutions. As we agreed on many of the issues, our conversation went on pleasantly. While we were talking, an incident happened—the fire alarm sounded throughout the building. People all left their offices and quickly walked down the corridor. I asked Mr Mandelson, "Is it real?"

"It must be real," he calmly replied. Then sensing my nervousness, he added: "Maybe it's not real. We organise regular fire drills."

We walked out of the building along with many other people and found a quiet corner near the building. The two of us picked up where we left off and continued the conversation. This incident did not seem to interrupt his train of thought at all.

When I asked him about how to deal with the media, he encouraged me to do media interviews, for he was well aware that every effort to engage with the media proved to be productive. He also suggested that I should arm myself with professional training before facing the media.

There are press officers or media officers in the British government but they do not serve as spokespeople. Often, secretaries and under-secretaries of government offices assume the responsibility of spokesperson. The Prime Minister acts as the primary spokesperson for the government on important issues and he is supported by two or three special media advisers. The UK's government offices do not hold routine press conferences. When important news breaks, the Prime Minister speaks to the media at 10 Downing Street, making his news release a principal channel of policy communication. Observing the British government and its officials, they have developed a pattern of communication skills. For example, when confronting a news issue, they often start with describing the issue or risk they face, then move on to the measures they have put in place, and finally elaborate on the results they expect to achieve, preferably ending with a few concluding remarks.

I have discussed with some British professionals the basic principles of dealing with the media. They emphasised three points: First, do not hide information or provide deceptive information, otherwise, you will be on the defensive once the real story is revealed. Second, try to provide known information as soon as possible to avoid an information vacuum. Third, keep close communication with the media and win their trust.

PUBLIC OPINION SHOCK FOLLOWING THE "3·14" UNREST IN TIBET

On 14 March 2008, a group of political agitators instigated riots and looting on the main roads in Lhasa, capital of the Tibetan Autonomous Region. They brutally beat up and killed innocent people, including Tibetans and even some police officers got hurt, causing serious casualties and property damage. The police forces stationed in Lhasa, along with reinforcements, responded quickly and brought the unrest under control while maintaining great restraint in the way they dealt with the rioters. There were a number of international journalists who witnessed the riots in the initial stage and they made factual reports.

It was soon revealed that the 14th Dalai Lama's group residing overseas masterminded the "3·14" Lhasa riot, a serial criminal act of violence involving beating, destruction of property, looting and arson, and they wanted to pressure the Chinese government through the use of terror and chaos in the run-up to the Beijing 2008 Summer Olympics. The Xinhua News Agency reported on the incident the very night the unrest broke out and informed the public of the incident and the casualties as well as the cause and who orchestrated it. Unfortunately, in the following week, further information was coming outside the official channel. During the same period, a whirlwind of coverage of the riots was sweeping across the world. Many stories were clearly based on speculation and groundless assumptions. Disinformation from Tibetan exiles was widely adopted and reported by the Western media. Consequently, the perceptions and views of the wider international community were manipulated and influenced by the misinformation and distorted reports from the Western media and public opinion regarding China became very negative.

A Beijing-based journalist with the *New York Times* published a long article the day after the 3·14 unrest entitled "Violence in Tibet as Monks Clash with Police". According to his account, Buddhist monks and other ethnic Tibetans felt compelled to start protests and demonstrations and thus clashed with armed forces of Han nationality, which ignited the unrest. But he did not mention the brutal acts of the mobs, who killed civilians and burned and looted stores. Instead, the journalist described the unrest as "peaceful protests" and mentioned how the "protesters" were beaten up and killed by the police. This partial and distorted story was widely communicated to the world.

Then on 16 and 17 March, criticism of China for "human rights violations" and "religious persecution" grabbed the headlines in the Western media, which mostly used untruthful or incomplete information. In the following 10 days or so, the *New York Times*, CNN, BBC, and *The Times* published hundreds of special reports. They attributed the unrest to the Chinese government's long-term intervention into Tibetan Buddhist affairs and expressed sympathy for the "Tibet independence forces" which, well aware how the Western media operated, made painstaking efforts to satisfy their information thirst by not only offering fabricated news stories but also providing translations in multiple languages to facilitate their coverage.

The Western media orchestrated strong public opinion on "the Chinese government's suppression of religious freedom." The most unimaginable mistake they made was that, when there was no photo or footage to support their false stories of the Chinese government crushing protests in Lhasa, many of the Western media outlets used footage of protests in other countries and pictures taken elsewhere or cropped photos to fit their narrative. To tarnish the Chinese government and the military, some of them went so far as to fake images and videos. For instance, there was a photo of someone throwing rocks at a military vehicle, and CNN crafted it as if a military vehicle was heading into the crowds. N-TV, a German television news channel, used footage of Nepali police officers dispersing monks when reporting the unrest in Lhasa. The *Washington Post* also posted a photo of Nepali police officers dispersing crowds in Katmandu, yet claimed it was students in Lhasa engaging in peaceful demonstrations. They were not bothered that the people in those images did not look like Chinese at all.

It is arguably a scandalous act perpetrated by the Western media to produce such a stream of fake news. Unfortunately, most people in the West fed with such disinformation could not distinguish between what was real and what was not, and were easily persuaded to believe that the "Chinese government put down protests." Public opinion in turn morphed into a kind of political pressure under which some Western dignitaries misjudged the situation and expressed inappropriate remarks about China. This would inevitably hurt the feeling of the Chinese people and affect bilateral relations. Such a vicious circle served the interests and purposes of the Dalai group and the "Tibet independence forces" which, feeling encouraged, would just make more fabrications and provocations.

Confronting the negative public backlash on China and the furious response by the Chinese people at home, my embassy faced serious public relations challenges. I first made a diplomatic démarche to express China's stance on the unfair criticism. I then visited British media outlets one by one to clarify the situation. Every visit was met with a sincere attitude and attendees at my meetings included not only editors-in-chief and senior journalists but in some cases senior management and board members also attended. We had long discussions about China, often with fierce debate. I used facts and figures to refute their distorted reports and views, and often won the arguments as they were not as familiar as I was with the real situation. On top of that, crafting photos and misreporting stories was indisputably a press scandal and they all knew it was taboo.

Yet, I often felt tongue-tied when they challenged me with one last question: "Where is the Chinese voice?" "If your side is so confident in your argument, how come you didn't provide images and information immediately? Why didn't your people come out in the open and take interviews?" An editor told me that he could receive a dozen pieces of information from the "Tibetan exiles" and their sympathisers every day. Some journalists also admitted that they did not verify the authenticity of their sources. But they argued once something had happened, the public would be craving information, putting the media under heavy pressure, so they would report whatever they could get their hands on. Although I disagreed with some of their arguments, I did reflect on an important point— what we needed to do to counter disinformation and misinformation was to convey to the public first-hand messaging in a more proactive and timely manner.

At this time, Chinese embassies in other countries also criticised the Western media's falsification of the news, for which some media outlets offered apologies. Nevertheless, false and skewed reporting and stories had already spread all over the world and serious misunderstandings about China prevailed in many countries.

Jimmy, a Beijing-based journalist with CBS, had a phone conversation with me while he was attending a meeting in London. I questioned him: Why had so many Western media produced fake news about what happened in China? He agreed that this kind of distortion was wrong and he explained that although those journalists didn't have enough information, most of them believed that there was a crackdown and bloodshed in Tibet and were convinced that they could obtain real pictures very soon. Scrambling to report the news, they chose to use other pictures temporarily. Furthermore, the Western media habitually criticised China for abusing human rights, so they truly thought that things like this could happen. Then, he asked: "Have you considered why the Western media does not treat other countries like this and only unscrupulously targets China?" He held that people would not easily buy into such stories if China improved its transparency and provided authoritative information on a more timely basis.

The excuse of "scrambling to report the news" was unacceptable to me. Whatever the reason, creating fake news was against the professed professional ethics of any media. Such acts were inexcusable, as they had maliciously defamed China and severely prejudiced China's international image. Still, Jimmy's question reminded me once again that action was urgently needed on our part.

"PROGRESSING FANTASTICALLY YET COMMUNICATING BADLY"

While negative public opinion related to the "3·14" riots was still haunting us, the Beijing 2008 Summer Olympics international torch relay was officially kicked off on 24 March and was set to reach London on 5 April. It was a great event in China-UK relations, so several British media outlets sought to interview me. They provided the outlines of issues they wanted to discuss, mainly about the Beijing Olympics and the recent unrest in Lhasa. I thought taking interviews would be a good way for me to directly convey views and information about China to the British people.

The British people enjoy reading and have a habit of following news and current affairs. As a nation of over 60 million people, the number of newspapers, magazines, books, TV and radio programmes, and audio/video products the country has is higher than the world average. Let alone the great influence they have on people's daily life. As the modern media industry originated in the UK, the British media not only influence their own people and people in the Western world, but also the wider international community. *The Times, the Financial Times, the Guardian, The Sun,* the BBC, etc. have established an international reputation over the years and have wide viewership at home and aboard.

British journalists are professional and sharp. They claim to be standing on behalf of the people to challenge the government and the policies. To deal with the media, the government needs to constantly improve its capabilities and skills. As a result, the two formed into a competing and yet inseparable interdependent relationship. This complicated relationship has also cultivated an increasingly specialised public relations (PR) consultancy and training services sector.

I was introduced to David Hill, who had been a spin doctor for former Prime Minister Tony Blair. We met two or three times and I wanted to learn about the UK's media environment, the characteristics of its local media, and how to deal with them. I noticed that he placed special emphasis on professional training and suggested that to successfully interact with the media, I needed to learn the skills and conduct targeted exercises before each interview. Mr Hill cited his personal experience as a consultant to UK dignitaries. For example, if an important statesman is about to give a five-minute interview, he would spend at least 25 minutes drilling over the few key questions. Hill would challenge the statesman from a variety of angles to prepare him for difficult questions and train him to stick to his original position, thus enabling him to articulate his views and prepare information successfully. After the challenging exercises, the interviewee could handle any tricky questions with ease. Mr Hill told me: "The media may ask anything and you need to be well prepared. The key thing to stick to is: What is your message?"

I benefited a lot from the conversation and realised that I must receive professional training. Through my exchanges with other countries' ambassadors, I discovered that they also attached importance to professional training and preparation when taking media interviews. So my embassy started doing research and considering which specialist agency to reach out to for training assistance.

British PR companies provide highly professional services. Once a contract is made, they start researching and analysing the relevant media reports and commentaries, and developing customised plans to serve clients' specific requirements. However, just like lawyers, PR consulting companies are expensive and the quoted price of Mr Hill's company was beyond the embassy's budgetary constraints. I had to give up on this idea.

A friend introduced me to a smaller communication risk company, and I became friends with its Egyptian-British owners Mr Sameh El-Shahat and his younger sister Ms Samah El-Shahat, who used to be a journalist. Through their father, who had once met Premier Zhou Enlai, the El-Shahats cherished friendly feelings towards China. We hit it off immediately. Speaking of China's international image, Sameh said: "We have never seen a country like yours which has progressed fantastically but communicated badly." Their remarks touched me because it showed that they were aware of the difficulties and challenges facing the embassy. So I decided to use part of the granted special funds allocated for the embassy's olympics-related activities for their special training. They often worked long hours with me, much more than we had paid for, and did not seem bothered when many other embassy staff attended their courses.

The El-Shahats and their team devoted their time to trying to understand Chinese culture, ideas and values. Furthermore, their family background made it easier for them to identify with developing countries like China and China's view. They held that the Chinese people should make an effort to share with the world their ideas and values so that people in the UK and other countries may relate to and accept them. Only in this way can we foster respect for China's image, spread China's story and gain more trust from the international community. They also argued that as China grows stronger, insufficient knowledge and a lack of understanding of Chinese ideology and values will only result in the international community developing a greater sense of being threatened by, and hostility towards, China.

I agreed and acknowledged that we, the Chinese, must improve our communication skills and powers of persuasion in order to deal with Western society which had limited knowledge of China and the Western media that has deep-rooted bias against China. As a diplomat, I have been posted overseas for years, so I am keenly aware of how rarely the voice of the Chinese people can be heard in the Western world as well as in the wider international community. We often lack representation at critical moments and on vital issues. Therefore, we need to develop awareness when dealing with the media and enhance our ability to communicate effectively. As the saying goes: "He who sups with the devil should have a long spoon." When dealing with tough opponents, especially if you cannot change the rules, it is important to understand how they conduct themselves and what their objectives are, then draw on their strengths to get your points across. Only in this way can we leverage local communication channels better and convey China's messages, explain the ideas of the Chinese people and tell our story.

STRICT TEACHERS

The El-Shahats were strict teachers. They were very chatty and cheerful when we had tea together, but once the class began, they would tell me that they were journalists now and not friends any more.

The first lesson was an interview simulation. They raised a string of questions, which we normally considered "sensitive", in an "unfriendly manner", relentlessly questioning China's political system and its domestic and foreign policies. For me, these were the routine questions when facing Western media; I effortlessly and eloquently refuted all those critical questions.

After the simulation, I would join them to watch and analyse the video footage. They asked me to carefully observe my own image on the TV screen. When a tough question was brought up, I appeared extremely serious with my facial muscles contracting. My expression was amplified on the television screen, which further intensified the atmosphere.

They told me, the general public who would be watching would find me lacking in composure and self-confidence as if I had something to hide. People would therefore find it hard to trust me. Samah shared her experience with me and said some journalists would deliberately provoke their interviewees in order to catch them off guard. Normally, the calmer the interviewees are, the easier it is for the audience to focus on the messages they are trying to convey. She suggested: "When taking a question from a journalist, try to refrain from appearing defensive. If a journalist labels you as 'blah blah…' and you try hard to deny the labels, you fall into the trap of self-justification." Instead, a more effective method is to illustrate who you are and disprove the labels by using solid facts.

The suggestions were very helpful. Why do we receive interviews and face the media? We do so to communicate our information and views to the public. If an interview is likened to a game, the journalist challenging you with questions is your opponent. But the objective of the game may not necessarily be to outperform one another but to win over the public behind the camera. The media is a bridge and a medium of communication. If you do not trust the media, you might as well give up speaking to it altogether. However, once you decide to accept a media interview, you must concentrate on the public who stand behind the media and focus on convincing the public rather than quarrelling with the journalists.

The first step of the professional training was to learn how to face journalists in a relaxed manner and confidently communicate with the target audience, the public. I could tell from watching the footage that I looked more amicable and trustworthy when I smiled as I answered the questions. This rule is actually applicable in normal interpersonal relations.

The second lesson of the professional training was on linguistic expressions, namely, designing the key points of answers and responding to questions convincingly. The point is how to stay away from the routine of "I'm right, so I'm right." The Western public has little background knowledge of China, as not many have access to such information. For instance, a truck driver or a housewife in the UK learns about what is happening in the world by watching television, listening to the radio, going to the pub or talking to friends. But the television programs rarely present first-hand information about China. For me, communicating naturally with the British public was not an easy job both in terms of technical skill and the art of expression. Sometimes, telling a story is more effective than expressing an argument. One's views can be better understood and accepted when using expressions or metaphors the listeners are familiar with.

When I started to dicuss issues about China with the El-Shahats that were most frequently mentioned by Western media, I took out a thick book of "white paper" containing talking points covering a wide variety of issues. As I went through it with them, some of the answers were convincing and they agreed with the argument. But, from time to time, they disagreed. They would point out flaws in the reasoning and discuss with me how to better express the points. It was an exhausting and gruelling process. Some of the sentences sounded quite OK to me, but Sameh would say: "You've lost me." Having listened to my explanations, he would comment that although the wording sounded nice, the meaning was elusive in English. The essential messages became obscure when a lot of adjectives or slogans were used. He suggested that I should use real-life stories and cases to illustrate my points. We discussed the connotations of some concepts and reorganised the sentences. We sometimes would ponder on a specific verb or adjective over and over again.

The training was thorough and strict, including paying attention to some details, such as how to set the tone, make a pause and use gestures. For example, when I spoke, the harsher my words were, the slower my tone should be. That also corresponded to a traditional Chinese saying: "It does not require a loud voice to speak the truth". In addition, while emphasising a point, I was supposed to pause for a moment to draw the audience's attention and allow it to resonate with them. But to pause too often was not good, as it would disrupt the flow of the speech. I was also told to use a few gestures; otherwise, I would look stiff. The appropriate use of gestures would make me sound natural and compelling. My expressions and tones also mattered in front of the camera, so I was asked to adjust myself according to the context of the question. Television interviews are the art of watching and listening and thus an art of expression. In an interview, even when you are specific about the messages and policies you want to convey, whether you are successful or not depends also on the expressive force of your language.

We stuck to the schedule—conducting interview simulations, watching video replays, making corrections, engaging in discussions and doing exercises. When my schedule permitted, I would even spend an entire day practicing and discussing with my colleagues what we had learnt. Little by little, I made progress. The intensive training helped me to see my own weaknesses and pushed me to improve quickly. For example, it taught me to keep a cool head under pressure and be better prepared as well as how to flexibly respond to familiar or unfamiliar topics. My performance improved and I was able to deal with and even refute a variety of questions. Sameh smiled and commented: "Now, you are able to take the initiative and challenge me, instead of passively responding to my challenges." I also came to master some useful techniques like how to use humour and self-mockery, how to present the facts and reason things out, and how to disprove the journalists at the most appropriate time to gain the upper hand.

The El-Shahats led a professional team. Before I took an interview with a media outlet, they would go through its recent reporting on China as well as recent coverage by other media outlets and commentators on the same issues. They would also research for background information on the interviewer and their previous stance. From this massive amount of information, they compiled a condensed summary of about 20 pages of key information, which formed the groundwork for a response plan. With such thorough preparation, the possibility of me running into unexpected questions during the interview was significantly reduced, and there was less probability of failure or me being put on the back foot.

With the help of professional consultants and training, I developed a better understanding of how the British media operated and mastered some techniques for dealing with them. In an information era, the success of public diplomacy depends on not only whether you have a good story to tell, but also your ability to tell it well. Those who do a better job at it have a greater chance of success. It is certainly a formidable task to influence and change the West's prejudice against China. Ultimately, it will be the concrete achievements of China's development that will convince the rest of the world. Nevertheless, by improving our professional skills and successfully conveying China's views and messages via the Western media, we may be able to influence the public on some specific issues. If we continue with this endeavour, over time, we will be able to make a difference.

MY MAIDEN APPEARANCE ON BBC BREAKFAST

In late March 2008, *BBC Breakfast* requested an interview with the Chinese ambassador to discuss the upcoming 2008 Beijing Olympic Games. I was told that it had the highest audience share among all the UK's morning news programmes. The El-Shahats agreed to provide technical support and it marked our first cooperation on a real interview.

As we started working on the plan, Sameh asked me: "Why do you want to accept the interview request?"

I said: "They came to me first. And I also need to express some views and our position to the British public."

To which they asked: "What is the most important message you want to convey and the most important problem you want to address?"

The point they were trying to drive at was that, to prepare for an interview, I should start from what I wanted to say rather than what they might ask. So I replied: "The UK media seems to believe that China is holding the Olympics not because people want it, but to serve the interests of the state apparatus. They have no idea how the Chinese people look at it or what's on their mind."

"Alright, now we are clear about your purpose, let's start preparing you for the interview," they said.

The BBC interview was scheduled for the morning prime time slot and would last for five minutes. Considering that the anchors in this type of morning news programme throw questions at their guests very fast, we estimated that I could answer three to four questions.

Before I had any training, to prepare for an interview, I would brainstorm with my staff, guess the questions and prepare for specific answers. For a five-minute interview, I would come up with over 20 possible answers, covering almost every aspect I thought might be raised. However, I could not always memorise all those answers, so I would seize upon any ideas that flashed through my mind during an interview, compromising the integrity of my responses.

This time, we used a more scientific method to prepare. The first step was to identify the possible direction of the questions. My teachers suggested not to prepare five times as many answers as the number of questions that could be asked in the allotted time. Instead, they recommended I only prepare four key points. In other words, we should assume the four issues most likely to be raised and prepare accordingly. Based on their research, the El-Shahats' team came up with the key concerns and hottest issues the UK public and media had about China. I also brought forward the key information that I would like to tell the British public. Combining these two trains of thought, we were able to identify the areas and issues most likely to be raised, which were also what I wanted to talk about to achieve my aims for the interview.

We put the issues on the table and eventually selected four areas: why China wants to host the Olympics; the torch relay; Tibet issues; and China's political system.

For the next step, we moved on to developing key points for my answers. It was important that we constructed key points for answers in each area and identified appropriate ways to express them. We spent half a day examining China's position on each of these questions. When I read out our standard official answers, my teachers often shook their heads. "You lost me."

For example, when talking about the Beijing Olympic Games, the standard slogans were: "Green Olympics," "Culturally-enriched Olympics," and "High-tech-empowered Olympics." They could not get it until I gave a more detailed explanation. However, it was obvious that I had to spend a lot of time explaining the meanings of these slogans in order to get these ideas across. Besides, too many definitions would overshadow the inherent nature of the Beijing Olympic Games as a sporting event and miss the compelling message. Instead, people would be left confused about what exactly the Chinese wanted to achieve. Sameh said, in the morning most people are in a rush to go to work. Those watching news on the television just want to get as much information as they can in as little time as possible. People would find it hard to concentrate if a foreign ambassador sits there, spending time trying to preach Big Truth.

"Perhaps you can put aside official rhetoric this time and think about how the ordinary Chinese people think and what they are doing. You can also picture a scene which shows how the Chinese people support, anticipate and participate in the Olympics," they suggested. "After all, your audience is ordinary British people who know little about China, so there is no need to use overly complicated language to make your point. Telling the stories of ordinary people will be good enough."

I thought about it for a moment and then began to share how I felt when I was on vacation in Beijing earlier that summer. I spoke of how taxi drivers could not wait to see the opening of the Olympics and how "*da ma's*" (middle-aged Chinese women) living in Beijing's *hutongs* (alleys) were diligently studying English. My stories were received with applause. They told me that it would be good if I could share these stories, especially the one about the *hutongs*, these lively stories portraying real lives can convey profound messages which would otherwise be difficult to explain even in 10 minutes. That was it! We had found a way to achieve my goal. Then we worked on the rest of the key points in the same way, citing stories or examples for each of them in concise, natural language and making sure that each answer took no more than a minute and a half.

The third step was to conduct rehearsals with the aim of training me to use the four key points to answer any question from the anchors.

Given my tight schedule, Sameh suggested that we conduct

exercises over the phone. The minute my alarm clock went off in the morning, his call came in. I smoothly answered the four questions he raised in one sitting, using clear logic, and I thought it went well.

However, after I finished, Sameh asked: "Your Excellency, where are the four key points we prepared? Why didn't you use them?"

"You didn't ask," I replied.

Indeed, since the questions he threw at me could not be linked to the key points we had prepared, I just let the questions take over and completely forgot my key points.

"We cannot expect the anchors to ask questions according to the key points we have prepared. You need to be flexible and resourceful. I'm sorry, but you have failed the first round of rehearsals. You were not able to bring up the key points you wanted to convey. Moreover, your tone was stiff and your remarks harsh. The early morning TV audience would be put off if they saw a foreign ambassador apparently in a bad mood, responding to their concerns," commented Sameh.

I found this all a little bit frustrating. Still, I accepted his comments and went over my answers in my head. His next call came in when I was in the car being taken to work. This time he asked questions from yet another different angle. I tried to answer his questions with the four key points we had prepared, but in every answer, I was fumbling and just could not attend to one thing without neglecting another. At the end of the exercise, I told him that I knew I had failed again.

During a break in a morning meeting at the embassy, I called Sameh and we conducted another exercise. His questions had changed again, and I still did not make much progress. Even though I was able to present the key points prepared, my answers were beside the point. My poor performance during the three rehearsals increased the pressure on me, so I changed my schedule that afternoon to give myself more time to calm down and figure out what had gone wrong.

By reviewing the different questions in the first three exercises, I realised that I must first identify how to link my narrative to the questions. In an interview, racking one's brain for an effective point to answer the question can be unnerving. Instead, one needs to change the angle and try to convey the intended messages based on the journalist's questions. But, of course, it won't work if one completely ignores the question and focuses on one's own thoughts or gives a totally irrelevant answer. This kind of response cannot win over an audience.

As long as we were able to correctly ascertain what the public's and journalists' concerns were, no matter what form the questions took, it should not be impossible to connect them to the prepared points of response. I should not expect the journalists to raise questions perfectly in line with my prepared answers, nor should I worry about whether I can squarely answer the questions. What is more important is that I take the initiative and convey the messages I want the audience to know. It can be very stressful taking a media interview, especially on live television, so it is important that I know my prepared key points by heart to ensure that I can effortlessly and naturally express myself.

In the afternoon, while reviewing my prepared key points, I tried to memorise as much as possible the elements in them so that I could divide them into independent points, like LEGO blocks. In this way, I could reassemble them in any order I wanted. Having figured this out, my hard work paid off in the next round of rehearsals. No matter how the questions were framed, I could lead them to my pre-set answers, using only one or two connecting sentences. Repeated exercises reinforced my memory, and exhausting as it was, I could sense the progress I was making. As my nervousness faded, I came to enjoy the process of trying to outwit the questioner.

When we worked through the last exercise that night, Sameh declared that I had passed the test and told me not to think about it any more, and that everything would work out just fine. I felt reassured and, with a light heart and looking forward to the next day's interview, I went for a walk in the park.

On the morning of 28 March 2008, I awoke to a lovely day. Together with the Embassy Press Counsellor Liu Weimin, I arrived early at the London-based BBC building and there were only a few employees around, including a professional makeup artist who was there to prepare me.

My interview came between segments in the news programme, and as I was ushered into the studio, the two anchors were still delivering other news. I was led to my seat on stage during a pre-filmed advertisement. When the camera turned to us, the female anchor asked the first question, and afterwards she and her male colleague took turns to raise questions. They were polite, but their questions were sharp. I reminded myself that I was not only facing these two anchors, but also the public having breakfast in front of their televisions. Smiling throughout, I tried to answer their questions as concisely as I could.

The anchor went straight to the point, saying that when the Chinese government was dedicated to delivering a spectacular 2008 Summer Olympic Games, the public saw "violent scenes" from Tibet in the media. Then she turned to me and asked whether the government was worried that these unpleasant scenes would spoil the year, which was very important for China.

Instead of responding to her aggressive statement directly, I first expressed thanks to the anchors for having me there, as Sameh told me during the exercise that the first question would always be challenging or even provocative. Whatever the interviewer said, I should always start by saying: "Thank you for inviting me." It would not only show my good manners but also create a break for myself and for the audience, allowing me those few vital seconds to change the mood and atmosphere.

Next, I led the topic to the essence and purpose of the Olympics. I said that people had been discussing the Beijing Olympic Games for a while, as if it had been a United Nation's heads of state conference, responsible for solving many international and domestic issues. However, for the Chinese people, it was about sports, and China's TV programmes were very much focused on the sporting competitions.

The anchor interrupted me, stating that it was difficult to separate sports from politics in real life. I did not let her distract me and stuck to my stance by saying: political issues are more important and more complicated. We cannot solve them on a football pitch or in a swimming pool. As a big family of 56 ethnic groups, China faces many challenges, just like the UK, and we are working continuously to improve and solve our own problems.

Then the anchor pressed on, asking what the Chinese government planned to do to handle the unrest in Lhasa, Tibet. I stressed that the first objective was to stop the violence. For the Chinese government, the priority was to calm down the people and prevent further damage.

The next question was why the Chinese government would not allow Western journalists to interview freely in Tibet. I explained that the decision was made for the sake of safety. There were some Western journalists as well as international tourists who had been in Lhasa during the early stage of the unrest, who had just been evacuated from the area.

The anchor threw another question at me: Is the Chinese government going to speak to the 14th Dalai Lama? I said that as early as the 1970s, the Chinese government approved of his relatives' returning to China to start a dialogue with the central government, and the Buddhist Association of China once invited him back in the 1980s. In spite of the unrest at that time, the Chinese government continues to keep the channels for dialogue open.

We proceeded quickly from one issue to another. Soon we came to the topic of the Beijing Olympic torch relay. I was asked "would there be any different arrangements" concerning the torch relay due to the riots that had erupted in Lhasa, for example, whether there would be any change in terms of freedom for press reporting or security arrangements. I did not know much about the arrangements for the media, but I did emphasise that China would want reliable security. I also told the anchors that Tibet was a stop when the torch relay came to the Chinese mainland.

The anchor then asked me one last question: How do the Chinese people feel about the Olympics coming to their country in August? I said confidently that people were excited in anticipation. I did not forget to mention that even the *"da ma's"* (middle-aged Chinese women) living in the *hutongs* of Beijing were learning English. I also stressed that the torch relay should help promote relations between China and the UK and let Londoners experience some of the atmosphere of the 2008 Beijing Olympics. The Chinese people would also see London on TV, which might help change their traditional impression of men wearing dark coats and carrying an umbrella.

As the anchors thanked me for taking the interview and said goodbye, I presented them with the 2008 Beijing Olympics mascots Beibei and Yingying, and said that I hoped they could convey China's best wishes to the world.

Seventy percent of our prepared key points overlapped with the questions asked, which gave me reason to be more confident and time to think. I was a bit nervous during the interview but my debut as the Chinese Ambassador on British television was favourably received. Most importantly, although after the "3·14" Lhasa riots, negative views of China prevailed in British society, my interview had successfully conveyed first-hand positive messages from China. Indeed, a few interviews cannot remove all the prejudice and misunderstandings and we need more people to join the cause of improving China's international image by delivering Chinese stories and messages to international society.

THE 2008 BEIJING OLYMPIC FLAME ARRIVES IN THE UK

London was the first Western city to host the Beijing Olympic torch relay. It was an important mission of the Chinese Embassy in the UK to make sure that the torch relay went smoothly and to take this opportunity to further promote understanding between China and the UK, and the West.

In anticipation of the moment, I often mentioned the story of "three questions on the Olympics" in my speeches. A century ago, in 1908, a young student from Nankai University posed three questions about the Olympics in an article published in *Tianjin Youth*: "When can China send an athlete to the Olympic Games? When can Chinese athletes get an Olympic medal? When can China host the Olympic Games?" Three similar questions were posed in *Shen Bao (The Shanghai News)* on 17 July 1910 in an announcement entitled: "Preface to the China Sports Meeting": "When will China send representatives to the Olympic Games? When will a Chinese become an Olympic champion? When will China host the Olympic Games?"

Amidst about a century of turmoil in the country, the three questions were answered one by one. In 1932, the Chinese sprinter Liu Changchun arrived alone by ship in Los Angeles, USA, for the 10th Olympic Games. Although he failed to win a medal, Liu became the first Chinese athlete to compete in the games. Then, on 29 July 1984, Xu Haifeng won China's first Olympic gold medal in the 50 metres individual free pistol, scoring 566 with 60 shots at the Prado Olympic Shooting Park during the 23rd Olympic Games in Los Angeles. However, the third question was not answered until 13 July 2001, when Mr Juan Antonio Samaranch, then President of the International Olympic Committee (IOC), announced that Beijing, China had won the hosting right for the 29th Summer Olympics.

I still remember that night when we heard on the evening news that China had won the right to host the Olympic Games. There was a feeling of elation in my family and we all erupted into cheers. My daughter, who was a middle school student at that time, went out and joined the cheering crowds in Tiananmen Square. I was worried sick when she had not returned home until early the following morning. When she finally showed up, her face was glowing with excitement, and when she saw me waiting desperately at home for her, she said: "Are you dinosaurs from the cretaceous period? China is going to host the Olympics!" During the following seven years, the Chinese people eagerly anticipated and prepared for the 2008 Beijing Olympic Games. The young people celebrated, expressing their hopes and excitement in a variety of ways as they looked forward to the arrival of this grand event.

But did the rest of the world know and understand the feeling of the Chinese people?

On 24 March 2008, the Beijing Olympic flame was ignited at Olympia in southern Greece, the site of the ancient Olympic Games. The ceremony was attended by the Greek President and Prime Minister, along with the President of the IOC and Liu Qi, then Secretary of the CPC Beijing Municipal Committee and

President of the Beijing Organising Committee for the Games of the XXIX Olympiad (BOCOG).

An incident occurred during the ceremony. I was watching it live on television in London and saw a man wearing black, later found to be a member of *Reporters Sans Frontières* (Reporters Without Borders, RSF), who had forced his way into the venue with a protest banner, and some "Tibet independence" activists tried to disrupt the torch lighting process. Well-trained Greek police immediately apprehended and removed the perpetrators. Some of the activists could still be seen in the distance holding banners in protest against the 2008 Beijing Olympic torch relay. Watching the scene, I could sense the gathering momentum and realised that the torch relay in Europe could not be expected to go peacefully.

Good triumphs over evil. The lighting ceremony was not affected, as the Greek High Priestess, wearing a traditional linen dress, handed the torch to the first torchbearer, Greek taekwondo athlete Alexandros Nikolaidis, kicking off the international torch relay that would end at the opening ceremony of the Beijing Summer Olympic Games.

On 30 March 2008, the five-day relay in Greece concluded successfully and the torch handover ceremony was held at a stadium in Athens. Local police were in place to ensure security. A dozen police officers with loaded weapons were spaced every 100 metres or so along the street and security was maintained throughout the torch relay. Countries which were going to host the Beijing Olympic torch relay became aware that there were going to be unprecedented provocations, but there was also unparalleled resolve to safeguard the Olympic torch and the dignity of the Olympic Games.

The national flags of China, brought by the Overseas Chinese Association attending the handover ceremony, flew proudly in the air looking extraordinarily fiery against the crystal blue sky of Athens. The Olympic flame arrived in Beijing the following day before starting its global tour. It was going to traverse the longest distance, cover the widest area, and involve the largest number of torch bearers in the history of Olympics torch relays.

On 2 April 2008, the Olympic flame arrived in Almaty, Kazakhstan, an important stop on the ancient Silk Road. Attaching great importance to the event, the government of Kazakhstan organised a grand commencement ceremony at the Medeu Skating Rink and Ski Resort in Almaty. Then President of Kazakhstan Nursultan Abishevich Nazarbayev attended and addressed the ceremony. The torch relay's first leg at Almaty was successfully concluded in six hours.

The Olympic torch relay then proceeded to Istanbul, Turkey and Saint Petersburg, Russia, on 3 and 5 April, respectively. These two legs were broadcast on television. The torch was welcomed by a sea of flowers and cheering crowds along the way.

At 7:20 pm on 5 April, charter flight CA2008 "Beijing 2008 Olympic Flame," arrived at Heathrow Airport in London. Tessa Jowell, then UK Minister for the Olympics, and I went to the airport to welcome the torch's arrival. On leaving the plane, Jiang Xiaoyu, General Director of the 2008 Beijing Olympic Torch Relay Operations Team and Executive Vice President of BOCOG, held the Olympic flame lantern in his two hands as he walked down the steps, marking the commencement of the fourth overseas leg of the torch relay in London.

London was to be the host city of the 2012 Summer Olympics, which spoke volumes for the importance of this leg of the torch relay. However, there was already serious public negativity towards the upcoming 2008 Beijing Olympic Games in many Western countries and distorted media reports blaming the Chinese government for the "3·14" riots generated a lot of anger among the people. Consequently, the torch relay was met with a solemn and grim atmosphere.

THE ROCKY TORCH RELAY

The London leg of the torch relay had a planned route of 50 kilometres, which was the longest of the 22 overseas stops. The torch was to pass through many of London's famous historical sites and tourist locations, including Marble Arch, Hyde Park, 10 Downing Street, the British Museum, Saint Paul's Cathedral and Tower Bridge, before reaching the ceremonial site at Peninsula Plaza near the Millennium Dome after about seven and a half hours. A total of 80 bearers were to carry the torch during the leg. But trouble started long before the relay began as 'Tibet independence' organisations wrote letters to torchbearers trying to dissuade them from participating in the relay.

Before the relay started, Beijing sent a message to the Embassies that Chinese Ambassadors should not become torchbearers and they should focus on overseeing the torch relay process. However, it was publicly known in the UK that I as the Chinese Ambassador had already signed up for the torch relay early on, which was seen as an important gesture of support to the torch relay's local organiser. If I was to withdraw, it might trigger unnecessary political consequences.

I asked our press officer to test the water at a gathering with journalists, suggesting that Ambassador Fu Ying was still considering whether she would be able to personally be a torch bearer as she had many other responsibilities that day. Word spread fast and within an hour the British media had posted news about "the Chinese Ambassador giving up on torch-carrying." Such reporting, claiming that I had withdrawn from the torch relay, was also appearing on some overseas Chinese news websites. The embassy soon received inquiries from some British torchbearers, who told us that they were being pressured to pull out of the relay as the Chinese Ambassador had already decided to do so.

Taking these factors into consideration, I could not permit my withdrawal to be used to undermine the morale of the UK torch relay team. That night, I explained the situation over the phone to my colleagues in Beijing in charge of the matter, and the next day the embassy announced that "Ambassador Fu Ying is a torch bearer!" The BBC and several other media outlets had to correct their story about my withdrawal.

The night before the torch relay, I paid a visit to the hotel where the Chinese torch delegation was staying and met with Chinese journalists for a briefing. I was completely honest with them about the challenging situation awaiting the Beijing Olympic torch relay and I wanted them to be active in reporting the positive stories. As the host country of the 2008 Olympic Games, China had the priority rights to broadcast the torch relay through international media channels. China was given two camera positions on the broadcast van in front of torchbearers; the BBC had one. I hoped very much that the Chinese media would be the first to broadcast the Beijing Olympic torch relay, as whoever reported the news first, either via text or images, would have the decisive influence on world opinion.

On the morning of 6 April 2008, the sky looked gloomy as tiny snowflakes fluttered and twirled in the air.

At 10:30 am, the inauguration ceremony for the London leg of the Beijing Olympics torch relay was held at Wembley Stadium. Three attendants lit the first torch from the lantern in which the Olympic flame was placed. Jiang Xiaoyu held high the torch bearing the lucky clouds symbol to show everyone before handing it over to the Deputy Mayor of London, Nicky Gavron. She then passed it to the first torchbearer Sir Steve Redgrave, a British rower who had won five gold medals in his six consecutive Olympic Games appearances. He turned around and started running towards the stadium's open door. The short but solemn ceremony was not open to the public and the empty stadium felt somewhat desolate.

In the square outside the stadium, artistic performances had already begun entertaining the spectators for more than half an hour and the fluttering snow could not dampen people's enthusiasm. Artists from various countries staged a fabulous gala of hip-hop, Indian, Irish, and Chinese red silk dancing. Hundreds of spectators, including ethnic Chinese and Chinese students, enjoyed the entertainment while eagerly waiting to catch sight of the torch. When Lord Redgrave came into view with the torch held high, the crowds cheered. The British are a nation that loves public events, and London is a city known for successfully hosting all kinds of large public gatherings. For the torch relay, every district arranged their own welcoming events, including a gala or dance performance.

However, just like the low-hanging dark clouds, the organisations supporting "Tibet independence" and other anti-China groups had come prepared to obstruct the torch relay. They obtained a map of the relay route beforehand and had their own plan to disrupt the relay in an attempt to snatch the torch at different points along the route. They seemed obsessed with the belief that getting hold of the torch and extinguishing the flame would mean that the Beijing Olympic torch relay could be blocked.

As soon as the relay started, they leapt into action and the BBC followed them closely, capturing striking pictures of the troublemakers with exaggerated body movements, and the torchbearers' startled expressions. The story was immediately broadcast worldwide and "Disruption of the 2008 Beijing Olympic torch relay" soon emerged as a hot topic and headline news. Many Western television stations focused on this story, turning it into a major live news event. By fixing their cameras on the tensions along the torch relay route, the BBC and all other Western media outlets deliberately overlooked the warm welcome and support many people along the route extended to the Beijing Olympic Games.

Throughout the relay from the morning until late afternoon, troublemakers had not stopped disrupting the torch relay and harassing the torchbearers, taking advantage of London's underground rail and bus networks, and leapfrogging from one location to another to find shortcuts to block the torch convoy. I was on the bus at the tail of the convoy, with Jiang Xiaoyu and his command team to handle emergencies and incidents.

Just after 11:00 am, the convoy approached the relay section where I was due to be the torch bearer and this location had been publicised by British newspapers for days in advance. The embassy received information that a large group of protesters was waiting in ambush in a narrow alley near the location. Here, the convoy had entered a narrow street where it could only zigzag forward slowly, leaving the torch bearer a vulnerable target. It was clear that the troublemakers intended to create breaking news by disrupting the Chinese Ambassador's torch-carrying run, and with excellent preparations, they were quite sure they could achieve it.

When I had previously checked out the relay route, I examined my own location with two young counsellors from the embassy. They wanted to make sure that I could carry out the torch relay run with safety and dignity, insisting that this was not a matter of personal vanity but rather an issue of the country's image. I agreed. No way would I allow the torch to be snatched from my hand. When we realised how unfavourable the route looked, we decided to find and check out some alternative routes. As suggested by our young colleagues, we kept the new routes to ourselves until the last moment.

When the convoy slowed down along the original route, sure enough, many unidentified people stealthily checked out our convoy buses one by one, looking in through the windows seemingly looking for somebody. Jiang Xiaoyu and I talked it over and decided to give up on this section altogether. The last torch bearer of the previous section was told to run on to the next section. Here more people started to crowd in and the convoy was jammed. Our team waited calmly and it took them quite a while to drive out of the area. As for me, I left the convoy quietly without being noticed and got into a police vehicle provided by the London Metropolitan Police.

The police safeguarding the torch relay were from Scotland Yard, a highly professional organisation, and regardless of the personal views of the police officers on duty that day, they conscientiously fulfilled their task to protect the torch and torchbearers. Weeks before the torch relay, senior officers from Scotland Yard and I jointly inspected the route. They informed me of the various security arrangements, including mounted police on wide roads and officers on bicycles on narrow paths, along with a mixture of other available emergency response measures.

Fully prepared as they were, they had not expected to encounter such persistent and serious disruptive activities that occurred on 6 April and few of the plans formulated beforehand were working. Hours of ongoing disruptions caused by protesters infuriated the police and the pressure on them was mounting as the situation became increasingly chaotic. I spoke to the head of Scotland Yard over the phone, who was on duty at their headquarters and observing the situation via CCTV and video links. We both agreed that it was not the time to back down or give up, and he reassured me of their commitment to protecting every torchbearer and the torch. In light of the dire situation, Scotland Yard adapted their tactics and resources, and deployed more police officers to handle the chaos. By the afternoon, groups of reserve police officers were called in to join the operation.

During the torch relay, the Chinese attendant runners served as bodyguards to torchbearers, forming an inner circle of protection, the British police formed the outer circle of protection. Without their tireless efforts, it is hard to imagine how the convoy could have continuously broken through the mob and moved forward. However, the British police were constrained in their methods and were not permitted to use compelling force or detain anyone, so they were left with very limited means to deal with the situation. As a result, the same cohort of protesters were able to come back again and again, and repeatedly disrupted the torch relay team.

When I did not show up at my designated relay section, the guest commentators sitting in the BBC studio began to comment that the "Chinese Ambassador had withdrawn from the relay after all."

The torch relay convoy reached Chinatown at 10:55 am. This relay section belonged to Defence Attaché Zhang Jianguo, who was the second torchbearer of the Chinese Embassy. As planned, this was also one of my alternative routes and I made the last-minute decision to use this one. Zhang was shifted to a later section in the suburbs, where, as it turned out, he completed his run without any trouble. When the convoy reached the entrance to Chinatown, the narrow paths could not accommodate large buses and the convoy drove on to wait at the exit together with the leading van, with only the torchbearers and attendant runners passing through Chinatown.

When I got out of the police vehicle at a three-way section of Chinatown, the young attendant runners came up to me with bright smiles on their faces. One man approached me and said: "Madame Ambassador, you look amazing today!" That was really nice of him to say so. Although I was way beyond the age when appearances mattered and at that moment I was too exhausted both physically and mentally to "look amazing", it still touched my heart. The kind of optimistic attitude that only young people possess made me feel revitalised.

They guided me towards my starting point. When the incoming torchbearer Bai Jian, a middle school PE teacher from Anshan, Liaoning, saw me, he was both surprised and delighted. I could see in his eyes the pride and sense of responsibility shared by all the Chinese torchbearers that day. I solemnly took over the torch from him, feeling the weight. I could hear applause around me as my appearance was also a surprise for the crowd waiting to welcome the torch relay here. Chinatown glowed with lanterns and lights, filled with a cheerful and festive atmosphere. The road was lined with people of all ages, old and young, ethnic Chinese and overseas Chinese, waving the national flags of China and the UK. I ran slowly along the street, wearing the red-and-white torchbearer uniform with the Olympic torch held high in my hand. The crowds erupted into thunderous cheers. By then, the sky had cleared up and the sun was shining. I was more than happy to see that so many people had come out onto the streets to welcome the arrival of the Beijing Olympic torch. The place was filled with laughter. Whenever I go back to London's Chinatown, I always think of that day, feeling confident that the courageous Chinese people would not be stopped by any obstacles.

AMBASSADOR AS A TORCHBEARER

I came out of Chinatown and passed the torch into the receiving hand of Dame Kelly Holmes. Surprised at first, she immediately grinned happily. It was an important day for both of us, as we had both been put to the test.

The image of me, the Chinese Ambassador, passing on the torch, was soon sent back to the BBC studio, finally putting to an end to the guessing game about "the withdrawal of the Chinese Ambassador." Those trouble-makers who failed to disrupt my torch relay were enraged and shifted their attention elsewhere. When the relay convoy arrived at Downing Street, where the Prime Minister's office was located, a bigger crowd of protesters surrounded the area. They loudly chanted slogans in a bid to pressure then Prime Minister Gordon Brown into withdrawing his promise to welcome the torch relay here in a gesture of support for the Beijing Olympic Games. At that moment, a team of ethnic Chinese also arrived to support the Olympic relay. They played traditional Chinese musical instruments—gongs and drums—and performed a lion dance to express their good wishes. The two opposing teams created a huge noise outside Downing Street and the police officers, both on foot and on horseback, were trying hard to maintain some semblance of order.

Prime Minister Brown is a man who keeps his word. Despite the turbulence that day, he did not buckle under pressure. When the 34th torchbearer, Denise Lewis, a renowned British track and field athlete and the 35th torchbearer, Ali Jawad (a British Paralympic powerlifter) both arrived in front of 10 Downing Street. Mr Brown walked out of the door cheerfully, shaking hands and taking photos with them. He then witnessed the torch handover, accompanied by applause and cheers from the crowds on the roadside, while the protesters also shouted even louder from across the road.

The presence of Prime Minister Brown sent an important message; the Head of the British government welcomed the Olympic flame and supported the Beijing Olympic Games, thereby confirming the positive political tone of the torch relay in London.

By the time the Beijing Olympic torch had been securely carried to the Peninsula Plaza beside the Millennium Dome in Greenwich, it was already past six o'clock in the evening. Princess Anne, the British IOC representative, attended the ceremony and witnessed the successful conclusion of the London torch relay.

The torch flame had not been extinguished even for a moment during the disturbances that had lasted the entire day. Despite all the twists and turns, I saw more people welcoming the Beijing Olympic torch on the route. London's district communities followed through with a wide variety of planned welcoming performances. Children enthusiastically danced despite the cold weather. There were a newlywed couple running out of a church together with the wedding participants to take photos with the torch convoy in the background. The torch team captured footage of many moving moments. But to my regret, these wonderful images never appeared in any media.

Although China had the exclusive rights to be the first to release messages and images of the Beijing Olympic torch relay, the images we captured were not broadcast on time due to the time differences and internal procedures. The BBC's live broadcast was much quicker to lead the news and its coverage swept the world from the very beginning. Since they only showed disruptions and scenes of attempted torch-snatching while disregarding the positive gestures many Londoners extended to the Olympic torch, only stories about the chaos spread across the world.

In an interview with a Chinese journalist at the end of the torch relay, I shared my feelings implicitly: "Today marks an encounter between Beijing and London." This was indeed an encounter with splashes and sparkles. The Beijing Olympic torch relay met grave difficulties rarely seen in London. That being said, I can say with certainty that both the Chinese and British teams satisfactorily fulfilled their missions. The moment I saw the Chinese attendant runners, accompanied by the British police and Defence Attaché of the Chinese Embassy Tang Busheng, stepped into the venue in Greenwich and handed the Olympic flame back to Jiang Xiaoyu unscathed, I felt a great sense of relief. I shook hands with each of the young Chinese attendant runners, who fought hard for an entire day. I felt proud of our country and people for their courage and resilience. I also expressed my sincere gratitude and appreciation to the police officers from Scotland Yard.

A young colleague of mine, while watching the live broadcasts of the BBC and CNN overnight in his Beijing office, sent me a short email that read: "Congratulations! You've made it! Tears welled up in my eyes as I watched it to the end. It was not just a tough torch relay, but also a symbolic moment reflecting the hardship China endures while going global."

The British and other Western media overwhelmingly reported negatively about the Beijing Olympic torch relay. On 6 April, the *Sunday Times* posted a commentary entitled "Stand Up, for Today You Can Force China Through a Tunnel of Shame," which incited people to protest against the torch relay. On the BBC's *News 24* that afternoon, an interviewee linked the torch relay with the "3·14" unrest in Lhasa, Tibet and attributed the disruptions of the Beijing Olympic torch relay primarily to human rights issues in China. A search on the Associated Press (AP) website on 7 April revealed that, of the 186 pictures available, 96 displayed either people supporting "Tibet independence", holding banners and flags in protest against the Beijing Olympic Games or making bizarre facial expressions and gestures opposing China. In contrast, one could barely find any images showing people welcoming the Beijing Olympic torch. The same was true for Agence France-Presse (AFP) and Reuters. One could not find any images of those enthusiastic crowds of local ethnic and overseas Chinese supporting the Beijing Olympic Games or the national flags of China they were waving, not to mention international supporters of the Olympics.

The torch relay disruption seemed to be a well-prepared and orchestrated stunt. A Tibetan separatist revealed in an interview with the *New York Times*: "At first there was a profound sense of despair after the Chinese government was awarded the honour." Then he added: "But after five minutes, we realised this would be a monumental opportunity for the Tibetan people to be put in the international spotlight." This article also revealed some detailed methods used by the "Tibet independence" forces to attract media attention. They saw resorting to media as the best way to arouse public attention. Since they themselves had no news channels, they put intensive efforts into creating information the media craved. "Tibet independence" forces also regularly held "training camps" to teach activists how to organise protests and deal with the police. All this was aimed at "ambushing" the torch relay overseas and undermining China's image.

Although my Embassy colleagues and I were exhausted by the end of the day, I invited some of them to join me in a meeting to reflect on, and summarise the experience and lessons from that challenging day. Later, the Beijing Olympic torch relays in Paris and San Francisco were also confronted with serious disruptions from "Tibet independence" forces. Faced with this situation, the torch team and Chinese Embassies and Consulates in the countries of the later stops readjusted their strategy and involved more ethnic and overseas Chinese, including Chinese students studying abroad. In this way, the torch team was better able to counter disruptions and the situation gradually improved. Scenes showing the welcoming activities came to dominate the relay and the image presented by the international media also began to change.

When the torch flame arrived in Canberra, Australia, which was the only stop in the South Pacific and where I had served as the Chinese Ambassador for over three years, the scale of the supporting crowds was unprecedented. People from different parts of the country, including ethnic and overseas Chinese, and Chinese students, swarmed onto the streets to welcome the torch flame. Singing and dancing merrily, they waved the Chinese and Olympic flags. The protests by the "Tibet independence" forces were completely submerged in the joyful atmosphere, and the 80 torchbearers completed the relay without disruption. The Australian media exclaimed that "it was a day never seen before" as Canberra, a small city of 300,000 citizens, saw 30,000 people out on the streets celebrating the relay.

The Beijing Olympic torch relay came to an end in Ho Chi Minh City, Vietnam, on 29 April 2008, before returning to the Chinese mainland after traveling through 19 overseas cities.

MY ARTICLE IN *THE SUNDAY TELEGRAPH*

After the strife in London, I mulled over what had happened and why. It dawned on me that it might not be entirely true to say that China lacks the channels and the opportunity to influence international opinion. It can at least be said that we are not making the best of our limited opportunity to speak up. Timeliness is also a matter of politics in this kind of major public incident. We must learn how to proactively and comprehensively provide information. The more promptly we do so, the easier it is for us to gain the advantage which can, in turn, reinforce our active role.

Conversely, a delayed response only drags us deeper into a defensive position. We cannot afford to turn a blind eye, nor is there any point in us complaining. Instead, it is imperative that we enhance our awareness of, and ability to respond to, public opinion crises.

I wrote an article entitled "Thoughts About the Torch Relay" for *The Sunday Telegraph*, the UK's weekend edition of *The Daily Telegraph*. The article was inspired by a discussion I had with David Rowat Barclay and Frederick Hugh Barclay, co-owners of *The Daily Telegraph* and their editors. They suggested that if I did not like what the newspapers said, I could just write an article to tell the readers my view. At the time I was too busy to write. However, while watching the torch relay in Paris and San Francisco live on television, I jotted down some thoughts going through my mind and they came to six pages.

Remembering their suggestion, I retrieved some of those notes from the wastepaper basket in my office, compiling them into an article and handed it over to the newspaper. The editor changed the title to "Western Media Has 'Demonised' China". The general rule with newspapers was that a writer is responsible for the contents, and the editor of the column is responsible for proofreading it, to ensure there are no language mistakes, and can also determine the title. This article, when published, also caught the attention of the Chinese media, which reposted it under the title "If the West Could Listen to China".

The article stirred up active discussion as it informed many people in the UK of the opinions of the Chinese and triggered some debate. *The Telegraph* was surprised by the number of comments left under the online version. This made me realise that we needed to speak up. Indeed, as long as we make an effort and make use of the opportunities presented to us, we can make the Chinese voice heard and we can inform the people of our thoughts and ideas which they may be unaware of. This article was reposted in many other countries. When I paid a visit to Kenya, a local guide told me that he had read the article in the local newspaper and it had left a deep impression on him of how the Chinese people felt at that time.

Here are some paragraphs from the article.

In the darkness of a London night, waving the chartered plane goodbye, I had a feeling that the plane was heavier than when it landed. The torch will carry on, and the journey will educate the more than a billion Chinese people about the world and the world about China.

A young friend in China wrote to me after watching the event on the BBC: "I felt so many things all at once—sadness, anger and confusion." It must have dawned on many like him that simply a sincere heart was not enough to ensure China's smooth integration with the world.

The wall that stands in China's way to the world is thick. In China, what's hot at this moment on the internet, which has 200 million users there, is

The questions raised at the end of the article were for the Western media. It also reflected some of my thoughts on the communication gap between China and the West. Starting from this article, I became more proactive, together with my colleagues at the embassy, in promoting knowledge about China and its policies as well as the viewpoints of the people. We followed up every report and comment concerning China made by British media and expressed our opinions when necessary. As a result, we became better known in society, the embassy spokesperson frequently received questions from the media, and I began to receive more requests for interviews and published more articles.

Our efforts won more respect from the media and the public who valued our comments and opinions. BBC journalists learnt to set boundaries and would confirm information with or interview the Embassy in cases of a major report on China. I have learnt an important lesson from my experiences that year. The arena of international communication is like a football match. You may win or lose the match if you take to the pitch. But you are doomed to lose if you never take part. If a team never competes, anything people say about it is believed. On the stage of public opinion, staying silent or avoiding debate only leaves more room for prejudice, mistakes and misunderstanding. In times of peace, a country's ability to sway international opinion is also an important strategic resource.

FACE-TO-FACE WITH VETERAN JOURNALIST JON SNOW

Following my interview on *BBC Breakfast* and the publication of my article in *The Sunday Telegraph*, more British media outlets sent me requests for interviews. In May 2008, I received an interview request from Jon Snow of Channel 4 News—at the time, word had it that the 14th Dalai Lama would be visiting the UK and meeting then Prime Minister Gordon Brown. It is a general rule in journalism that when a hot topic pops up it heightens public attention and becomes the focus of media attention. Therefore it also creates a good opportunity for taking the initiative and correcting misinformation on a subject.

I decided to accept an invitation by Mr Snow, whose news programme had a good reputation in the UK. I learnt through background research that Snow sympathised with the 14th Dalai Lama and was a seasoned journalist with a sharp tongue. Moreover, as our conversation was to be a special segment, it would be an exclusive interview that would be longer than usual and difficult to handle. Therefore, I decided to again receive advice and training from the El-Shahats. Following the methodology we used previously, we analysed and evaluated potential questions in the interview, summarised the points I needed to make and, in particular, carefully studied several tricky points.

For example, Mr Snow may ask: "If the 14th Dalai Lama meets with Prime Minister Brown after he arrives in London, what will be the response of the Chinese government?"

He knew that China opposed any meeting between the 14th Dalai Lama and foreign leaders. Predictably, if I did speak out against the meeting in the TV interview, he could make an issue of it by claiming that China had "intervened" with the agenda of the British leader, which in turn may even have provoked a confrontation between the Chinese Ambassador and the British people.

How to answer this question was a challenging issue. In the

beginning, the El-Shahats and me had a serious disagreement. In my view, I had to explicitly voice opposition against Brown's meeting with the 14th Dalai Lama. This was the position of the Chinese government and I needed to deliver this important message through the interview. But the El-Shahats insisted that a foreign ambassador had no authority to make such a request. They explained that the British people would definitely not accept my views—after all, which country would allow its leaders to bend to the instructions of a foreign ambassador? "Both Snow and the British public will think that you have no right to dictate whom the Prime Minister should or should not meet," said Sameh.

I unfolded a map to tell them about the history of Tibet and the related issues, and explained that the British Prime Minister's meeting with the 14th Dalai Lama would indeed be an intervention in China's internal affairs. Though convinced by my reasoning, they still frowned on the unequivocal expression of "no" on television, and worried I would not have enough time to reason things out in an interview. But I told them that if I could not explicitly voice China's opposition, I might as well not take the interview because my purpose would not be achieved that way.

Eventually, the El-Shahats understood the necessity for me to express objection; but they recommended that I articulate my position in a way that the British people could understand. So we needed to find an appropriate word to convey my message. They emphasised that to gain the public's understanding is the foundation for realising the purpose of communication. But how to say "no" without sounding offensive? We were stuck. It took us nearly an hour to finally find a word suggested by Sameh: "unfortunate." The British people are habitually reserved in wording and tend to use understated expressions, which is very different from the Americans' straightforwardness. The word "unfortunate" appears to be a neutral approach, but it does express a repudiation of any misconduct. In the context of this issue, the word embodied an explicit intention to discourage the meeting. Therefore, it should be enough for the public to get my point.

Sure enough, Mr Snow asked about the British Prime Minister's intended meeting with the 14th Dalai Lama. I replied that it would be "unfortunate" if that happened. Mr Snow found it hard to refute my answer and could not press it further, so my mission was accomplished in a concise and clear-cut manner.

Another difficulty in my preparation was how to describe the identity of the 14th Dalai Lama. After years of PR efforts, he has constructed an image for himself in the Western world and many in the UK regarded him as a religious leader and wise man rather than a political figure. Therefore, how was I to explain to the British public his political identity and intentions, and how could I make them understand China's position and the concerns of the Chinese people? I needed to give a compelling argument.

There are several outstanding and complex issues in the dialogue between China and the West. They include human rights, democracy, and the Tibetan issue, which have constantly generated heated debate. In communication it is important to pay attention to the interconnection between facts and values, and when emphasising the facts one should also articulate the related values. The Dalai group is expert at packaging its agendas with Western values and using narratives related to human rights and religious freedom to gain support. It was necessary for me to find the flaws and weakness in their arguments and fight back from a value-based standpoint. To make personal attacks against the 14th Dalai Lama would not have worked and could even have backfired as it might have generated more sympathy for him among the British audience.

I thought about British history and the principle of the separation of church and state, which the country established through drawing lessons from history. The complex conflicts between kings and church leaders have spanned the country's history. One such famous example was Henry VIII, the second monarch of the Tudor Dynasty, who broke with the Pope, set up his own church, and managed to get rid of Rome's intervention in, and control over, the power of the king. Today, the British Queen is the secular leader of the Church of England. The British royal family and the Church of England hold that their king or queen is chosen by God, and over half of the British people agree about retaining the monarchy. However, secular laws provide that the king or queen is a natural person like every ordinary British citizen, and the system of "God and King in one" is denied in modern British society.

It then occurred to me that the rejection of such a system could be common ground between the British and Chinese people. When Tibet was ruled by the 14th Dalai Lama in the old days, they practiced theocracy and he now continued to carry that identity. I could talk from this angle to reveal the 14th Dalai Lama's special political identity and therefore his political intentions. In the UK and the West, the general public remember the history and the dark ages under religious rule, and oppose the combination of religion and government. Therefore, in the interview with Mr Snow, I first described the identity of the 14th Dalai Lama as "God and King in one" and then elaborated on the political intentions of him and his group which was to try to mix religion with politics and to split China. On that basis, I expressed China's opposition to what the 14th Dalai Lama said and did, arguing that his approaches should be rejected not just in China but also elsewhere in the world.

The opinions I articulated in the interview attracted lots of attention among the public, and I even received letters. A grandma wrote to me, saying that I had shown a different perspective on the issue. Different voices were now being heard in the country. In a media interview with the London representative of the 14th Dalai Lama, the journalist asked him: "Is the 14th Dalai Lama a religious figure or a political figure?" "Both, he is both," replied the representative without hesitation. The answer inadvertently proved my characterisation of his role as being both.

Mr Snow also asked me a question concerning the identities of the Chinese torch attendant runners. After the London leg of the 2008 Beijing Olympics torch relay, there were rumours that the Chinese attendant runners were police officers and questions were raised about why the British government allowed foreign police to carry out law enforcement in the UK. Snow asked me whether the runners who came from Beijing were police. I had anticipated this question and had given it some thought in the preparations.

Lying, intentionally or not, is a big no-no in any media interview. Lies cannot stand up to scrutiny and would have done more damage to my credibility than anything else. Therefore, an interviewee must try to find out the facts and be aware and clear about what they do and do not know. As far as I knew, the attendant runners had been recruited from all over China. Most of them were college students, and some were from police academies. During the torch relay, I had met several of them. They appeared to be under 20 years old, and their youthful curiosity and enthusiasm for the world left a deep impression on me. I thought I should stand up for them.

Snow laid a trap in the question by trying to make me choose between "yes" or "no." This is the typical *modus operandi* of the media. If I had said "no," it would have led me into a whirl of explanations, such as why they were equipped with many professional skills and how they were trained. These explanations would certainly have stoked up the hype. Hence, after rounds of discussions with my teachers, I decided to focus on talking about "who the runners were" rather than struggling to explain "what they were not."

I told Snow, the Chinese torch attendant runners were recruited and selected from across China. They were excellent young people whose identities were clarified when entering the UK. I added that the younger generation in China were raised as single children and their parents were very proud that they could guard the torch for the Olympics. But look what the media said about them! If their mothers heard this, how would they feel? I used an emotional angle to help the audience see the issue in another way and touch the soft spot in people's hearts to make them aware that it was wrong for the media to accuse them in that way.

Channel 4 News presented the interview in its entirety, and I was satisfied with the outcome.

Another element about the interview worth mentioning was my outfit.

Samah advised me to wear a skirt suit, which not only fitted my official capacity but also retained an air of femininity. After choosing a grey skirt suit, she recommended that I use a red accessory to match it, i.e., a pair of red high heels. At first, I found it difficult to accept this advice because I could not imagine how I would look in grey clothes with red shoes. I rarely wore red, to begin with; besides, images on TV are limited anyway. Who would notice the shoes? But my two teachers held their ground, saying that female charm could find perfect expression in red shoes.

They studied the programme's studio setting, which usually featured a large, indigo screen in the background showing footage related to the interview. The table in the centre at which Snow and I would sit facing each other, was transparent. During the process, a video camera would move back and forth between us and, from time to time, zooming out to show a panorama of the studio. Since the programme would start with a full-body scene of me and end with a panorama, the audience would get to see my red shoes more than once. Though unused to this emphasis on detail, I promised to think it over. After returning to my residence, I had pictures taken of me in a grey skirt suit coupled with, respectively, white, black and red shoes. To my surprise, it turned out the red shoes looked best in the pictures.

On the day of the interview, I wore the grey skirt suit over a red shirt, a pair of red coral stud earrings, with my feet clad in a pair of red high heels. Snow also wore a light grey suit that day, and I noticed that his tie featured bright colours and vibrant patterns. When we started talking, sitting on the sofa, I noticed that his socks were in the same print as his tie. It seemed that it made sense to pay attention to detail in the UK, and as the saying goes: When in Rome, do as the Romans do.

After the interview aired, it was not just our discussion that drew wide attention, but my outfit too: "When the ambassadress, with a pair of coral stud earrings, sat there saying that…" wrote one newspaper. I realised that "professionalism" involved attending to detail. Being appropriately dressed is not only a reflection of respect but also a way to charm.

According to the Mehrabian Rule, which was established by the US psychologist Albert Mehrabian, when the audience evaluates the performance of a speaker, facial expressions, attire and hairstyle account for 55%, while 38% relates to voice, tone and pitch, and only 7% is about the information and content the speaker delivers. Although this theory takes substance too lightly, it does reveal the importance of appearance from the perspective of public psychology in modern communication.

In late July 2008, I was on vacation in Beijing, just before the Beijing Olympics opening ceremony. At that time, the British media continued to cover the event negatively, commenting that it would not go well due to all the interruptions and resistance it encountered. So, to get first-hand knowledge of their views, I invited a dozen British journalists based in Beijing to a symposium and then had a meal with them.

They raised many questions, most of which were tricky, even harsh, including imperfections in services and facilities, post-Olympic use of the venues, press freedom for foreign journalists in China—all critical opinions. I patiently answered each question, noticing their cold attitude and occasionally expressed frustration. When dessert was served, I said: "Now that you've asked me so many questions, let me ask you a question: do any of you have any positive views on the 2008 Beijing Olympics?" The whole table went silent. No one said anything. Apparently, none of them was willing to say something positive in front of their peers, since the general tone of the Western media had been so negative about the 2008 Beijing Olympics.

However, at 8:00 pm on 8 August 2008, once the magnificent opening ceremony of the 2008 Beijing Olympics began, everything changed. The successful ceremony stunned the world and completely changed how the British media viewed the event.

At 8:00 pm Beijing time, it was 1:00 pm in the UK. I held a reception at the Embassy of China in London to watch the live broadcast of the opening ceremony. The embassy hall was set up with chairs, and big television screens were placed along the walls. I invited some British friends and representatives from the Chinese community to join all the embassy staff in attending a reception for the event. We watched the ceremony together. Everyone was enthusiastic and thrilled, marvelling at the magnificent performances with distinct Chinese style. The audience even burst into spontaneous applause as they got bound up in the thrills and emotions, forgetting that they were not there in person. After the broadcast ended, many friends lingered and some British people shook my hand, congratulating me on China's success. "This is like a debut for China to rise into a global power," said one elderly gentleman.

The next day, British newspapers carried full-page colour photos of the Beijing Olympics opening ceremony with most using the ceremony as their cover stories. The media appeared to have swept aside all the sourness, ridicule and smears, and replaced them with positive narratives, unanimously commenting that only the Chinese could stage the Olympics opening ceremony in such a way. This was a decisive lift for the national image of contemporary China.

Since London was going to host the 2012 Olympics, then Prime Minister Brown was invited to attend the Beijing Olympics closing ceremony. During the second half of the event, I returned to Beijing to accompany Mr Brown on his visit to China. When watching a football match in the Bird's Nest (formally called the Beijing National Stadium), I was spotted by several British journalists. They requested to interview me and I readily agreed. I thought for a while, picturing in my mind several tough questions they might ask. However, to my pleasant surprise, throughout the interview, they did not raise any critical questions and instead calmly asked how I felt about the 2008 Beijing Olympics and my expectations of bilateral relations.

A DEBATE WITH LIONEL BARBER

In February 2009, the then Chinese Premier Wen Jiabao paid an official visit to the UK. I recommended that he took an exclusive interview with Lionel Barber, the then editor of the *Financial Times*. Firstly, I knew Mr Barber and could trust his professionalism; secondly the timing was right. Battered by the international financial crisis resulting from the US subprime mortgage crisis, global economic prospects looked grim and Europe was in trouble. Against this backdrop, the big question everyone wanted to know was: What was China's position, and how was it going to deal with the crisis, as a large country that had maintained continuous growth at a fast pace for years.

On 1 February, Premier Wen took the interview with Barber at the Mandarin Oriental Hotel in London, where he was staying. In a small classical and elegant room, the interview went on for an hour and Premier Wen elaborated on the economic development in China and the country's position on dealing with the international financial crisis. Later, the *Financial Times* published on 2 February 2009 a high-profile coverage of the interview on its front and second pages. It was a successful communication at a critical moment and people in London financial circles paid much attention to it. Even weeks later, some business friends still brought it up with me, noting that the candour and composure of the Chinese Premier during such a crisis was crucial in calming the nerves and the atmosphere in international financial markets.

However, stumbles are inevitable on the way to success, and a serious disagreement appeared between Barber and I over a specific phrase the Premier used during the interview. When talking about the cause of the international financial crises, Barber said that although the crisis originated in the US, some believed that part of the problem was the imbalance of the world economy, such as China's US$2 trillion of foreign exchange reserves. He asked for a comment. Premier Wen replied that such a view was ridiculous and that it was confusing right and wrong when people who had been overspending blamed those who lent them the money. He used a Chinese saying to describe the situation: like Zhubajie, shifting the blame to those who had actually done him a favour. Zhubajie is a Chinese fictional character from *Journey to the West*, who was said to be reincarnated on earth in the shape of a pig. The interview was consecutively translated and the interpreter translated "Zhubajie" directly as "pig". It did not seem to be a big deal at the time but, upon reflection, it would have been inappropriate to liken a country or a person to a pig, and more importantly, it was not Premier Wen's intention. Such wording in coverage might be misleading or even be used to stir up hostility. After the interview had ended, a senior official in the Chinese delegation asked me to speak with Barber to revise the English translation.

I went after Barber and stopped him on the front stairs of the hotel and explained the issue, hoping he would agree to modify the translation. But he bluntly declined my request because the word he heard from the interpreter was "pig". He said that the interview was recorded, and according to the principle of originality, he had no authority to alter anything. I argued that your "originality" should refer to the original wording in Chinese, and "Zhubajie", as originally used by Premier Wen, was a fictional character in Chinese mythology, not a "pig" in the literal sense. I told Barber that he should convey the original meaning in Chinese, which emphasised "a person who shifts the blame to those who have actually done him a favour."

The February weather in London was quite chilly. I ran out in such a hurry that I did not put on a coat. I stood there continuing to argue with Barber, feeling more and more cold but he still refused to budge. I had to tell him my bottom line: you and I agreed beforehand that in case of major differences, the Chinese side had the right to withdraw. If you insist on publishing the interview with this phrase, I will have to publish another article to clarify the points, which would make things complicated. The agreement I referred to was an "exit plan" set up before the Chinese side agreed to take the interview, as even though I trusted Barber, I was always prepared for the unexpected. So, I made this deal with him, retaining some leeway for the Chinese side. Now, as we could not reach agreement, we both needed to back down a little and see if we could find a compromise.

He seemed to waver, I went on to tell him the outline of the novel *Journey to the West*, including what Zhubajie looked like, how he was reincarnated from Marshal Canopy to a pig-shaped earthy person, and his role together with his brother "Sunwukong" (Monkey King) in monk Tang Sanzang's journey to retrieve the Buddhist scriptures. I then asked his advice on how to better translate the term. As such playful characters are common in Shakespeare's plays, it was not difficult for Barber to understand it. He was persuaded and said that, given the figure's mythological nature, we might use the name in the novel. I liked the idea and suggested that we could use "mythical person Zhubajie". After some thought, he agreed and asked whether "Mr" should be put in front of the name. I did not think it was necessary. Finally, "mythical person Zhubajie" was adopted in the interview when it appeared in the newspaper.

When Barber and I had serious arguments, it was not because we were hostile towards each other or because Barber was deliberately making things difficult for China. Rather, we argued because we both adhered to our professional principles and interests. But as long as we were willing to be sensitive to each other's concerns and find a compromise, there were always ways to resolve differences. The British are a principled people, although sometimes a little stubborn. But they attach importance to reasoning and friendships, once made, last. During my stay in the UK, I talked with Barber regularly, listening to his views on current affairs. As a veteran editor he followed closely what was going on in the political landscape in the UK and around the world. I benefited from talking with him and he also gained more knowledge and understanding of China from talking with me.

In February 2010, just before leaving my post and returning to China, I did an exclusive interview with Barber for "Lunch with the FT", a famous column in the *Financial Times*. The column, a combination of knowledge and fun, started in 1994 and involves the editor inviting a celebrity to have lunch and chat openly and freely. The chat would be turned into a published interview, which includes the editor's narrations and comments, and is published in the "Life and Arts" section. Nearly 1,000 people have so far been interviewed, making the column a voluminous encyclopaedia of who's who.

Barber invited me to the lunch in the Goring Hotel in London. He was friendly and was mostly interested in my personal experiences, views and anecdotes. Our conversation ranged widely over various topics that included the meaning of democracy, the values of different countries, freedom of speech and the cognitive disparities between China and the West. I shared with him my reflections on serving as the Chinese Ambassador to the UK and expressed my gratitude to the British people who had generously donated to the relief efforts in the wake of the Wenchuan earthquake in Sichuan Province in 2008. Later, his long article appeared in the weekend edition of the *Financial Times* on 30 January 2010. Despite a few minor imperfections and small errors in quoting what I said, his narrative was positive. Many of my British friends told me that his article had given a vivid image of the Chinese Ambassador, and it proved to be a successful promotion.

I remained in contact with the *Financial Times*. In early 2015, I received an invitation from Zhang Lifen, founding editor of FT Chinese.com, to give another interview to "Lunch with the FT".

MY PRE-G20 LONDON SUMMIT INTERVIEW

On 29 March 2009, I took an interview with *The Andrew Marr Show* on BBC One. The 60-minute Sunday morning talk show is broadcast at 9:00 am, during which the renowned host Andrew Marr has one-on-one special interviews with world leaders and celebrities on world affairs. My interview focused on the G20 London Summit, which was due to start in a few days. Marr had already interviewed the Australian Prime Minister Kevin Rudd, the Russian President Dmitry Medvedev, and the British Foreign Secretary David Miliband.

The G20 was established in 1999, originally as a meeting for finance ministers and central bank governors. Following the 2008 international financial crisis, it was elevated to a summit of heads of state and government focused on improving global governance in the financial sphere. As one of the major countries, China has made a constructive contribution to the institutional development of the G20, playing a role in global economic governance. As London was the first European city to host the event, the UK and the international community paid great attention to it, expecting the summit to help address the European debt crisis.

Marr made an opening statement to the camera at the outset of the programme, squarely focused on the expectations and speculations of the international community on China's presence at the summit. He noted that *The Economist* magazine had voiced the concerns of European countries: Will the summit turn into a G2 consisting of China and the US only, rather than an economic cooperation forum for 20 countries? Will it witness the first meeting between the Chinese President Hu Jintao and the US's new President Barack Obama?

Marr then turned to me and welcomed me to the show. His

questions were mostly about China's development and its role in the international arena. He asked:

> "If there is one country in the world which has still got money, big amounts of money to spend if it chose to, it's China. And people have speculated about China deciding to build a Western-style health service or a welfare system or something really big. Could we see that coming out or being announced at this conference?"

Marr was expressing an expectation of the British people and many in Europe that China would boost spending and "pay" to help tide them over the crisis. Although I did not know at that moment the specific plan of the Chinese government, I was quite aware of China's basic policy direction. Therefore, I needed to let the UK and the wider international community know the basic thinking of the Chinese people.

I replied:

> *"I think people in China feel flattered, overly flattered, when we are said to be rich, wealthy and to have huge reserves. And also, there is a misunderstanding about China's reserves. The foreign reserves are not the government's money. The Premier cannot write a cheque against it. It's the money that the Chinese people and the businesses have left in the safekeeping of the central bank, and the central bank has to look after it and take good care of it. And regarding the reserves, the size is big. But if you remember, there are 1.3 billion people in China, and when you divide it by that number it comes to a small amount. It's about £1,000 per capita. So people should remember that China is still a developing country and our per capita GDP is only US$ 3,000, although we are number three in the world in aggregate terms."*

Marr also asked if China would launch a new and large fiscal stimulus with the intention of seeing an end to the dollar as the world's reserve currency and securing larger voting powers in organisations like the International Monetary Fund (IMF). To me, his questions were a bit far-fetched, but they were indeed topics of discussion in the UK at the time.

I gave a vague response to his question about the US dollar, saying that there had been interesting discussions about the reserve currency and its replacement, and that this was now also a topic in China. In terms of the voting power in the IMF, I said: "China is fulfilling its quota in the IMF, which is under 4%, but if people want China to contribute more, we hope there is going to be a reform to increase the quota. We'll be happy to do more." Referring to an article that Chinese Vice Premier Wang Qishan had written for *The Times*, I added that "we will take an open attitude if the IMF is looking for alternative contributions, and maybe if the IMF issues a bond, we'll see how good it is and if we can contribute."

Unsurprisingly, before the end of the interview, Marr brought up an old topic:

> "You face, of course, many questions about human rights in China. If China is going to become part of this global system and there will be much more transparency in banking and so on, do you accept that it's going to be impossible and wrong for China to carry on screening newspapers, screening the internet and censoring news from outside? That you're going to have to be part of an open system in every way?"

The Western world has always been biased against China on human rights issues, displaying their double standards.

There would have been no end to arguments if I had started debating with him on specific issues, but I could not completely skirt the question. I replied:

> *"Andrew, I have to say that we in China often find it arrogant for the West to think that the human rights development in China has to be taken care of by the West —an assumption that you have a supreme, superior system everybody has to copy."*

"That sounds like a no to me. Is it, Ambassador?" asked the seasoned host.

I said:

"I think it's important that we have an equal dialogue on human rights and acknowledgment and acceptance that China has made huge progress regarding human rights. And as far as the issue of open society is concerned, China has become a very lively and open society, and everyone who has been to China would have seen it."

I hoped, to the British public who were watching the interview, the answer made my position clear.

The interview was somewhat demanding for me as, at the time, British society's central concern was about financial issues, but I had limited financial knowledge and was not fully aware of what policies were being considered by China. However, in the wake of the financial crisis, the West's view of China began to change, as they expected more support from China. It was clear, the public needed to hear China's voice before the G20 summit, and the interview was perfectly timed.

Speaking of the 2009 G20 London Summit, I want to share my impressions of US President Obama's press conference at the end of this summit. I had been following his public presentations and found that he communicated with people excellently by making his core arguments concise, neat and coherent. The audience could easily capture the key information he intended to convey, and his style suited the public-speaking culture in Western society.

In July 2008, when Obama was a US presidential candidate, he visited Europe and created a "whirlwind" in Berlin, Germany. Over 200,000 people reportedly gathered in front of the Brandenburg Gate to hear his speech. But one year later, when Obama arrived in Europe as the US President, the circumstances had changed completely. On the one hand, as the spillover effects of the US subprime mortgage crisis severely hit Europe and the world beyond, Europeans were angry with the US and worried whether the new administration led by Obama could weather the storm. While, on the other hand, they also hoped that the US could come to Europe's rescue. From the moment that Air Force One landed in the UK, the European media closely followed Obama's visit. For the US President, his mission was to mobilise international society to jointly fight the crisis, while coping with the mounting pressure and trying to defend America's image in front of the European public.

Located in Docklands, the Exhibition Centre London (ExCeL) is situated close to the River Thames. Nearby, the uniquely shaped O2 Arena (originally called the Millennium Dome) and Canary Wharf, which was transformed from a derelict area of shipping docks and berths into the city's new financial powerhouse, demonstrates the integration of traditional quality and innovation. ExCeL was chosen as the venue for the summit and on 2 April, the G20 leaders' summit began. The enormous venue was separated into two spaces, one for the meeting and the other for the media. The press conference hall in the media space housed over 2,000 journalists from across the world. At the end of the hall was a long, narrow stage on which Prime Minister Brown was scheduled to announce the summit's outcome at the end of the meeting at about 4:30 pm and there would be some other leaders giving press conferences.

That day, I stayed in the sitting room in the meeting space together with other members of the Chinese delegation and watched the leaders' discussions on television. Later on, I was amazed and impressed by how Prime Minister Brown brilliantly presented the outcomes. The discussions were, in fact, loosely organised, where the leaders were talking past each other. But in his summary, Prime Minister Brown highlighted the contribution commitments by all the countries at the meeting to address the financial crisis, thus successfully sending a signal to the world that the G20 countries would make concerted efforts to fight the crisis. This was exactly what the world had been expecting.

At just before 7:00 pm, three hours after the meeting had ended, Obama stepped onto the stage. He probably had a fair amount of time to rehearse for the press conference, and the huge number of journalists who had gathered there waiting for him reflected the heightened international attention. Obama went on stage and started by thanking journalists for their patience. Then, after brief opening remarks, he began taking questions. The journalists were eager to ask and the questions were pointed, but he kept wearing his smile and showed humility through his body language. While answering questions and engaging with the audience, he walked slowly from one end of the long stage to the other, trying to pay attention to every corner of the hall.

Obama was confident in his response to the questions, which demonstrated his excellent media training. Of all the responses he made to the questions shooting at him from the crowd, he was mainly stressing three core points. The first point: the US had made mistakes. He was bombarded by questions about American responsibilities and how the US could have allowed the subprime mortgage problem to go so far. Obama did not try to shirk America's responsibility for causing the financial crisis which had swept the world, nor did he try to conceal the mistakes his country had made in financial regulation. He was newly elected to office, and it is not uncommon for a US leader to criticise the previous administration. The second point: other countries slipped too. Clearly much of Europe was mired in debt, not least because of the shocks from the US. The crisis also exposed their grave mistakes in financial regulation and fiscal policies. He hoped that all countries involved could recognise the importance of enhancing global financial regulation and accelerating reform of the international financial system. The third point, the US was committed to promoting economic growth and increasing employment, and it was ready to work together with all other countries to overcome the crisis. This might have been the primary purpose of Obama's attendance at the summit—to mobilise the international community to jointly fight the crisis. To a certain extent, his responses eased Europe's dissatisfaction with the US and effectively shifted the attention of the international media to the importance of jointly combating the crisis.

Obama's performance made me guess that he had a strong team behind him, which had thoroughly studied the concerns of Europe and the entire international community and accurately calibrated his responses. No matter what the journalists asked, Obama just responded to them by focusing on these three core points throughout the press conference. The next day's news reporting proved that the messages he wished to convey were effectively spread.

As I have found out, professional training can sharpen one's ability to engage with the public and help to achieve the purpose of communication. Therefore, training people in how to deal with the media has become a mature profession in the UK and, for example, many ambassadors from other countries to the UK receive such training. The US Ambassador to the UK told me that he gave over one hundred interviews in a year and did a rehearsal each time. His embassy allocated a budget for this purpose. For important interviews, specialised consultants were recruited to provide training while, for most routine interviews, he asked staff at the embassy to carry out simulated rehearsals. Certainly, there was one thing we all related to: It takes courage to receive training.

The knowledge and skills I learnt in the UK became valuable assets in my work later on. After returning to China, I continued to apply these methods and did rehearsals in order to make further improvements.

On 17 August 2011, I gave an interview to the German magazine *Der Spiegel* in Beijing. At the time, I was the Vice Foreign Minister in charge of European affairs. This was my first interview with a foreign journalist after returning to China. The magazine's editorial team took the interview seriously and after it was done, they were so satisfied with the content, they decided to give the published interview four pages instead of two as originally planned.

Der Spiegel had a reader base in Germany consisting of mostly intellectuals and it also had a certain level of international clout. Overall, it was right-leaning and tended to view China from a negative perspective. At that time, although Germany had become an important economic and trading partner of China, the biases held by the German media ran deep. The German people and many in Europe held strong opinions about China despite having little first-hand knowledge of what was going on there. So an interview with the magazine would be a good opportunity to convey the Chinese story.

The German media are known for their rigour in practice and their respect for interviewees. For example, before an interview is published, they allow the interviewee to review it and if any inaccuracy in references or concepts is found, the interviewee can request adjustments. This kind of attitude helps avoid misinterpretation and therefore gives interviewees a sense of security. The media of other countries are rarely as helpful.

I remember an unpleasant interview with an Australian magazine in 2003 when serving as the Chinese Ambassador there. My interviewer was a female journalist whose family had emigrated from Eastern Europe and she had bad memories of the past. Therefore she was hostile towards countries led by a communist party. I was inexperienced at the time and did not thoroughly research her background before accepting the request. After discovering her hostility during the interview, I tried very hard to persuade her to look at China objectively by giving her many examples and facts in an attempt to show her a fuller picture of China. I had hoped to be able to influence the fundamental tone of her writing and although the scheduled time for the interview was 40 minutes, I gave her nearly three hours. I tried in earnest and even brought out some of the latest publications in China to illustrate the current situation. But she remained indifferent to whatever I said and insisted on expressing suspicion about everything to do with China, seemingly determined to label China as a "wrong country". Clearly, she came to interview me with a predetermined conclusion.

She never contacted the embassy after the interview. It was not until the interview was published that I saw what she had written. She listed the alleged wrongs of China like peeling an onion and finally concluded that the ambassadress was a "die-hard Communist". She made no mention of China's current situation, policies or position, which I had spent a lot of time talking about. Instead, she used the article to express her own position and views. Since then, when deciding whether to accept an interview request, I always do background checks on the media outlet and the journalist to properly assess their intentions.

Der Spiegel sent journalist Susanne Koelbl for the interview. I noticed that she was in China for three months where she received training, meaning that she had some first-hand knowledge of China and might not view China in a rigid and obsolete light. Koelbl was young and did not appear to be a renowned veteran journalist. But a journalist's seniority is not important to me; instead, I am more interested in their knowledge and basic qualities, preferably: that they be open-minded, a good communicator, savvy and reasonable. My hope is always to have a nice conversation which allows the interviewer to write a good and informative article for their readers and where I too am able to achieve my purpose of communicating China's messages and views.

Koelbl sent me an outline for the interview which was a framework of a possible question list. Journalists rarely ask questions in strict accordance with their outlines and they tend to keep more leeway for spontaneous questioning. Nevertheless, a serious journalist does not deviate too far from the outline because they want to conduct an effective interview and prefer to let the interviewee be well prepared so that they can delve into an in-depth conversation.

In China I was without the kind of professional help for preparation that I used to have in the UK, so I decided to apply the basic techniques I had learnt. I brought together a team of young diplomats from the Department of European Affairs of the MFA to work on the preparation. Based on Koelbl's outline, we developed a list of 10 key questions which were mainly the often-mentioned criticisms of China found in the German and European media. They included "China's reform of the political system," "China's military threats," "China's human rights issues" and "China's economic collapse." We also included some topical issues the Germans were concerned about at that time.

Each team member was responsible for one question and gathered facts and data on the issue. Based on the information, the team started preparing key points of recommended answers according to China's declared policies and positions. This involved extensive work but I was too busy to join in and the materials were mostly prepared by the team. At the weekend, I brought together the team members to practice some drills.

In the first round, the team was divided into two groups, one acted like journalists and raised questions and the other gave answers while I observed and contemplated the issues. It turned out that those who raised the questions performed as well as real journalists and their questions were sufficiently pointed and tough. By contrast, those who gave answers mostly read straight from their routine talking points and appeared defensive. Despite the accuracy of their answers, they were not persuasive. Afterwards I swapped the roles of the two groups and the results were similar. Those giving answers still seemed to struggle and were not able to effectively confront the issues when the "journalists" pressed them on the questions. Perhaps this was because they did not have sufficient knowledge about the issues or there was not enough information. We needed to research further and gather more information. But that was certainly not the only problem. When people are confronted with probing questions from journalists, their ability to think can be affected—even I can be easily led astray by questions and fall into defensive arguments, if not well prepared.

After the first round of the exercise proved to be unsatisfactory, I managed to find time to look into the materials myself. Fully prepared, I moved on to the second round of the exercise in which my whole team played Western journalists and shot random questions to which I gave answers. They quickly entered into the role and pressed forward with increasingly tough questions, never letting up. As for me, although I said a great deal with a firm attitude, I could feel that I was on the defensive as if I was being controlled by their questions. My attitude was antagonistic, making my words anything but convincing. If the real interview was to go like this, it would not have any good effect and I would be better off not doing the interview. Feeling frustrated, I asked my team to leave and I stayed on alone for a while. I quietly thought about what had gone wrong. What China was doing was clearly successful but why were we on the defensive in our reasoning? How could I break this vicious circle?

I had an answer for every critical question, which clarified that China was not what they said it was. But I could not always try to defend and justify. I asked myself: Why was I behaving as if I was in the dock having to defend myself faced with journalists' doubts? Worse still, the more I tried to explain, the more likely it was that I would be subjected to more questioning. Just as a Chinese idiom says: "For one thing cited, ten thousand may have been left out." As a result, it would have been too easy for me to lose track of my own line of thinking and become entangled in further defensive explanations.

I reviewed the process of the exercise back and forth, and finally realised that the problem lay in my own way of taking the questions. I was not firm enough with my own line and allowed the questions to lead my thought process. For instance, when a question was raised about China's growing defence budget, claiming that the Chinese military posed threats, I would explain the purpose of the increased defence budget which included improving the living conditions of the military and upgrading hardware. Then the interviewer could enquire further by asking more details about the composition of China's defence budget or directly raise an issue related to specific advanced weaponry. Setting aside whether or not I had all the requisite knowledge, even an expert would be dogged in such a situation.

Moreover, an interview is not a presentation, and there is not enough time to cite numerous facts and statistics to explain specialised issues. Therefore, answering questions in this way makes it very hard to achieve a good result.

I finally realised that I had to decode the journalist's set pattern of asking questions. I had to see that the foundation of the negative questions about China was problematic as it came from a position of negating anything about China. If I could not fundamentally challenge the erroneous starting point, it would not be possible to have a dialogue on an equal footing. It would be like proceeding with a wrong formula, how would it be possible to get a correct result?

This shift in mindset enabled me to see more clearly what needed to be done. This new awareness also revealed the solution to me. I asked the team to come back to the meeting room for another exercise. This time, I was no longer "in the dock", instead, I took the upper hand from the very beginning and no matter how biting their questions were, I was able to avoid becoming defensive. Sometimes I even gained ground by raising questions in return. For example, when being asked why China was building aircraft carriers and whether they would threaten the world, instead of struggling to explain the history and purpose of China's aircraft carriers, I simply asked the journalist why the UK or the US carriers were not considered a threat. This was like pulling the rug from under their feet, forcing the interviewer to step back from the "moral high ground" and allowed the European audience to realise how unfair their double standards and biases were.

The subsequent exercise progressed well, during which I could find new entry points for every question and firmly hold my ground. My team was delighted with the breakthrough and we continued with two rounds of rehearsals to perfect my responses.

On 17 August 2011, my interview with Koelbl took place in a reception room in the MFA's south building. I felt relaxed, with a sense of control, because I had worked out the method to face her questions and prepared the key points. The real interview followed the outline she had previously submitted and Koelbl's critical attitude in her questions was also predictable. I was able to find a way to move from being defensive to being proactive and doing so in a natural manner. For example, when she asked about Ai Weiwei, I turned the tables on her by asking: In addition to Ai Weiwei, which other Chinese artists are known to the German people? Although sounding polite, my question caught her off guard and made readers realise that they needed to see a fuller picture of China. As she kept criticising and questioning China, the subtext running through my answers was: "You are biased against China."

Throughout the intensive interview, which lasted more than an hour, Koelbl and I remained calm. At the outset I asked her permission to call her by her first name Susanne, which enabled us to narrow the distance between each other. She was professional and seldom looked displeased when facing pushback from me and instead seemed to enjoy the intense conversation.

Having exhausted her list of questions, she came up with a question that I did not expect and had not encountered before: "Then, in your view, what can be learnt from China by the West today?" This was a simple and yet substantive question, which also indirectly suggested that she had accepted my responses and acknowledged that China had its own logic and success. However, her realisation could not have been achieved through a single conversation. It was her experiences in China that had opened her eyes and given her a deeper understanding of the progress the country had made. This was an unexpected question which I had never thought about how to answer, but there were always surprises in interviews. I hesitated a bit and then replied: "Maybe it is humility. In China, we often quote Confucius: 'When three people walk together, there must be a teacher for me'."[1]

AFTERWORD

When the book's first seven chapters had almost been completed, the 19th National Congress of the CPC was successfully held in Beijing.

"Never forget why we started, and we can accomplish our mission," General Secretary Xi Jinping earnestly told the entire Party while delivering the Report to the Congress.

"The original aspirations and mission of the Chinese communists were to seek happiness for the Chinese people and rejuvenate the Chinese nation. This founding aspiration, this mission, is what inspires the Chinese communists to advance," he stated.

Recent years have witnessed the rapid development of China, improvement in the people's livelihood and new achievements in socialist modernisation. One important reason that China's political system and the CPC leadership have demonstrated vibrant strength is that the Party has always adhered to its abiding mission of serving the people wholeheartedly.

I remember in 1967, when I got my first army-green canvas satchel, I used red silk yarn to embroider the slogan "Serving the People (*Wei Renmin Fuwu*)," an inscription by Chairman Mao

Zedong, on its cover. For me and many of my contemporaries, "serving the people" is a lifelong quest.

As a spokesperson for the NPC sessions, the audience I intended to get my points across to was the Chinese people and, to some extent, also the worldwide public. When I stepped into the NPC building, the Great Hall of the People, what I had in mind was how to better understand the people's concerns and how to play the role of a bridge between the NPC and the Chinese people, as well as a bridge between China and the rest of the world.

Over my 30-plus years as a diplomat, I made a lot of effort to tell China's story to foreigners, explaining China's perceptions and policies, and illustrating how China had pursued reforms and development, and how it had opened up and learnt from the outside world. I often needed to explain how China had chosen its path. In contrast, during my five years working for the NPC, I had been more in touch with domestic affairs and learnt a great deal about the concerns and pursuits of different people in society.

In the information age, the boundary between domestic and international communication has become blurred, especially for the major countries. An international issue can quickly reach the domestic audience and produce an impact, and many stories related to international politics also stem from countries' internal affairs. All this means that when we talk to the domestic audience, we need to consider the possible reaction by the international audience, and when we speak to international society, we need to take into consideration the opinions and feelings of people at home.

The Party's media and public communications work are crucial issues in state governance and they concern national stability and security. As Party General Secretary Xi Jinping has stated, the responsibility and mission, in terms of international communication, is to "connect China with the world." He said: "As China opens wider to the world, one important mission of the work on communication and ideology is to guide people to have a more comprehensive and objective understanding of contemporary China and the rest of the world." Since the 18th CPC National Congress, the Party Central Committee with Comrade Xi Jinping at its core has attached great importance to international communication and laid out a series of important arrangements and theoretical expositions. General Secretary Xi Jinping has stressed on many occasions that efforts should be made to strengthen our capability for carrying out international communications. For example, we need to enhance the creativity, appeal and credibility of our international discourse; tell China's story well, make China's voice heard and explain China's characteristics well.

I have been thinking about how to follow the objectives set out by General Secretary Xi Jinping, using the skills I have learnt, to make a tangible contribution to the pursuit of credible public communication and the effort to foster capabilities in this area. I have therefore written this book to share my experiences and the lessons I have learnt. I hope this book will provide a source of reference for the younger generation to explore their way in practice.

SPEAK IN A TIMELY AND HONEST WAY

There is a rule in journalism and communications: First impressions last. In modern society which is rife with a variety of intermediaries for spreading news, there is always a "hunger" for information. The demand by the international community for China-related news is particularly high. When something happens, the first information which makes its way through the communication channels usually influences people the most and can quickly shape a prevalent perception. Therefore, government departments and news agencies need to provide first-hand information in a proactive and timely manner, so that they can take the lead in shaping public opinion. However, if the information first given is wrong, fictitious or incomplete, it is still widely perceived as truthful and is usually repeated over and over again. When this happens, considerable efforts and resources are needed to clarify and make corrections which, however, are often wasted or worse, trigger a backlash.

To avoid being put on the defensive, we should strive to take early steps and employ the most effective ways to lead the tide of opinion. The earlier, faster, more extensive, accurate and comprehensive your release of information is, the more likely you are to gain the high ground and earn public trust. It is also important that you take into consideration the demands of both domestic and foreign audiences. However, some people tend to suppress or block the distribution of information whenever an incident occurs as if the problem will somehow disappear or be easier to handle if nobody knows it. But this is not a good idea as, one way or another, the truth will come out eventually. Then over time, this kind of approach erodes credibility and people will not trust any information you provide, even when it is true and accurate. Therefore, we need to maintain a strong sense of responsibility and provide a sufficient amount of information to people. In the case of sensitive issues, as long as sufficiently clear messages are released promptly, false information will not have any chance of influencing the public.

Modern society has a growing demand and expectation for transparent governance and effective information disclosure. In China, as basic education is accessible nationwide and the citizens are better educated and equipped with more knowledge, the demand for information in our society has also grown. It is our responsibility and duty to convey true and accurate information to the public promptly. Spokespersons need to be aware of their responsibility for safeguarding people's right to know, and communicate with media and the public with humility while striving to respond and address people's concerns in a timely manner.

The speed with which we are seeing information disseminated, the complexity of realities and the difficulties in pursuing the truth have all become more significant. No one can be sure that they command sufficiently accurate and comprehensive information. Therefore, spokespersons must not rush unprepared into a press conference. Nor should they blurt out whatever comes to mind. Before speaking on any occasion, I often question myself: Am I clear about the issues of concern? Have I found all the facts? Spokespersons should get into the habit of doing repeated research, confirming the information and pondering over what they will say. When facing the public, they must respect facts, be logical and avoid being influenced by other factors.

Of course, a judgment call is inevitable when it comes to what the "truth" is. Moreover, it takes time to learn the "truth" which must also stand the test of time. Therefore, it is better if communicators only talk about the facts they know and refrain from talking about uncertainties until things become clearer. Sometimes, we cannot tell the entire truth or speak out immediately due to national security or policy considerations. But a general rule is that you should tell the truth as much as possible within the limits of your authority. From my observation on international occasions, some speakers may not be able to give adequate information; however, their eloquence, confidence and sincerity of expression often win recognition.

I have learnt that whatever the question is, the most compelling way to get my message across is to tell real Chinese stories, including facts, statistics, the difficulties and challenges, and how we accomplished it. After all, real-life stories are the most convincing and engaging. Indeed, in a world with a history full of fighting and killing among great powers, the rise of an emerging power certainly arouses speculation, doubts and even misunderstanding. We have to work out how to transcend longstanding differences in culture, language, way of thinking and interests between China and other countries, and work on clarifying China's intentions and role in ways that the rest of the world can understand. We need to let our voice be heard in places of need. General Secretary Xi Jinping said: "We should respect the rules of journalism and communication, and create new means and measures, to effectively strengthen the penetration, guidance, influence and credibility of the Party's work on media and public communication." We still have much to learn and improve in our understanding and respect for the rules of journalism and communication. So we must find better means and approaches to effectively enhance our work on media and public communications.

At the press conferences of the NPC sessions, I was often confronted with questions regarding various hot-button issues in China and abroad. For some of the questions, I knew the facts and was prepared, which enabled me to answer without difficulties; but some were new issues and unexpected, therefore I could only offer improvised answers based on my policy knowledge. Spokespersons are ordinary people who are neither omnipotent nor omniscient. There is always something they do not understand or know, and this is where sincerity matters. In this kind of situation, a simple statement is enough: "I am not aware of the specifics, but I will try to find out more about it."

What is also worth mentioning is the "margin of error". In the case of an emergency, spokespersons may not know any more than the public does. In this kind of situation, they should try to get as many of the factual details as possible. But if they mishandle anything or make some honest mistakes, shouldn't society be more tolerant and patient?

PROMOTE UNDERSTANDING OF CHINA

In the early years of my diplomatic career, China had relatively few contacts with the outside world. Whenever some hot issues concerning China emerged and aroused wide attention, China's voice was weak and rare. I remember in 1985, when I was studying in the UK, I would often leaf through all kinds of newspapers in the library, occasionally finding a short article about China, which was often irrelevant.

Nowadays, there is much more information available about China. And lately, many books and articles on China have been published, mostly written by scholars and experts specialised in international strategy and security studies as well as in the economic area, analysing and predicting the potential influence this emerging power will have on the world. However, the fundamental problem has not changed as, among the international publications, there is very little first-hand information and knowledge about China written by Chinese.

Generally speaking, in the global and information database, knowledge about contemporary mainland China has always been scarce, let alone for one to find systematic and complete data on any specific issue. While serving as the Chinese Ambassador to the UK, I often visited prominent universities. I noticed that although there were many books about China in the libraries, they were mostly publications on Chinese history or printed during the Republic of

China (1912-1949). Likewise, when I visited the US in 2017, I saw in the Library of Congress many non-English-language magazines on the shelves of the Asian Division. Yet, on closer inspection, I found no publication from the Chinese mainland. Therefore, it can be concluded that there is a wide "information deficit" about China and, as a result, the media and the public tend to develop perceptions of today's China based on outdated information, and even politicians have to assume and conceive ideas about China based on biased or incomplete materials.

A Western journalist once told me in private that three types of articles about China were favoured by editors-in-chief. The first described China as "too large" to be normal, with various super-scale phenomena. The second represented China as "too weird" to be similar with other countries. And the third claimed that China was "too bad", behaving against the so-called mainstream values of the West in many aspects. These views have developed as a result of non-objective reports about China that have been seen over many years.

Nevertheless, this country that is "too large, too weird and too bad" in their eyes has step by step achieved great success over the past four decades. In spite of the changing international situation, China has unswervingly followed the right direction of development while upholding CPC leadership.

During the second decade of the 21st century, China has further consolidated its position as a major country in the world and started to play an increasingly important role in international affairs. Quality Chinese products have been widely recognised and the Chinese people are traveling to all parts of the world. China's fair approach toward international affairs and its strong voice are more and more acknowledged by the international community. Instead of simply copying the Western model, China has secured continuous success in building socialism with Chinese characteristics. The Western media can no longer report news about China in the simple, mechanical manner it used to. Whether out of curiosity, the need for career development or self-reflection, increasing numbers of people are hoping to know more about China.

In recent years, while traveling overseas and attending

international meetings, I feel that China's rapid development and its successful construction and governance efforts are pushing the world to change its attitude towards the country. It is obvious that all concerned parties are sensing the pressure of changes in the international political structure. The China-related topics that are influencing this tendency are drawing more and more attention. I often hear people discussing at length about China's latest domestic and foreign policies. As China grows stronger, they wonder what kind of role it will play in the international arena and how it will influence the future of the world.

I have also taken part in discussion with congress members and scholars from other countries on these issues. I talked about China's development, its challenges, and the fact that the Chinese people were fully aware of the arduous task that lay ahead and understood that our focus was at home, and that we needed to continue running domestic affairs well. However, China also had to fulfil its international obligations. I explained to them President Xi Jinping's concept of building a community with a shared future for mankind and the idea of seeking common security. I emphasised that China would remain committed to international security cooperation based on mutual respect and mutual benefit, and that we looked forward to building strong reciprocal partnerships with other countries that were adaptable to new situations. Many of them were willing to listen to me and valued my views.

As China is progressively approaching the centre stage of the international arena, the view of China has become more diversified.

Most people have realised that the rise of China is inevitable and have recognised the coming opportunities. For many developing countries, China's road to success is worth observing. While extending help and support, China brings them new opportunities to overcome the difficulties that hinder their domestic development. In this increasingly rigid and conservative world, the global governance propositions China puts forward, and the public products China offers are like a breath of fresh air blowing in from the East. They ignite a new hope that there will be reform of the international order that will render greater fairness and justice.

Some worry that China may seek hegemony as other great

powers did in the past. The incumbent great powers and traditional forces worry that China may challenge or even replace their world leadership and are therefore taking an increasingly guarded and protectionist attitude. To some extent, such views have also been shaped and spread with the help of misinformation and disinformation about China.

In China, there is growing awareness about the need to improve the international narrative and effective efforts are being made. With more platforms, new media tools and better infrastructure, China is now capable of better presenting the real picture of its national development and people's lives to the rest of the world. In international communication, we have evolved from simply talking about "what China is not" or "what China does not do" to explaining "who we are," "what we will do," and "what we will become."

Nevertheless, the old opinion carries inertia and is slow to change, and the stereotypes formed over the years are unlikely to change in a short period of time. There is still much misunderstanding about China internationally, some derived from deep-seated geopolitical memories of the Cold War, the zero-sum concept and ideological bias while some are rooted in the fear of world power shifts, while others stem from lack of understanding due to differences in language, culture and means of expression. Still, there are also a handful of anti-China forces and people behind them who live on attacking and smearing China, and they collect, fabricate and spread negative information about China with no respect for what is real and truthful.

As China has become prosperous and its political system is demonstrating vitality, the US has realised that its goal of pushing for political changes in China by bringing it into the world system cannot be achieved, hence it has become more and more uncomfortable and there is a rising sense of repulsion against China ideologically. Some even advocate that China is America's primary strategic competitor. In the *National Security Strategy of the United States of America* and similar papers, the US has stated that it will shift its global strategic focus from non-conventional security threats and global challenges that include combating terrorism, back to the traditional great power competition. This has indicated its attempt to develop a new thinking and make preparations to contain and obstruct the rise of China.

These changes have complicated China's international environment for communications when it is trying to better connect with the world. Therefore, it has become more urgent for us to consider how to clearly and systematically present China's image to the world. For our communicators, in order to keep abreast of the changes, they need to learn and gain experience in practice, including learning about China's national developments and people's aspirations. In this way, they will be able to raise capabilities and make China's voice better and more often heard by the international community. We may also consider how to make our communication more effective and targeted, how to turn overseas questioning into communications, and how to promote the understanding of China's political ideas and cultural quintessence in a more engaging and persuasive way.

One of the prerequisites for China to participate in and influence world affairs is to be able to effectively share with the international community its knowledge, information and policies so that the world can have a full and accurate understanding of it. While we need to work on removing the old prejudices, we also need to prevent the emergence of new ones. Prejudice among countries is generated in the same way as among people. If someone is always being labelled as being something yet makes no effort to refute it then inevitably more labels start getting attached, and they turn into "generally acknowledged facts".

For a modern country to promote its policies and earn international credit, well-thought-out news strategies are indispensable. Before announcing any major decision, it is wise to assess and prepare for potential international reactions. In other words, for major countries, its political statements and conduct should not only be understood and supported by the domestic public, but also be convincing to the international community. This is not always easy to achieve. For example, whenever China experiences an important event, introduces an important measure or releases an important policy, the media worldwide pay attention to it and it soon becomes news. However, if there are no informed Chinese officials, experts or scholars immediately available to give translations, interpretations and clarifications to the international media, the foreign journalists or scholars act on our behalf. It is difficult for China's national conditions and policy intentions to be accurately and comprehensively reflected in this kind of situation. Furthermore, some of our new views or propositions, when translated into foreign languages, may be difficult to understand due to political or cultural differences inherent in the contexts and vocabularies. These are some of the new problems we need to consider when trying to improve our international communication.

China remains committed to peaceful development, it pursues a peaceful independent foreign policy and practices an inherently defensive national defence policy. In dealing with the rest of the world, we actively engage in world affairs, promote the building of a community with a shared future for mankind, and foster a new type of international relations. We are honest with our goals and approaches, and do not oppose in private what we openly agree to. Therefore we have nothing to hide in explaining China's strategic goals and policies to the world. It is important that we keep pace with the changes in international situations and try to meet the demands for more information about China from people across the world by proactively offering information and telling China's story to the outside world. When there are misunderstandings or misconceptions, we need to reflect on what more needs to be done and whether we can be more active in delivering our messages and making sure that they reach the audience who care about, and pay attention to, China.

The target audience for China's story is the general public in the world who form the foundation of the international community. They have fewer preconceived opinions and learn about China from what they see, read and experience, and from their interactions with Chinese people. But, if they cannot obtain first-hand information about China, they can be easily influenced by misinformation.

We need to raise our awareness of the importance of proactively carrying out international communication. We need more Chinese people to engage in explaining China's policies by accepting interview requests from the international media, writing articles for them and attending international forums. We need the Chinese media to provide timely information overseas. And we also need more high-quality Chinese materials and books to be translated and made available. To this end, there is the need to accelerate reforms and adjustments in political, procedural and financial terms, encourage and train more talent, and motivate more people to take part in the effort to promote international communication.

Different societies are composed of various groups of people. In international communication, we face countries that may have somewhat different social systems. Many countries have diversified opinion circles and their own way of international communication. For example, in the US, the government, the Congress, think tanks, higher education institutions and the media all have their unique ways of exerting influence and promoting their interests. Hollywood, a typical symbol of America's cultural soft power, is also an important part of its opinion shaping and international clout. When we promote international communication, we should keep in mind the demands of different audiences and foster the awareness of, and capability for, delivering messages via multiple channels. We should not only communicate with countries at the governmental level but also build the capability and channels of communication at non-governmental levels.

In recent years, the demographic composition of the people that China deals with overseas has been changing, as more and more young people are directly engaging with the Chinese people. The younger generation did not experience the Cold War, and the past ideologies have less influence on them. As time goes by, the young people, and even the younger generation, will be in a better position to shake off the yoke of the outdated Cold War mentality. This trend presents a valuable opportunity for China and the rest of the world to improve communication and mutual understanding.

TAKING PEOPLE TO MY HEART

When we conduct exchanges and communication, we face a specific audience. Whether it is delivering a speech, giving an interview or attending an international forum, although the audiences differ, they have one thing in common—they are human beings, they are people with thoughts and cultural habits. It is my belief that in domestic or international communications, one should always keep the "people" factor in mind.

There are three progressive levels of "taking people to heart", which are: knowing people, valuing people and respecting people.

The first is to know your audience, especially those "present", that is, the people you actually talk to at a specific time and place. For example, the journalist who interviews you, the press professionals at a press conference or the guests and audience you face while giving a speech or attending a forum. Those "present" are the people who establish the most direct and intimate ties with you. In this sense, it is always good to be able to get to know them, the more the better.

What is the main concern of the journalist or moderator during an interview? What is the political tendency and stance of a news agency? Has it voiced any opinions on relevant issues recently and what did they say? Just as the interviewer should do good research on the interviewee, the interviewee also needs to do research on the interviewer.

At international forums, the moderators and guests also have their specific concerns or perspectives. It would be good to know background information, such as the focus of the forum, the topics for discussion, your fellow panellists' concerns and interests, and their positions on China.

When making a speech, we need to have a clear picture of the audience's composition. Are they mainly domestic or international? Are they students, scholars, professionals or policymakers? We also need to find out what kind of policies and situations are of major concern to them or what questions they are mostly interested in. This not only is beneficial for us to deliver a more targeted speech but also enables us to be better prepared for questions raised in the Q&A session.

These issues are "required homework" for my team and myself before attending any forum. Sometimes I would organise a simulation, asking each of my team members to play the role of a panellist and collect their views beforehand. Such preparations are even more crucial for press conferences for which, as I mentioned in earlier chapters, much of the preparation was focused around the concerns of the media and the public.

To quote from Sunzi: "If you know the opponent and know yourself, you need not fear a hundred battles."[1] Knowing your counterpart is a prerequisite for effective exchanges and responses. When sitting on the stage answering questions, you only have a limited time to think and organise your thoughts into words. Adequate preparation is therefore important to ensure you can deal with unexpected circumstances. By telling China's story, we aim to let others know about us. What matters is not only what we want to say but also what people want to know. Only by connecting "the speaking" with "the listening" can we reach the objective of communication.

The second is to value the audience, including those who agree and those who disagree with you. Sometimes when I attended international forums or gave interviews, I could feel that my counterpart disagreed with China's policies or political system. If there was someone with a deep-rooted misunderstanding or prejudice against China, I would have to deal with sharp and provocative questions. Some would want to tempt or provoke me into saying things which could justify their preconceived views or judgment.

In the context of media relations, what is going on between the interviewer and the interviewee is a contest of wisdom, as each side is trying to earn the general public's recognition. Especially when we face the Western media, we cannot expect them to let us use their platforms to voice our ideas easily and we have to try to overcome the difficulties and the high threshold. As long as we accept the invitation and come to their platforms, we should be ready for a tough fight and be well prepared to address tough questions.

Those who raise difficult questions may be acting out of prejudice or in the hope of stimulating a debate so as to allow the programme to attract more attention. The interviewer is also taking a risk when asking provocative questions as it is tantamount to putting oneself into a contest. For the responder, this is a challenge but can also be an opportunity. Like playing tennis, the harder the ball is hit towards you over the net, the greater the chance for you to leverage its strength as you hit it back. In this sense, the best strategy when tackling provocative questions is not to shy away or flinch from them but instead to respond directly, using your prepared facts. It is essential that we correctly judge the question to establish whether it is based on false facts or faulty logic, and what are the real facts. If the logic is wrong, how can we identify the loophole and pull the rug from under their feet. To get our ideas across and eventually achieve the goal of effective communication, we must focus on answering questions seriously without creating ambiguity.

The third is to show respect for people and humanity. I have always believed in this. This year (2018) marks the 120th anniversary of the birth of the late Chinese Premier Zhou Enlai. In dealing with interpersonal relationships and handling domestic and external affairs, one characteristic that distinguished him from many others was his innate respect for everyone, which was reciprocated by all those who met him, friends and opponents alike.

In December 2016, at the US-based New York University (NYU), I delivered a speech entitled *"The Human Element in International Behaviour"* in which I expressed some thoughts on this issue. I had noticed through years of diplomatic experience that in the modern civilised world, "when judging an international act, regardless of how passionate the purpose is or what the moral principles are, in the end, it is the consequences for the people, for the families and children, that is the central consideration."

Serving the People is the concept that has inspired me, especially when serving on the NPC, and "people" was a keyword in my press conferences. Under the leadership of the CPC, from the media to government departments to the NPC, we all work to serve our people, listening to their voices and responding to their concerns. The principle of respecting humanity and respecting people guided my practice from which I have learnt to nurture a sense of responsibility, stay humble and act respectfully. It has also motivated me to be tenacious in carrying out my endeavours.

In the international environment, most of the audience we speak to are ordinary people. Since our purpose is to win over their understanding, we have every reason to state our views and positions respectfully.

PLACE EQUAL EMPHASIS ON "DAO (MORAL PRINCIPLES)" AND "SHU (SKILLS)"

In communication, we should place equal emphasis on "Dao" and "Shu." "Dao" refers to the ideas and values we uphold, which determines what positions we adhere to, who we serve, and what goals and ideals we pursue. "Shu" refers to the technical skills and the approach we adopt, which are also important. "Telling China's story well" highlights the importance of skills. "What to tell? How to tell it? And how to tell it well?" Stories are for people, so we need to tell stories that people are interested to hear, using the stories to appeal to, move and convince. General Secretary Xi Jinping asked the leading Chinese officials to raise their ability to communicate with the media and improve their skills to explain policies. To meet his request, we need to work hard to learn and adopt good methods and improve our skills.

As part of modern state governance, effective communication requires special attention to the skills, the "Shu". I see professional training as the necessary path to grasp the skills which help us to face the media with confidence, but it is also a persistent process for self-improvement. I am a beginner who is still learning and exploring for improvement. With some clumsy and hard effort, I have achieved some progress and put some of my knowledge and experience into this book. But it is not possible for me to write down everything in every detail and it may not be necessary either as technique and skills are something personal. People can develop their own method and habitual way of doing it.

When I started this book, I was unsure whether I should include some technical and trivial details but in the end I decided to include some of them with the hope of reproducing my real experience and making this book more like an "operation manual". Some of my practical methodology and even some of my lessons may serve as a guide for those who follow in my footsteps. Indeed, "Dao" and"Shu" are mutually complementary. "Those who have Shu (skills) but are without Dao (moral principles) cannot achieve success." We cannot talk about skills only，methods and skills need to be guided by moral principles and they should be applied to serve a higher purpose. Learning and improving one's skills can be a tediously hard process and it takes a strong conviction to make it. The reason why some people are willing to endure the hardship and surmount the difficulties is that they hold a belief and a sense of responsibility, and they want to tell China's story well, which in a way is also a kind of "Dao".

To make China's voice heard in the world, it is not enough to tell China's story well. In the final analysis, it is what we do and what we achieve which matter the most. Under the guidance of *Xi Jinping Thought on Socialism with Chinese Characteristics for a New Era*, our country will be able to continue delivering successes and achievements while earning greater understanding and trust from the international community, which will lay a foundation for building a community with a shared future for mankind.

NOTES

FOREWORD

1. According to the *Constitution*, the National People's Congress（NPC）of the People's Republic of China (PRC) is the highest organ of state power. Its permanent organ is the Standing Committee of the NPC. The NPC and its Standing Committee exercise the legislative power of the state. The NPC is composed of deputies elected by provinces, autonomous regions and municipalities directly under the central government, special administrative regions and the armed forces. All ethnic minorities should have appropriate representation within it. (excerpted from the *Constitution of the PRC*)
2. Ranking by the number of times the questions were asked, they were: the functions of the NPC and the development of the socialist rule of law (19 times), diplomatic affairs (9 times), taxation and economic affairs (7 times), hot topics in society (7 times), national defence budget (5 times), environmental protection (5 times), anti-corruption (4 times), women's rights (4 times), political system reform (4 times), Hong Kong affairs (3 times).

1. WALKING INTO THE PRESS CONFERENCE

1. The Four Consciousnesses refers to: consciousness of the need to maintain political integrity, think in big-picture terms，follow the leadership core, and keep in alignment.
2. The "two sessions" refers to annual plenary sessions of the two organisations that make national-level political decisions, namely the NPC and the national committee of the CPPCC.
3. According to the *Civil Code of the PRC*, a natural person has the capacity for civil rights from the moment of birth to the moment of death, enjoying civil rights and assuming civil obligations in accordance with the law ; A legal person is an organisation with capacity for civil rights and capacity for civil conduct which independently enjoys civil rights and assumes civil obligations in accordance with the law.
4. On 24 May 2013, General Secretary Xi Jinping presided over the collective study of the Political Bureau of the 18th Central Committee of the CPC, and the theme for the learning was: vigorously promoting the construction of ecological civilisation.
5. *Ya Li Shan Da* is an internet buzzword in Chinese to describe the pressure as big as a mountain. It is homonymous with the name of Alexander the Great in Chinese.
6. On 15 August 2005, Comrade Xi Jinping, then Secretary of the Zhejiang Provincial CPC Committee, first put forward the scientific conclusion that "clear waters and lush mountains are invaluable assets" during his inspection in Anjiyu Village, Zhejiang Province.
7. http://politics.people.com.cn/n1/2016/0318/c1001-28210015.html

2. THE NATIONAL DEFENCE BUDGET, PERSONAL INFORMATION PROTECTION AND ANTI-CORRUPTION

1. "Death tax rate" was a term first used by renowned fiscal-policy expert Li Weiguang, who claimed that the tax burden was excessively heavy in China, saying that a corporate tax rate of 40% was deadly for Chinese companies, hence the term "death tax rate". The State Taxation Administration disagreed with the view and stated in a press release that the term "death tax rate" may misguide the public, and called for a fairer view on the macro taxation.

3. THE PROTECTION OF WOMEN AND CHILDREN AND CHINA'S INTERNATIONAL ROLE

1. *China Labour Market Development Report 2016: Female Employment in the Process of Gender Equality*, Beijing Normal University Publishing House
2. Data provided by the *US Bureau of Labor Statistics*
3. In 1953, when the CPC Central Committee issued the *Decisions on Mutual Aid and Cooperation in Agriculture* and the *Decisions on the Development of Agricultural Production Cooperatives*, the mutual aid and cooperation movement started in China's rural areas. At the end of 1956, the agricultural cooperative transformation was basically completed. Agricultural production cooperatives then continued to expand their activities and grew to become people's communes in 1958. Thereafter, such cooperatives experienced a tortuous journey of development for more than two decades.

6. FRIENDLY AND FIERY MOMENTS AT INTERNATIONAL FORUMS

1. *Capitalism, Socialism, and Democracy*, Joseph Schumpeter, 1942, Harper & Brothers.

7. RECALLING MY TIME SPENT IN THE UK

1. Quoted from Chapter 7, *The Analects of Confucius*. The meaning is that it is always possible to listen and learn from others but one must be careful to distinguish between good examples of people one can learn from and bad examples of people whose advice should be discarded.

AFTERWORD

1. Quoted from *Strategic Offence* of *The Art of War* by Sunzi.

ACKNOWLEDGMENTS

People say that ancient Roman poet Virgil compared writing poetry to "a she-bear gradually licking her cubs into shape."

I started mulling over the idea of this book in December 2015 and wrapped it up in January 2018. Over the two years, both my team and I felt like we have been "licking a cub into shape." We have toiled and suffered amid our sweet expectations.

I want to extend my gratitude to everyone on my team. Every time I lost confidence, it was their encouragement and support that kept me going. Their rigour and honesty in proposing both suggestions and critical opinions have been incredibly beneficial to me and have gone a long way to improving this book in terms of its structure and contents.

Liao Mengxia, my chief assistant, has collected numerous materials over the past two years. Zuo Yilu, Wang Huaisheng and Xiao Qian, along with the members of the NPC press conference team, were very attentive in collecting materials, sorting information and tracking the schedule of the 2017 NPC Press Conference. It was this preparation that laid the foundations for this book. Bian Yongzu participated in the part concerning economics, while Song Bo contributed to the section on the Valdai Forum. After revising each chapter, Zheng Yan and Yao Jinxiang patiently helped with sorting everything out and proofreading. During the finalising of the book, An Gang carefully polished and edited it. I am also grateful to many other friends and colleagues who have extended a helping hand. This book would not have been possible without their hard work.

My thanks also go to Xin Chunying, Li Lianning, Kan Ke, He Shaoren, Zhang Yuhua, Zhao Xibing, Fang Hong, Liu Bing and other colleagues, and my husband Hao Shiyuan and other family and friends. As preview readers before publication, they provided me with many professional and detailed suggestions for improvements.

Finally, I would like to thank other colleagues at the NPC and the MFA for helping and supporting me over the past five years.

ABOUT THE AUTHOR

Fu Ying started her career with China's Ministry of Foreign Affairs (MFA) in 1978 and has long been engaged in Asian affairs. She served successively as Director of Division and Counselor in the Asian Affairs Department of the MFA. In 1992 she joined the UN peacekeeping mission in Cambodia. She was appointed Minister Counselor at the Chinese Embassy in Indonesia in 1997, Chinese Ambassador to the Philippines in 1998, and Director General of the Asian Department of the MFA in 2000. She then was appointed Ambassador to Australia (2004-2007), and Ambassador to the United Kingdom (2007-2009). She served as Vice Minister of Foreign Affairs for European Affairs and then for Asian Affairs (2009-2013).

Fu Ying was elected deputy to China's 12th (2013) and then 13th (2018) National People's Congress (NPC). She was the Chairperson of the Foreign Affairs Committee and spokesperson of the 12th NPC (2013-2018). She was the Vice-Chairperson of the Foreign Affairs Committee of China's 13th NPC (2018-2023). Fu Ying is also the Founding Chairperson of the Center for International Security and Strategy (CISS).

ABOUT THE TRANSLATOR

Dr Chen Chunhua is a senior independent interpreter/translator and co-founder of "Transyes", a Beijing-based language service provider. A market-proven, seasoned conference interpreter who has provided professional services to state leaders, govermental/non-governmental organisations and multinational corporations, she holds a PhD in Political Science from the George Washington University, a Master's degree in International Trade Policy from the Middlebury Institute of International Studies at Monterey, and a Master's degree from the Sino-EU Interpreter Training Center. She is also certified by the European Union's Department of Interpretation.

ABOUT ACA

We hope you enjoyed this intimate, frank and rare behind-the scenes look at how a senior Chinese spokesperson engages with the media.

ALAIN CHARLES ASIA publishes an exciting range of China-focused non-fiction. From the soaring highs and grim lows of China's tumultuous history to the vivid life stories of its major and minor player, ACA has books for anyone eager to learn more about this vast, diverse nation.

To let us know what you thought of this book, or to learn more about the diverse range of exciting Chinese fiction in translation we publish, find us online. If you're as passionate about Chinese literature as we are, then we'd love to hear your thoughts!

alaincharlesasia.com
@aca_pub